Learning to Pass

New CLAiT 2006

File management and e-document production •
Creating spreadsheets and graphs •
Database manipulation •

Units 1–3

Ruksana Patel

www.heinemann.co.uk
✓ Free online support
✓ Useful weblinks
✓ 24 hour online ordering

01865 888058

Inspiring generations

Heinemann Educational Publishers
Halley Court, Jordan Hill, Oxford OX2 8EJ
Part of Harcourt Education

Heinemann is the registered trademark of Harcourt Education Limited

Text © Ruksana Patel, 2005

First published 2005

10 09 08 07 06 05

10 9 8 7 6 5 4 3 2 1

British Library Cataloguing in Publication Data is available from the British Library on request.

10-digit ISBN: 0 43508271 X
13-digit ISBN: 978 0 43508271 0

Typeset by Thomson Digital, India

Original illustrations © Harcourt Education Limited, 2005

Cover design by Wooden Ark

Printed in the UK at Bath Colour

Cover photo: ©

Acknowledgements
Every effort has been made to contact copyright holders of material reproduced in this book. Any omissions will be rectified in subsequent printings if notice is given to the publishers.

The author would like to express her deep gratitude to Abdul Patel for working through the book several times and for his support, incredible patience and invaluable feedback during the writing of this book. A special thank you to Fayaz and Fozia Roked for their help, encouragement and support. Thank you to Gavin Fidler, Elaine Tuffery and to Lewis Birchon for his invaluable input which has improved the quality of the book and for his constant support, advice and patience during the production process.

The publisher would like to thank Daydream Education (tel. 0800 068 0232
web. www.daydreameducation.co.uk) for kind permission to reproduce the image on pages 16, 37, 126 and 257.

Microsoft product screenshots reprinted with permission from Microsoft Corporation.

Picture credits
Image on page 3 © Corbis, image on page 4 © Corbis, image on page 5 (top) © Corbis, all images on the CD-ROM file handout.pdf © Getty/Photodisc.

Contents

Who this book is suitable for

This book is suitable for:

- *candidates working towards: OCR Level 1 Certificate or Diploma for IT Users (New CLAiT), and OCR ITQ qualification*

- *complete beginners, with no prior knowledge of Windows XP, Microsoft Office Word 2003, Microsoft Office Excel 2003 or Microsoft Office Access 2003*

- *use as a self-study workbook – the user should work through each unit from start to finish*

- *tutor-assisted workshops or tutor-led groups*

- *individuals wanting to learn to use Windows XP, Word 2003, Excel 2003 and Access 2003 (default settings are assumed).*

Although this book is based on Windows XP, Word 2003, Excel 2003 and Access 2003, it may also suitable for users of Microsoft Office 2002 (XP) and Microsoft Office 2000 applications. Note that a few of the skills may be slightly different and some screenshots will not be identical.

How to work through this book

1   Read the explanation of a term first.

2   If there are some terms that you do not understand, refer to the Definition of terms for the relevant unit on the accompanying CD-ROM.

3   Work through each Unit in sequence so that one skill is understood before moving on to the next. This ensures understanding of the topic and prevents mistakes.

4   Read the **▶▶ How to...** guidelines which give step-by-step instructions for each skill. Do not attempt to work through the How to... guidelines, read through each step and look at the screenshots. Make sure you understand all the instructions before moving on.

5   To make sure that you have understood how to perform a skill, work through the Check your understanding task following that skill. You should refer to the How to... guidelines when doing the task.

6   At the end of each section, there is an Assess your skills table. This lists the skills that you will have practised by working through each section. Look at each item listed to help you decide whether you are confident that you can perform each skill.

7   Towards the end of the book are Quick reference guides, Build-up and Practice tasks. Work through each of the tasks.

If you need help, you may refer to the How to... guidelines or Quick reference guides whilst doing the Build-up tasks. Whilst working on the Practice tasks, you should feel confident enough to use only the Quick reference guides if you need support. These guides may also be used during an assessment.

Contents

> More general advice on preparation for the assessment and the Unit 1 Definition of terms can be found on the CD-ROM that accompanies this book.

Chapter 1

Learning to use a computer and file management

For the first part of Unit 1, you will need to understand how to use a computer safely and how to manage files and folders.

To learn the basics of using a computer, we will use Windows XP. There are two different versions of Windows XP: Windows XP Professional and Windows XP Home Edition. You can use this book for either version of Windows XP.

This chapter is divided into two sections:

○ *in Section 1, you will learn about the different parts of a computer and basic health and safety practices when using a computer*

○ *in Section 2, you will learn how to manage computer files and folders.*

A CD-ROM accompanies this book. On it are the files that you will need to use for the file management tasks. Instructions for copying the files are provided at the beginning of Chapter 1 Section 2 on page 24. The solutions for all the tasks can be found in a folder called **worked_copies_unit1**

Note: There are many ways of performing the skills covered in this book. This book provides How to... guidelines that are easily understood by learners.

1: Use a computer

LEARNING OUTCOMES

In this section you will learn how to:

○ understand and use computer hardware and software

○ understand health and safety practices when using a computer

○ switch on a computer and monitor

○ understand windows, icons, buttons, menus and toolbars

○ use a password

○ use a mouse

○ use a keyboard

○ shut down the computer.

What is a computer?

A computer is a machine that is capable of taking in and processing information (referred to as data) at speed without making errors. A machine works the way it is programmed to function – it does not make mistakes. A computer is often referred to as a PC, which stands for personal computer. Remember, it is almost impossible to break a computer by using it and it is quite easy to correct any mistakes that you make. So don't be afraid to use a computer!

You will need to understand:

- *how a computer works*
- *the difference between hardware and software*
- *the different ways of storing data.*

The following pages give a brief introduction. These topics are covered in more detail on a separate handout called 'Unit 1 Handout Understanding Computers', which can be found on the CD-ROM accompanying this book.

Nowadays, many people use a laptop because it has the advantage of being portable.

FIGURE 1.1 A laptop computer is convenient and portable

What does it mean?

Hardware
Hardware are the physical parts that you can see and touch.

Software
Software are computer programs that allow you to use the computer, such as Microsoft Word. You cannot touch software.

Keyboard
Used to enter (input) information into the computer. Has more than 100 keys, including letters arranged in a set pattern, numbers and symbols.

Speakers

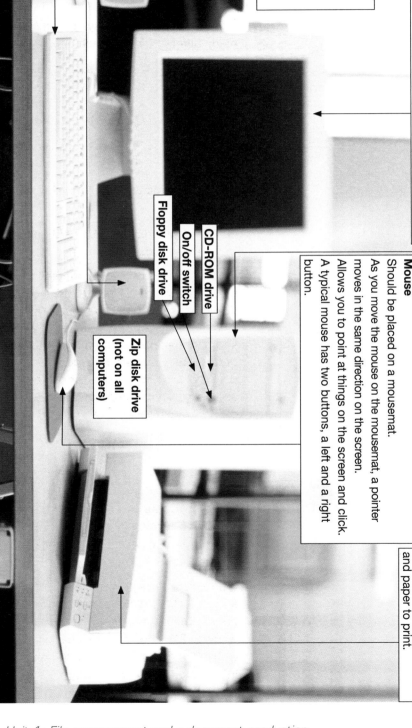

Monitor
Also referred to as **VDU (Visual Display Unit)** or screen because it looks like a television screen. Allows you to see data being entered into the computer.
The angle/position may be adjusted to suit you. May have an on/off switch and other settings buttons to allow you to change brightness etc. Thin, flat screen monitors are also available

Central Processing Unit (CPU) box
The most important part of a computer.
Contains the **memory** (brain).
Contains the hard disk drive which stores programs and data.
Other parts: printer, monitor, keyboard, mouse are connected using cables to the CPU box.
The CPU can be horizontal or upright as shown. An upright box is referred to as a tower.

Floppy disk drive

CD-ROM drive

On/off switch

Zip disk drive (not on all computers)

Mouse
Should be placed on a mousemat.
As you move the mouse on the mousemat, a pointer moves in the same direction on the screen.
Allows you to point at things on the screen and click. A typical mouse has two buttons, a left and a right button.

Printer
Allows what is seen on screen to be printed on paper, referred to as hard copy. Many types of printer are available, e.g. laser, inkjet.
Some print in black and white only.
Printers need ink cartridges and paper to print.

FIGURE 1.2 A typical computer system

Storing data

Data that is input into a computer can be saved to a variety of storage devices, as shown in the table below.

STORAGE DEVICE		DESCRIPTION
Hard disk		A fixed storage medium. A hard disk drive is usually inbuilt into the CPU box. Hard disk drives can store large amounts of data. On a networked computer system there are often many different drives, each one is given a letter.
Compact disc (CD)		A removable, portable, storage medium that holds large amounts of data but not as much as a hard disk. Types of CD are: ○ CD-R – data can be saved on to it but cannot be deleted ○ CD-RW – data can be saved, updated and deleted ○ CD-ROM – data can be read only, e.g. software programs.
Floppy disk		A floppy disk drive can be inbuilt into the CPU box or it can be an external drive. A floppy disk drive is often called the (A:) drive. A 3½ inch disk is inserted into the floppy disk drive and data can be saved on to it. The advantage of this removable storage medium is that it is portable and easy to use – it can be inserted and used in any computer that has a floppy disk drive. However, it can only store a limited amount of data.
USB disk		Also referred to as Flash Disk/Memory Stick/Flash Pen. Increasingly popular, this removable storage medium can store larger amounts of data than floppy disks and is portable. It is inserted into a USB port located at the front or back of a computer.
Zip disk		Zip disks are as portable and versatile as floppy disks but have the advantage of being able to store much larger amounts of data. Zip disks need to be inserted into a zip disk drive. Not all computers have an inbuilt zip disk drive, they can be external drives.

Referring to the diagram of a typical computer system on page 4, find the different hardware parts of your computer.

1 Is the CPU box upright or horizontal? (Not applicable to laptops.)

2 Does your computer have a floppy disk drive? If so, find the floppy disk drive – it may be in a slightly different place on your computer from that shown in the diagram.

3 Find the eject button which is usually under the floppy disk drive.

4 Does your computer have a CD-ROM drive? Not all computers do. Similarly, your computer may not have a zip disk drive. Find the button that allows you to open and close the CD-ROM drive.

5 Find the on/off switch on the CPU box (don't switch it on just yet!).

6 Does your monitor have an on/off switch? Are the buttons to adjust settings, e.g. brightness/contrast, at the front of your monitor? Are you able to adjust the positioning of the monitor? Be careful whenever you adjust the monitor, as the wires at the back may not be fully secure.

7 Find the mouse. Position your wrist over the mouse, keep the mouse on the mousemat and move it around slowly on the mat to get the feel of it. If your mouse has a cord, do not pull too hard as the wire may not be fully secure.

8 Does your computer have external speakers? They may be inbuilt into the computer.

9 Find the keyboard. Tap on the keys to get a feel for using the keyboard.

10 Find the printer. It may not be next to the computer. Is it a printer that will be used by more than one computer? If so, this is a shared printer.

Health and safety

When you use a computer, you should be aware of safe working practices to reduce the risk of strain-type injuries.

▶▶ How to... protect your eyes

○ *Use a monitor that:*
  - *is adjustable*
  - *has an inbuilt or additional anti-glare screen to protect your eyes*
  - *is positioned below your line of sight – you should be looking down at the monitor.*
○ *You should look away from the screen approximately every ten minutes to avoid eye strain.*

▶▶ How to... be aware of your posture

- Use a chair that can swivel and has an adjustable height.
- Your back and elbows should be supported.
- Both of your feet should touch the floor.
- Your knees and elbows should be at a 90-degree angle.

▶▶ How to... avoid repetitive strain injury (RSI)

- RSI can be caused if the keyboard or mouse are used incorrectly over a long period of time.
- RSI may affect the fingers, wrists, elbows and lower arms.
- When using a computer, make sure that your wrists are relaxed. Your wrists must be higher than your fingers, not lower.
- It may be helpful to use a wrist support in front of your keyboard and/or on your mousemat.

FIGURE 1.3 Check that you are seated correctly at the computer

Check your understanding *Basic health and safety*

1 Sit at your computer workstation.

2 Make sure your chair is at the correct height and angle. Your back should be straight and your feet should be flat on the floor.

3 Make sure that there is no glare on the screen.

4 Adjust the angle of the monitor. Your head should not be tilted back to look up at the screen.

Starting the computer

▶▶ How to... *switch on the computer*

Before you switch on a computer, you will need to check a few things.

- *Make sure that the light on the CPU box (or laptop) is not already on.*
  - *Some computers go on standby, so the light will be on even though nothing displays on screen. In that case, move the mouse or press any key on the keyboard. You should* not *press the on/off switch.*

- *Make sure that there is no disk in the floppy disk drive. If there is, press the eject button to remove it.*

- *When a computer is switched on, it will boot up (load up). The computer prepares itself for use by carrying out various checks, for example, the central processing unit checks that the monitor, keyboard, mouse and printer are all connected correctly.*

- *The monitor may switch on automatically when the computer is switched on. If not, you will need to press the on/off switch on the monitor.*

Check your understanding *Start the computer*

1 Start up your computer and monitor.

2 A login screen or desktop is displayed.

3 If a login screen is displayed (Figure 1.4), prompting you to enter your user password (or user name and password), work through 'The start-up screen' and 'Passwords' sections on pages 9–10.

FIGURE 1.4 An example of a login screen

FIGURE 1.5 An example of a computer desktop

4 If the desktop screen is displayed (Figure 1.5), work through 'The windows desktop' section on pages 10–11.

The start-up screen

- *When you start up your computer, a screen telling you to press **Ctrl + Alt + Delete** may display.*
- *Find these three keys on your keyboard.*
- *Press all three keys at the same time.*
- *Another screen prompting you to enter your user name and/or password may be displayed.*

Passwords

If your computer is networked:

- *you are usually told the user name that you will need to use*
- *you may be given a password or asked to choose your own.*

If your computer is stand-alone:

- *it may be set up so that you do not have to enter a user name and/or password every time you log in*
- *you may have a choice for your user name and password.*

▶▶ How to... *choose a password*

- A good password should consist of a combination of letters and numbers so that others cannot guess it.
- Avoid using obvious passwords such as your birthday or your car registration.
- On some computer systems your password may need to be a minimum number of characters.
- Passwords may be case sensitive (you may need to use lower case and/or upper case letters).
- Passwords should be changed from time to time for security reasons.
- Passwords should not be given to other users for security reasons.
- Passwords may be used on a drive, a folder or a file to protect confidential information.

▶▶ How to... *use a password to log in to a computer*

1. On the login screen, click on the **User Name** box.
2. Use the keyboard to enter your user name.
3. Click in the **Password** box.
4. Enter your password using the keyboard. Make sure you use lower and/or upper case correctly.

5 The password appears on-screen as dots so that others cannot see it.

6 Click on **OK** or the green arrow to proceed.

7 The computer will load up (boot up) and the computer desktop will be displayed.

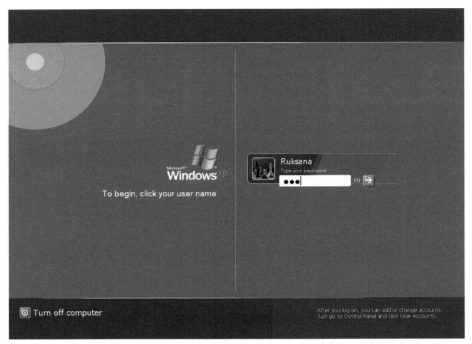

FIGURE 1.6 Your user name and password screen may be different to this one

Check your understanding
Enter your user name and/or password

1 Enter your user name and/or password (as required by the computer).

2 Make sure no one can see the keyboard when you enter the password.

The Windows desktop

Windows uses a **Graphical User Interface (GUI)**. This shows **icons** (small pictures) and **menus** (lists of items). Windows operating systems are easy to use, when you click with your mouse on an icon or menu item, you are actually giving the computer a command (or instruction) to do something.

When you start up your computer, the **desktop** screen is displayed (Figure 1.7). This is the work area for all tasks performed in Windows.

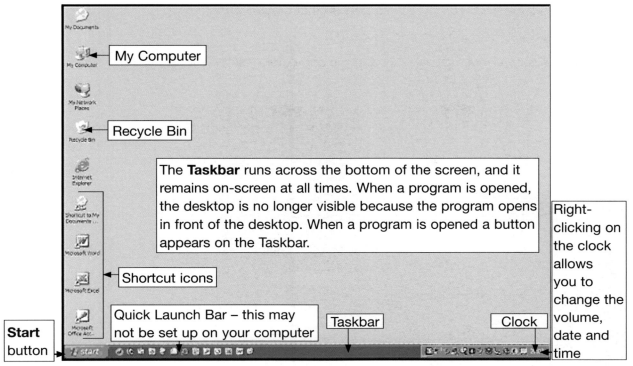

My Computer

Recycle Bin

The **Taskbar** runs across the bottom of the screen, and it remains on-screen at all times. When a program is opened, the desktop is no longer visible because the program opens in front of the desktop. When a program is opened a button appears on the Taskbar.

Right-clicking on the clock allows you to change the volume, date and time

Shortcut icons

Quick Launch Bar – this may not be set up on your computer

Taskbar

Clock

Start button

FIGURE 1.7 A desktop screen

Do not worry if your desktop screen is not identical to the screen prints shown in this book. The desktop icons, desktop background and the programs on the **Start** menu will vary from one computer to another, but the basic layout is very similar.

The desktop background may be a plain colour (as in Figure 1.7) or may have a picture as the background. Backgrounds can be changed in the **Control Panel**.

A program can be opened in various ways:

- *through the **Start** menu*
- *by double-clicking the shortcut icons on the desktop*
- *by single-clicking on the program icon on the **Quick Launch bar** if a shortcut has been created.*

The mouse

▶▶ How to... use a mouse

The mouse lets the computer know what you want it to do. A standard mouse works better if placed on a mousemat. This provides a smooth, non-slip surface. The mouse ball gathers dust and should be cleaned periodically.

Make sure the mouse cord is pointing away from you, then rest your hand on the mouse as shown in Figure 1.8. Left-handed users may place the

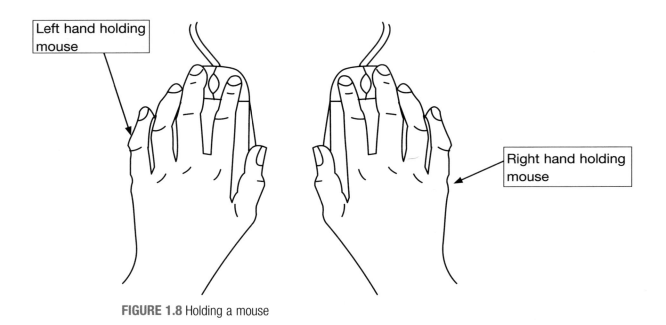

Left hand holding mouse

Right hand holding mouse

FIGURE 1.8 Holding a mouse

mouse to the left of the keyboard and can also change the button settings in the **Control Panel**.

Think of the mouse as an extension of your hand – you don't look at your hand when you use it, instead you feel what you are doing. When you use the mouse, you should look at the computer screen not at your hand.

MOUSE ACTION	DESCRIPTION
Point	Move the mouse on the mousemat until the pointer appears at the required position on the screen
Click	Press and release the **left** mouse button once
Double-Click	Quickly press the left mouse button **twice**, then release it.
Right-Click	Press the **right** mouse button once, a menu displays
Hover	Position the mouse pointer over an icon or menu item and pause, a toolbar **Tool tip** or a further menu item will appear (Figure 1.9). Save (Ctrl+S) **FIGURE 1.9** Save Tool tip in Microsoft Word

Mouse techniques

Note: unless otherwise instructed, always click using the left mouse button.

Check your understanding *Use a mouse*

Make sure that the computer is switched on and the desktop screen is displayed.

Hold the mouse

1 Place your hand over the mouse.

2 Use your thumb to hold the left side of the mouse and your little finger to hold the right side (left-handers reverse this instruction).

3 Position your forefinger on the left mouse button, but don't click the button!

Move the mouse

1 Still holding the mouse, look at the screen and move the mouse to the left slowly. Notice that the pointer on the screen moves to the left.

2 Move the mouse to the right slowly. Notice that the pointer moves to the right.

3 The mouse pointer on the screen moves in response to the direction that you move the mouse on the mousemat.

Select and deselect

1 Move the mouse pointer over the **My Computer** icon on the desktop screen. Click once on this icon, it becomes highlighted (different shade) – the icon has been selected.

2 Move the mouse pointer away from the **My Computer** icon to a blank part of the screen.

3 Click once – this deselects the **My Computer** icon, it is no longer highlighted.

Right-click

1 Move the mouse to a blank area on the desktop screen.

2 Right-click with the mouse.

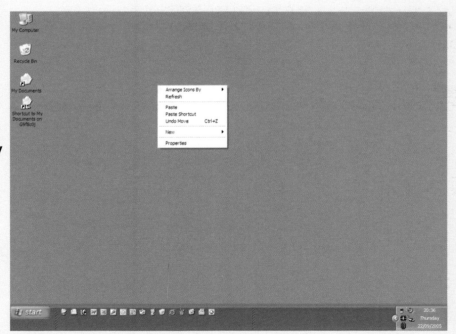

FIGURE 1.10 Right-click on the mouse to see a menu

3 A menu (list of items) is displayed when you right-click (Figure 1.10).

4 Click in a blank part of the desktop screen.

5 The menu disappears.

Mouse pointers

Windows uses different types of mouse pointer. The type of pointer displayed indicates what the computer is doing at the time.

POINTER	NAME	WHAT IT DOES
⬦	Arrow	Used to point and click at things
I	I-beam	Appears in a Word document, so you can click to place it between letters. Also referred to as a cursor
⧗	Busy	Usually looks like an hourglass. This shows that the computer is taking time to do something, wait until the busy sign finishes
↕ ↔ ⤡ ⤢	Resize	Drag to resize a window, changes depending on where it is placed. Can be diagonal, vertical or horizontal
✛	Move	Used to move pictures or objects around a page

Types of mouse pointer

The Start button

The **Start** `start` button is located at the bottom left of the desktop screen. This button can be used to start any program that is installed on the computer.

Check your understanding
Use the mouse to click the Start button

Make sure the computer is switched on and the desktop screen is displayed.

1 Hover the mouse over the **Start** button.

2 A **Tool tip, Click here to begin** ![Click here to begin tooltip], is displayed.

3 Click on **Start**.

4 The **Windows XP Start** menu appears.

5 Look at the programs on the **Start** menu. The contents of the **Start** menus shown in Figure 1.11 and Figure 1.12 may be different on your computer. The list on the left of the Start menu shows recently used programs. These will also vary between computers.

FIGURE 1.11 A Start menu

FIGURE 1.12 A different Start menu

6 Click anywhere on the desktop screen away from the **Start** menu to remove the **Start** menu from the screen (or click on the **Start** button again).

The keyboard

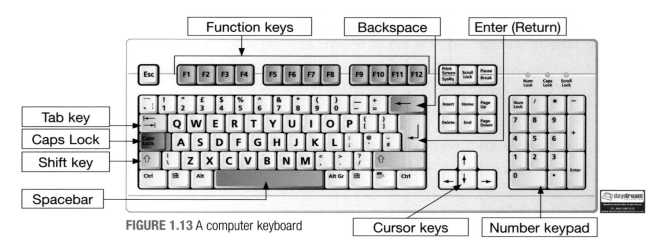

FIGURE 1.13 A computer keyboard

Some of the symbols and keys may be in a different place on the keyboard you are using.

▶▶ How to... *use the keyboard*

HOW TO...	ACTION
See where text will be entered	Look for the flashing straight line on the screen. Your text will be entered wherever this line is. This is the cursor (or I-beam)
Type one capital letter	Hold down the Shift key and press the required letter on the keyboard, then let go of the Shift key
Type word(s) in capital letters	Press down the Caps Lock to switch it on (a light may indicate that Caps Lock is on)
Type lower case letters	Check the Caps Lock is switched off. If not press down the Caps Lock key to turn it off
Insert a space between words	Press the Spacebar on the keyboard once
Delete a letter to the left of the cursor	Press the Backspace key
Delete a letter to the right of the cursor	Press the Delete key
Move to the next line	Press the Enter key
Move to the beginning of the line	Press the Home key
Move to the end of the line	Press the End key
Move to the beginning of the document	Press the Ctrl and Home keys at the same time
Move to the end of the document	Press the Ctrl and End keys at the same time
Create a new paragraph	Press Enter twice at the end of a paragraph. This will display one clear line space between two paragraphs

Using the keyboard

Symbols on the keyboard

- To enter a symbol which appears on the top half of a key on the keyboard, hold the **Shift** key down, press the key on the keyboard while still holding the **Shift** key, then let go of the **Shift** key.
- To enter a symbol which appears on the lower half of a key, tap that key.

SYMBOL	DESCRIPTION
.	Full stop
,	Comma
:	Colon
;	Semi-colon
(	Opening bracket
)	Closing bracket
=	Equals sign
_	Underscore – hold down the **Shift** key to enter an underscore (underscore is different from hyphen/dash)
?	Question mark
"	Speech marks
' ' '	Single quote mark and apostrophe
-	Hyphen or dash
+	Plus sign
*	Star (asterisk)
/	Forward slash
\	Back slash
@	At symbol
&	Ampersand (and)
!	Exclamation mark
£	Pound sign
#	Hash
%	Percentage sign
<	Less than symbol
>	Greater than symbol

Keyboard symbols

To practise using the keyboard, you will use Microsoft Word 2003.

▶▶ How to... Start Microsoft Word 2003

Make sure that the computer is switched on and the desktop screen is displayed.

1 Click on **Start**.

2 The **Windows XP Start** menu is displayed (Figure 1.14).

3 Click on **All Programs**.

4 The **All Programs** menu appears.

5 Click on **Microsoft Office**.

6 A list of Microsoft Office programs is displayed.

7 Click on **Microsoft Office Word 2003**.

8 A blank Microsoft Word document is displayed (Figure 1.15).

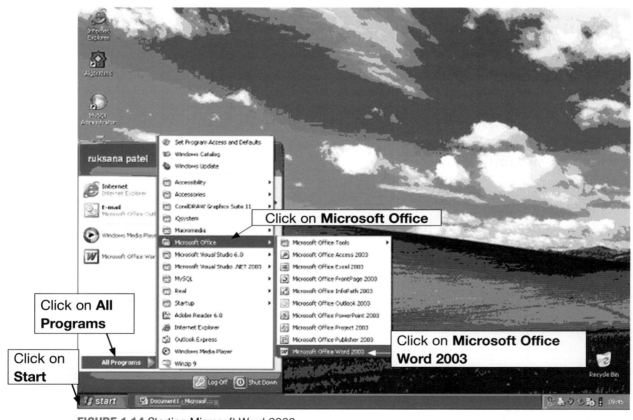

FIGURE 1.14 Starting Microsoft Word 2003

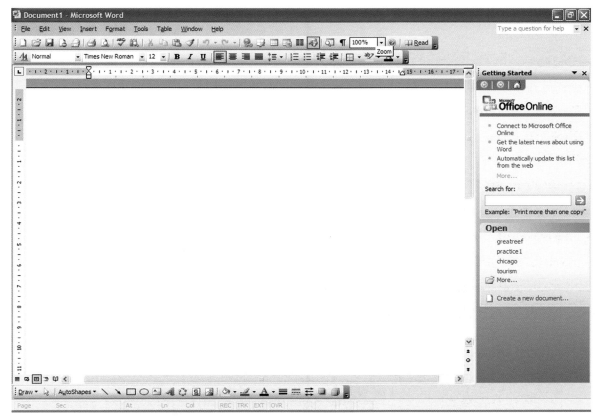

FIGURE 1.15 A blank Microsoft Word document

The Microsoft Word window will be covered in more detail in Chapter 2 (see page 45). For now you are simply going to use this document to practise your keyboard skills.

Check your understanding *Use the keyboard*

Refer to 'How to... Use the Keyboard' on page 16.

1 A blank Microsoft Word document should be open on your screen.

2 In the document, look for the flashing vertical line in the top left of the screen. This is the **cursor**. It indicates the position where text will be entered.

Enter text

Ignore any errors that you may make for the moment!

1 Practise using the keyboard by pressing some of the alphabet keys.

2 Press the **Enter** key to start a new line.

3 Press the **Shift** key, keep it held down and enter the first letter of your first name.

4 Let go of the **Shift** key and enter the rest of your first name.

5 Press the **Spacebar.**

6 Hold the **Shift** key, keep it held down and enter the first letter of your last name.

7 Let go of the **Shift** key and enter the rest of your last name.

8 Press the **Enter** key.

9 Press the **Caps Lock** key to switch it on, and enter the name of the town/city that you live in.

10 Press the **Enter** key twice.

Enter numbers

1 Enter some numbers by pressing the number keys above the alphabet keys.

2 Press the **Num Lock** key to switch the number keypad on.

3 Enter some numbers using the number keypad.

4 Press the **Enter** key twice.

Enter symbols

Refer to the **Keyboard symbols** chart on page 17.

1 Hold down the **Shift** key and enter the symbols displayed above the alphabet keys. Let go of the Shift key.

2 Enter the symbols that appear on other parts of the keyboard, e.g. / (forward slash), = (equals sign).

3 Use the **Shift** key and enter the symbols displayed on the top half of a key, e.g. £ (pound sign), + (plus sign).

4 Practise typing the commonly used symbols: , (comma) . (full stop) : (colon) ; (semi-colon) ? (question mark).

Delete text

1 Click with your mouse in the top row of text in your document.

2 Press the **Delete** key. This deletes text to the **right** of the cursor.

3 Click with your mouse at the end of the last line in your document.

4 Press the **Backspace** key. This deletes text to the **left** of the cursor.

Now, try moving around the page. Refer to 'How to... Use the keyboard' on page 16 to help you do this.

Close and exit a Word document without saving

As the Word document you have been working on is only a practice document, you do not need to save it.

▶▶ How to... *close a document without saving*

1 In your Word document, move the mouse to the red cross ☒ in the top right corner of the screen.

2 Click on ☒.

3 A **Microsoft Office Word** dialogue box is displayed.

4 Click on **No** (Figure 1.16).

5 The Word document closes and the desktop screen is displayed.

Shutting down the computer

When you have finished using the computer you should:

○ *close any files that are open*

○ *then close all programs*

○ *and, finally, shut down the operating system (or log off).*

The shut down process may vary slightly on different computer systems, but the basic process is similar. You will need to either shut down the computer or turn off the computer.

> **Microsoft Office Word** ☒
>
> ⚠ Do you want to save the changes to Document1?
>
> [Yes]   [No]   [Cancel]

FIGURE 1.16 Click on **No**.

▶▶ How to... *shut down the computer*

1 In the desktop screen, click on **Start**.

2 The **Windows XP Start** menu is displayed.

3 Click on **Shut Down** (Figure 1.17).

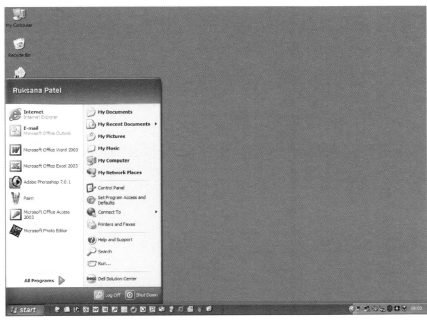

FIGURE 1.17 The **Shut Down** button in the **Start** menu

4 The **Shut Down Windows** dialogue box is displayed (Figure 1.18).

5 In the **What do you want the computer to do?** box, click on the drop-down arrow and select **Shut down**.

6 Click on **OK**.

7 The computer will switch off.

8 Switch off the monitor if required.

▶▶ How to... *turn off the computer*

1 In the desktop screen, click on **Start**.

2 The **Start** menu is displayed.

3 Click on **Turn Off Computer** (Figure 1.19).

4 The **Turn off computer** dialogue box is displayed (Figure 1.20).

5 Click on **Turn Off**.

6 The computer will shut down.

7 Switch off the monitor if required.

FIGURE 1.18 Shut Down Windows dialogue box

FIGURE 1.19 Turn Off Computer button

TIP!

Never press the on/off button on the computer or the plug at the electric wall socket if the desktop screen is displayed. Always close all open windows and shut down or log off your computer correctly.

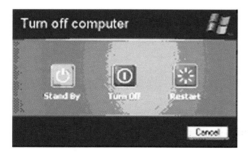

FIGURE 1.20 Turn off computer dialogue box

Check your understanding *Shut down the computer*

1 Close any open windows.

2 Shut down (or turn off) your computer.

On your computer you may be required to log off instead of shut down (or turn off).

ASSESS YOUR SKILLS – Use a computer

By working through Section 1 you will have learnt the skills below. Read each item to help you decide how confident you feel about each skill.

identify computer hardware:
- CPU box
- Monitor
- Keyboard
- Mouse
- Printer

- understand basic health and safety practices when using a computer

- start up a computer

- switch on a monitor (if required)

- use a password

- understand the desktop

- identify the **Start** button

- identify the **Taskbar**

- use a mouse

- use the keyboard

- shut down (or turn off) the computer.

If you feel you need more practice on any of the skills above, go back and work through the skill(s) again.

If you feel confident, move on to Section 2.

Files for this chapter

To work through the tasks in Section 2, you will need the files from the folder called **files_chapter1,** which you will find on the CD-ROM provided with this book. Copy this folder into your user area before you begin.

▶▶ How to... *copy the folder files_chapter1 from the CD-ROM*

Make sure the computer is switched on and the desktop screen is displayed.

1 Insert the CD-ROM into the CD-ROM drive of the computer.

2 Close any windows that may be open.

3 In the desktop, double-click on the **My Computer** icon.

4 The **My Computer** window is displayed.

5 Under **Devices with Removable Storage**, double-click on the **CD Drive** icon to view the contents of the CD-ROM.

6 A window displaying the contents of the CD appears.

7 Double-click on the **L1_Unit1_FM+DP** folder. Double-click on the **Source files** folder.

8 The **Source files** window is displayed (Figure 1.21).

9 Click on the folder **files_chapter1**.

10 The folder will be highlighted (usually blue).

11 In the **File and Folder Tasks** box, click on **Copy this folder**.

12 A **Copy Items** dialogue box is displayed (Figure 1.22).

13 Click on the user area where you want to copy the folder **files_chapter1**.

14 Click on **Copy**.

15 The folder **files_chapter1** will be copied to your user area.

16 It is advisable to copy and paste a second copy to another folder in your user area as backup.

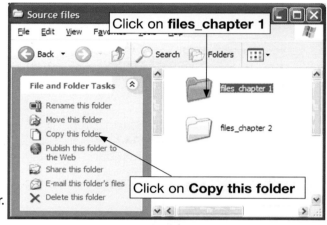

FIGURE 1.21 The Source files window

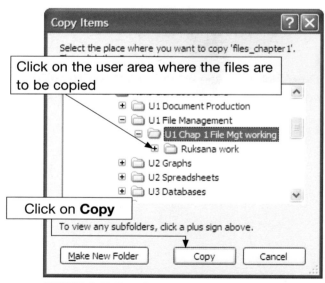

FIGURE 1.22 Copy Items dialogue box

Read only files

The files provided are set to 'read only'. After you have copied the files to your user area, remove the 'read only' properties as follows:

1 In your user area, right-click on the folder **files_chapter1**.

2 A menu appears.

3 Click on **Properties**.

4 A **Properties** dialogue box is displayed.

5 Click in the **Read-only** box to remove the tick/square (the box should be empty).

6 Click on **Apply**.

7 A **Confirm Attribute Changes** dialogue box is displayed (Figure 1.23).

8 Select **Apply changes to this folder, subfolders and files** by clicking in the second button.

9 Click on **OK**.

10 The **Confirm Attribute Changes** dialogue box closes.

11 Click on **OK** to close the **Properties** dialogue box.

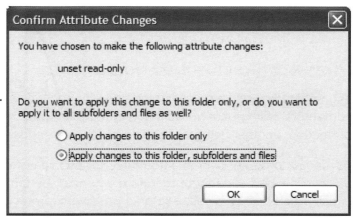

FIGURE 1.23 Confirm Attribute Changes dialogue box

2: File management

LEARNING OUTCOMES

In this section you will learn how to:

- create and name folders
- create and name subfolders
- rename files
- rename folders
- delete files
- delete folders
- move files
- copy files
- produce screen prints to show folder contents
- save screen prints.

▶▶ How to... recognise folder and file icons

ICON	WHAT IT LOOKS LIKE
Folder	
Word file	
Text file	
Image file (image file icons may vary on your computer)	

Folder and file icons

Password-protected documents

You should always be aware of the need for security when using computers. Using passwords to log in to a computer is one method of protection, another is to password-protect confidential documents.

On some computer systems you may not be prompted to enter a password when you log in; therefore you must be familiar with using passwords at other times, e.g. on a password-protected file, or folder, or a drive on the computer.

▶▶ How to... use a password on a password-protected drive/folder/file (optional)

Make sure your computer is switched on.

1 Go to the password-protected drive, file or folder.

2 Double-click on the drive, file or folder to open it.

3 You will be prompted to enter a password in the **Password** dialogue box (Figure 1.24).

4 Make sure no one can see your keyboard when you enter the password.

5 Enter the password. Use upper or lower case correctly.

6 The password appears in the box as dots for security.

7 Click on **OK**.

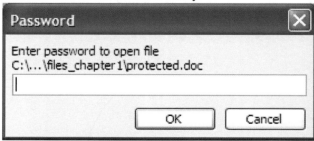

FIGURE 1.24 Password dialogue box

What does it mean?

User area
A user area is the workspace on a computer where you save your files.
One example of a user area is a folder called **My Documents**, Windows XP creates this area. In a centre, you may be given a work area on a network. This area may have a drive name, e.g. G drive. Alternatively, you may save your work on a floppy disk, which is usually the A drive. On your own personal computer, your user area may be the C drive.

What does it mean?

File
A file is a collection of saved data. To create a word-processed file, a blank document is opened, data is entered into this document, the document is saved with a particular name, and is then referred to as a file. Files may be picture files, spreadsheet files, text files, etc.

What does it mean?

Folder
A folder is a storage area within a user area in which files can be saved. A folder may contain files and other folders (called subfolders). Creating folders with suitable names allows computer files to be stored logically. This is like organising a filing cabinet by having separate drawers, with related files in each draw. Within each drawer, files can be organised further.

1 Make sure your computer is switched on and go to your user area.

2 Double-click on the folder **files_chapter1**.

3 The contents of the **files_chapter1** folder are displayed.

4 Look for a Microsoft Word document called **protected**.

5 To open the file, double-click on it.

6 You will be prompted to enter a password.

7 Enter the password **UseAPc1**. You must use upper or lower case correctly because passwords are case sensitive.

8 Click on **OK** to open the file.

9 To close the file, click on the **red cross** ⊠ in the top right corner of the Word window.

My Computer window

Windows gets its name from the fact that everything you do on a computer is shown in a window. All windows are similar.

○ There is the **Title bar** across the top (Figure 1.25).

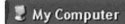

FIGURE 1.25 Title bar

○ There are three Window control buttons in the top right corner:
- • *Minimise*
- • *Maximise*
- • *Close* ⊠
○ If a window fills the screen, the centre button is **Restore Down** . Click on **Restore Down** to make the window smaller.

All the tasks about working with files and folders should be done through the **My Computer** window.

1 Make sure that the computer is switched on and the desktop screen is displayed.

2 In the Windows desktop, double-click on **My Computer**  .

3 The **My Computer** window is displayed.

4 Look at the examples of **My Computer** windows in Figure 1.26 and Figure 1.27 and compare them with the window on your screen – your screen may have fewer/more icons.

Menu bar | Toolbar

Title bar | Window control buttons

FIGURE 1.26 My Computer window

FIGURE 1.27 My Computer window

5 In the **My Computer** window, identify your user area.

6 Double-click on the relevant icon (or on My Documents) to go to your user area.

7 Your user area is displayed.

8 Find the folder **files_chapter1** which you copied to your user area in an earlier task.

9 Double-click on the **files_chapter1** files_chapter1 icon to view the contents of this folder.

10 The **files_chapter1** window is displayed (Figure 1.28).

11 Remain in the **files_chapter1** window.

FIGURE 1.28 The files_chapter1 window

Viewing folder contents

- *To view the contents of a folder, double-click on the folder icon. This displays any subfolders and/or files contained within the folder.*

- *Double-clicking on a file icon opens the file in the software that the file was created in. If you accidentally open a file, click on* [X] *at the top right of the window to close it.*

Check your understanding
View folder contents for files_chapter1

1 In the **files_chapter1** window, double-click on the folder icon called **try**.

2 The **try** folder is displayed.

3 Inside the **try** folder is one image file icon called **monitor**.

4 Click on **Back** | ⟵ Back .

5 You will be returned to the **files_chapter1** window.

6 Double-click on the folder icon called **task1**.

7 A subfolder called **t1files** and three text file icons called **autumn, spring, summer** are displayed.

8 Double-click on the **t1files** folder icon.

9 The subfolder **t1files** is displayed. The subfolder contains an image file called **daffy** and a text file called **winter**.

10 Click on **Back**.

11 You will be returned to the **task1** folder.

12 Click on **Back** again.

13 This takes you back to the **files_chapter1** folder.

14 Click on [X] in the top corner of the **My Computer** window to close the window.

Creating and naming folders

▶▶ How to... *create and name a folder*

1 On the desktop, double-click on the **My Computer** icon.

2 The **My Computer** window is displayed.

3 Double-click on the icon for your user area (or click on **My Documents** to find your user area).

4 Your user area is displayed.

5 In the **File and Folder Tasks** box, click on **Make a new folder** (Figure 1.29).

6 A **New Folder** icon is displayed (Figure 1.30). The words **New Folder** are highlighted.

7 Press the **Backspace** key to delete the highlighted words **New Folder**.

8 Enter the required folder name (Figure 1.31).

9 Press the **Enter** key.

10 Your new folder is created.

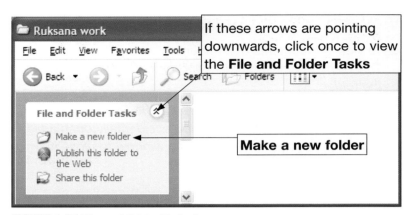

If these arrows are pointing downwards, click once to view the **File and Folder Tasks**

Make a new folder

FIGURE 1.29 File and Folder Tasks box

A New Folder is displayed

FIGURE 1.30 Creating a New Folder

TIP!

If the words **New Folder** are no longer highlighted or there is no flashing cursor, you may have accidentally pressed a key on the keyboard. If so, follow the instructions for 'How to... Rename a Folder' on page 33.

Enter the required folder name

FIGURE 1.31 Naming a folder

Check your understanding *Create and name a folder*

1 Open your user area and create a new folder.

2 Name this folder **work**.

3 Remain in your user area.

Creating and naming subfolders

▶▶ How to... *create a subfolder*

1 In the **My Computer** window, in your user area, double-click on the folder icon in which you want to create a subfolder.

2 The folder contents are displayed (the folder may be empty).

3 In the **File and Folder Tasks** box, click on **Make a new folder**.

4 A **New Folder** icon is displayed. This will be your subfolder.

5 Press the **Backspace** key to delete the highlighted words **New Folder**.

6 Enter the required subfolder name.

7 Press the **Enter** key.

8 Your new subfolder is created (Figure 1.32).

FIGURE 1.32 Creating a subfolder

Check your understanding   *Create and name a subfolder*

1 In your user area, create a subfolder in the folder **work**.

2 Name this subfolder **chapter1**.

3 Click on ☒ to close the folder **work** and return to your user area.

File extensions

Before you begin the section on renaming a file, you will need to check whether file extensions are displayed on your computer.

○ *In your user area, open the folder files_chapter1.*

○ *Are file extensions displayed after the filename? In Figure 1.33 a filename is shown with an extension, whereas in Figure 1.34 the filename has no extension.*

FIGURE 1.33 Filename with extension

FIGURE 1.34 Filename with no extension

If file extensions are displayed on your computer, you will need to remove them before starting 'How to... rename a file'.

▶▶ How to...   *remove the display of file extensions*

1 In the folder **files_chapter1**, click on the **Tools** menu.

2 From the menu, select **Folder Options**.

3 The **Folder Options** dialogue box is displayed.

4 To open the **View** option, click on the **View** tab (Figure 1.35).

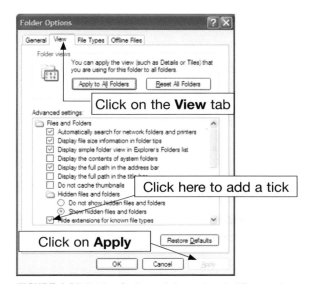

FIGURE 1.35 Folder Options dialogue box in View option

5 Click in the **Hide extensions for known file types** box to add a tick.

6 Click on **Apply**.

7 Click on **OK**.

Renaming files

▶▶ How to... *rename a file*

1 In the **My Computer** window, in your user area, double-click on the folder containing the file to be renamed.

2 The folder opens.

3 Click on the file to be renamed.

4 The file is highlighted.

5 In the **File and Folder Tasks** box, click on **Rename this file** (Figure 1.36).

6 Press the **Backspace** key to delete the existing name.

7 Enter the new filename (Figure 1.37).

8 Press the **Enter** key.

9 The file is renamed.

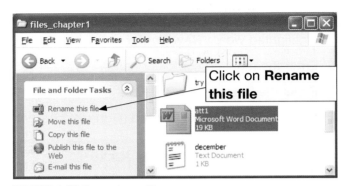

FIGURE 1.36 Renaming a file

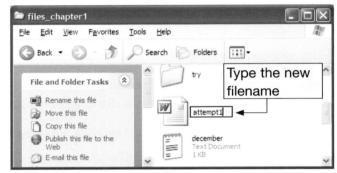

FIGURE 1.37 Typing the new filename

Check your understanding *Rename a file*

1 In your user area, double-click on the folder **files_chapter1** to open it.

2 The folder opens.

3 Find the file called **att1**.

4 Rename this file **attempt1**.

5 Remain in your user area.

Renaming folders and subfolders

You may want to change the name of an existing folder or subfolder.

▶▶ How to... *rename a folder or subfolder*

1 In the **My Computer** window, in your user area, click on the folder to be renamed.

2 The folder is highlighted (usually blue).

3 In the **File and Folder Tasks** box, click on **Rename this folder** (Figure 1.38).

4 Press the **Backspace** key to delete the existing name.

5 Enter the new folder name (Figure 1.39).

6 Press the **Enter** key.

7 The folder is renamed.

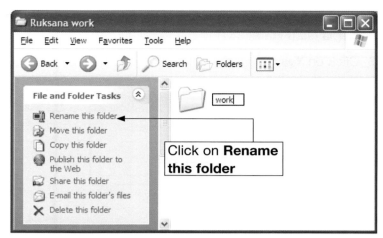

Click on **Rename this folder**

FIGURE 1.38 Renaming a folder

Enter the new folder name

FIGURE 1.39 Typing the new folder name

Check your understanding *Rename a folder*

1 In your user area, rename the folder **work** to **ictskills**.

2 Remain in your user area.

Deleting files and folders

▶▶ How to... *delete a file*

1 In the **My Computer** window, in your user area, double-click on the folder containing the file to be deleted.

2 The folder opens.

3 Click on the file to be deleted.

4 The file is highlighted.

5 In the **File and Folder Tasks** box, click on **Delete this file** (Figure 1.40).

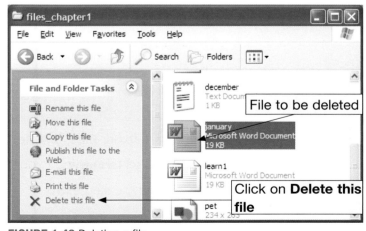

File to be deleted

Click on **Delete this file**

FIGURE 1.40 Deleting a file

6 A **Confirm File Delete** dialogue box is displayed (Figure 1.41).

7 Click on **Yes**. The file is deleted.

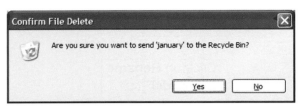

FIGURE 1.41 Confirm File Delete dialogue box

▶▶ How to... *delete a folder*

1 In the **My Computer** window, in your user area, click on the folder to be deleted.

2 The folder is highlighted.

3 In the **File and Folder Tasks** box, click on **Delete this folder** (Figure 1.42).

4 A **Confirm Folder Delete** dialogue box is displayed (Figure 1.43).

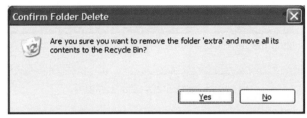

FIGURE 1.43 Confirm Folder Delete dialogue box

5 Click on **Yes**.

6 The folder is deleted.

TIP!

Here's a quick way to delete a file:

1 Click on the file to be deleted.

2 Press the **Delete** key.

3 A **Confirm File Delete** dialogue box is displayed.

4 Click on **Yes**.

TIP!

You can get back any files or folders accidentally deleted by going to the **Recycle Bin**:

1 On the desktop screen, double-click on the **Recycle Bin** icon.

2 Click on the file or folder icon that you had deleted.

3 Click on **Restore**.

4 The file or folder is returned to its original location.

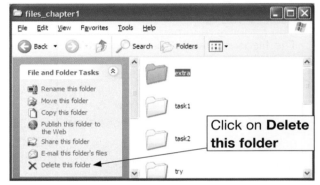

FIGURE 1.42 Deleting a folder

TIP!

Here's a quick way to delete a folder:

1 Click on the folder to be deleted.

2 Press **Delete key**.

3 A **Confirm Folder Delete** dialogue box is displayed.

4 Click on **Yes**.

Check your understanding *Delete a file and a folder*

1 In your user area, open the folder **files_chapter1**.

2 Find and delete the file called **january**.

3 Find and delete the subfolder called **extra**.

4 Remain in your user area.

Moving files and folders

▶▶ How to... *move a file*

1 In the **My Computer** window, in your user area, double-click on the folder containing the file to be moved.

2 The folder opens.

3 Click on the file to be moved.

4 In the **File and Folder Tasks** box, click on **Move this file** (Figure 1.44).

5 A **Move Items** dialogue box is displayed (Figure 1.45).

6 Click on the name of the folder in your user area where the file is to be moved.

7 Click on **Move**.

8 The file is moved to the new location.

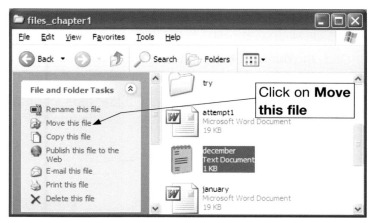

FIGURE 1.44 Moving a file

▶▶ How to... *move a folder*

1 In the **My Computer** window, in your user area, click on the folder to be moved.

2 In the **File and Folder Tasks** box, click on **Move this folder** (Figure 1.46).

3 A **Move Items** dialogue box is displayed.

4 Click on the name of the place where the folder is to be moved to.

5 Click on **Move**.

6 The folder is moved to the new location.

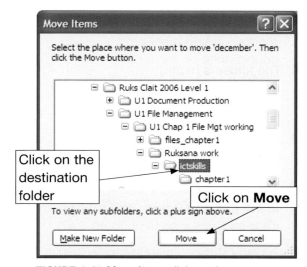

FIGURE 1.45 Move Items dialogue box

FIGURE 1.46 Moving a folder

Copying files

▶▶ How to... *copy a file*

1 In the **My Computer** window, in your user area, double-click on the folder containing the file to be copied. The folder contents will be displayed.

2 Click on the file you want to copy.

3 The file is highlighted.

4 In the **File and Folder Tasks** box, click on **Copy this file** (Figure 1.47).

5 A **Copy Items** dialogue box is displayed.

6 Click on the folder name in your user area where the file is to be copied (Figure 1.48).

7 Click on **Copy**.

8 The file is copied into the new folder.

FIGURE 1.47 Copying a file

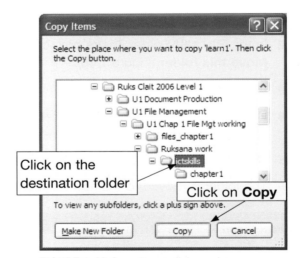

FIGURE 1.48 Copy Items dialogue box

Taking screen prints

Find the **Print Screen** key on your keyboard (Figure 1.49). This may be displayed as **Print Screen** or **Prt SC** or **Prnt Scrn** or similar. Now, find the **Alt** key on your keyboard.

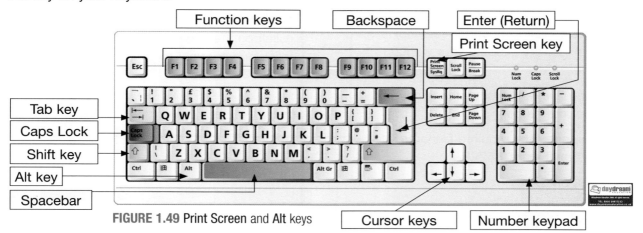

FIGURE 1.49 Print Screen and Alt keys

▶▶ How to... take a screen print to show the contents of a folder

1 From the **My Computer** window, go to your user area.

2 To open the folder that you want to take a screen print of, double-click on it.

3 On the keyboard, press **Alt** and **Print Screen** at the same time.

4 You have taken a screen print, but you will not see anything change on your screen.

5 Next, you will need to paste the screen print into a Word document.

6 Open a blank Word document. (If you need reminding how to open a Microsoft Word document, see page 18.)

7 In the document, enter your **name** and **centre number**.

8 Press **Enter**.

9 Click on the **Paste** icon.

10 The screen print is pasted into the Word document.

11 Now you will need to save the screen print.

▶▶ How to... save the screen print

1 In your Word document, click on the **File** menu.

2 The **File** menu is displayed.

3 Click on **Save** (Figure 1.50).

> **TIP!**
>
> If you press **Print Screen** only, this takes a screenshot of the whole screen instead of just the window.

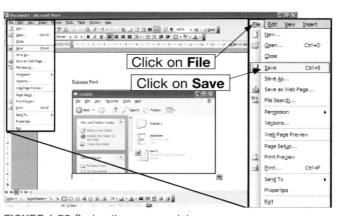

FIGURE 1.50 Saving the screen print

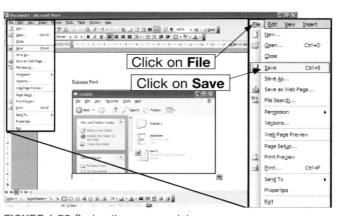

4 A **Save As** dialogue box is displayed (Figure 1.51).

5 Click on the **down arrow** to the right of the **Save** in box, then click on your user area.

6 Double-click to open the folder(s) in your user area, locate your working folder.

7 In the **File name** box, delete any text (e.g. your name).

8 Then enter the required filename into the box (Figure 1.52).

9 Click on **Save**.

10 The screen print is saved in your user area and the **Save As** dialogue box closes.

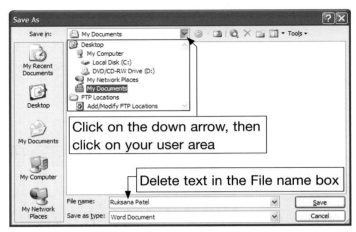

FIGURE 1.51 Save As dialogue box

▶▶ How to... *print a screen print*

1 In your Word document, click on the **Print** icon on the toolbar.

2 Your screen print will be printed.

3 To close the document, click on the red **Close** ☒ icon on the top right of the window. You will be returned to your user area.

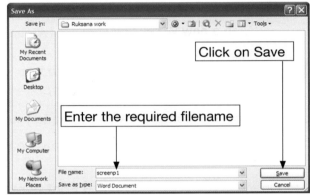

FIGURE 1.52 Enter the required filename

Check your understanding   *Take a screen print of your folder*

1 In your user area, open the folder **ictskills**.

2 Take a screen print of the contents of this folder.

3 Open a new Word document.

4 Enter your name in this document.

5 Paste the screen print into the Word document.

6 Save the Word document in your user area using the filename **screenp1**.

7 Print the file **screenp1**.

8 Close the file **screenp1** and exit Word.

9 Your screen print should display the contents of the **ictskills** folder as shown in Figure 1.53.

10 Remain in your user area.

Ruksana Patel

FIGURE 1.53 Your screen print of the **ictskills** folder should look similar to this

▶▶ How to... take a screen print of a subfolder

Repeat all the guidelines in *How to... take a screen print to show the contents of a folder, How to... print a screen print,* and *How to... save a screen print.*

▶▶ How to... close the My Computer window

○ Click on the Close ⊠ icon at the top right of the **My Computer** window.

Check your understanding *Take a screen print of a subfolder*

1 In your user area, open the subfolder **chapter1** (which is in the **ictskills** folder).

2 Take a screen print of the contents of this folder.

3 Open a new Word document.

4 Enter your **name** and **centre number** in this document.

5 Paste the screen print into the document.

6 Save the Word document into your user area using the filename **screenp2**.

7 Print the file **screenp2**.

8 Close the file **screenp2** and exit Word.

9 Your screen print should display the contents of the **chapter1** subfolder as shown in Figure 1.54.

10 Close the **My Computer** window.

FIGURE 1.54 Your screen print of the **chapter1** subfolder should look similar to this

ASSESS YOUR SKILLS – File management

By working through Section 2 you will have learnt the skills below. Read each item to help you decide how confident you feel about each skill.

- recognise file and folder icons
- create and name a folder
- create and name a subfolder
- change the display so that file extensions are not displayed (optional)
- rename a file
- rename a folder
- delete a file
- delete a folder
- move a file
- copy a file
- take a screen print to display the contents of folders
- start Word (and enter text)
- paste a screen print into Word
- save a screen print
- print a screen print
- close and exit Word
- close the **My Computer** window.

If you think you need more practice on any of the skills above, go back and work through the skill(s) again.

If you feel confident, move on to Chapter 2. You may wish to work through Build-up task 1 – File management now.

UNIT 1: File management and e-document production

In the second part of Unit 1, you will produce a word-processed document and make changes to a document that is provided.

You will use a software program, **Microsoft Office Word 2003**, which is part of Microsoft Office and which will help you to create, format and update documents easily. We will refer to it as Word from now on.

This chapter is divided into two sections:

- ○ *in Section 1, you will learn how to create a new document*
- ○ *in Section 2, you will learn how to edit (make changes to) a document.*

A CD-ROM accompanies this book. On it are the files that you will need to use for the tasks for editing a document. Instructions for copying the files are provided on page 72. The solutions for all the tasks can be found in a folder called **worked_copies_unit1**.

> *Note:* There are many ways of performing the skills covered in this book. This book provides How to… guidelines that are easily understood by learners.

1: Create a new document

LEARNING OUTCOMES

In this section you will learn how to:

- ○ start Word
- ○ identify the different parts of Word
- ○ set the page orientation
- ○ set the margins
- ○ set the line spacing
- ○ enter text, numbers and symbols
- ○ save a new document
- ○ set the text alignment
- ○ set the font size
- ○ set the font type
- ○ use spell check
- ○ save an existing document
- ○ use the **Show/Hide** tool
- ○ print a document
- ○ use headers and footers
- ○ use automatic fields in headers/footers
- ○ close a document and exit Word.

Preparing your work area

Now that you have learned to create folders and subfolders, it is advisable to prepare your user area so that you can keep your files organised.

An example of a folder structure for all units is shown in Figure 1.59. The main folder in **My Documents** is called **Ruks Clait 2006 Level 1**. Within this folder are subfolders for each of the units.

You may not need to create as many folders or you may prefer to create a folder for a unit when you begin a new unit or a new chapter.

For Unit 1, two subfolders have been created – one for Chapter 1 File management and another for Chapter 2 Document production.

Within each unit subfolder, there are further subfolders.

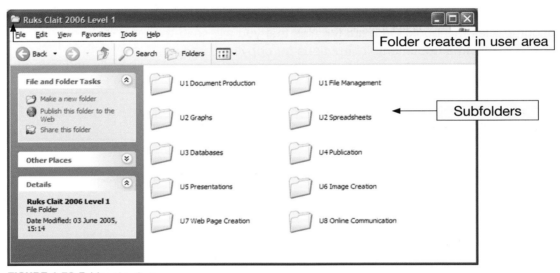

FIGURE 1.59 Folder structure

For example in the **U1 Document Production** subfolder, the four subfolders are:

- **U1 Chap 2 WP working** – *this is the working folder in which all files will be saved*
- **files_chapter2** – *the source files from the CD-ROM have been copied into this folder*
- **worked_copies_unit1** – *this folder has also been copied from the CD-ROM*
- **Copy of files_chapter2** – *this comprises a copy of the folder containing the source files.*

These subfolders are shown in Figure 1.60.

FIGURE 1.60 Subfolders in the **U1 Document Production** subfolder

What is word processing?

Word processing is using a computer to create and edit documents. To perform word processing, you need a computer and a word processing program such as Microsoft Word.

Word processing enables you to create a document, save it, display it on a screen, make changes to it and print it.

The advantage of word processing is that you can make changes to a document as many times as you want without retyping the entire document. You can correct, delete, insert, move and format text very easily. When you have made all the changes you want, you can print the file.

A document appears on the screen exactly as it will look when printed – this is known as WYSIWYG (What You See Is What You Get).

You will learn various word processing skills and techniques as you work through this chapter.

Word processing terms and actions will be explained throughout the chapter.

To remind yourself of the different mouse techniques, see Chapter 1, page 12.

Now, using the skills you learned in Chapter 1, switch on your computer and log in.

What does it mean?

User area
A user area is the workspace on a computer where you save your files.

Starting Word

▶▶ How to... *start Microsoft Word 2003*

1 On the desktop screen, click on **Start**.

2 The **Windows XP Start** menu is displayed (Figure 1.61).

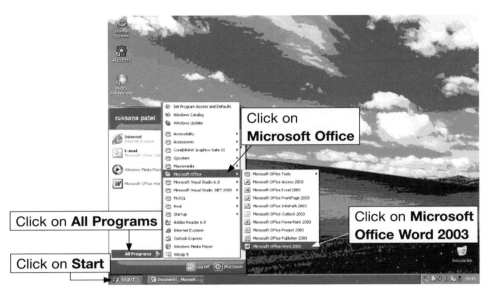

FIGURE 1.61 Starting Microsoft Office Word 2003

3 Click on **All Programs**.

4 The **All Programs** menu appears.

5 Click on **Microsoft Office**.

6 A list of Microsoft Office programs is displayed.

7 Click on **Microsoft Office Word 2003**.

8 A blank Microsoft Word document is displayed.

A quicker way to start Word is to double-click on the Word icon on the desktop (if a shortcut has been created) or to single-click on the Word icon on the **Taskbar** (if a shortcut has been created) (Figure 1.62).

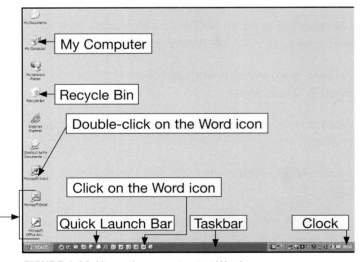

FIGURE 1.62 Alternative ways to start Word

1 Open Word, either through the Start menu or by using a shortcut icon.

2 A new blank document called **Document1** is displayed.

3 Keep this document open.

Getting familiar with the Word window

Word 2003 may open with the **Task Pane** on the right (Figure 1.63). Click on the black cross to close the **Task Pane**.

Take a few minutes to learn about the different parts of the Word window (Figure 1.64).

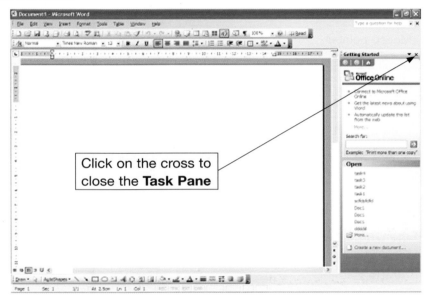

Click on the cross to close the **Task Pane**

FIGURE 1.63 The Task Pane

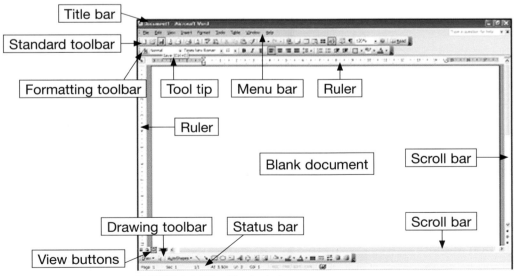

Title bar

Standard toolbar

Formatting toolbar | Tool tip | Menu bar | Ruler

Ruler

Blank document | Scroll bar

Drawing toolbar | Status bar | Scroll bar

View buttons

FIGURE 1.64 The Word window

PART OF WINDOW	DESCRIPTION
Title bar	Displays the title of the current document
Menu bar	A list of options; click on a menu item to see the drop-down menu
Ruler	Vertical and horizontal rulers can be displayed to help you view the page
Standard toolbar	Includes icons for commonly used tasks, e.g. save, print
Formatting toolbar	Includes icons for commonly used formatting, e.g. bold, centre
Tool tip	When the mouse is hovered on a toolbar button, a Tool tip displays showing the name of the button
Blank document	The main document window, where text is entered
Cursor	The position where text will be entered
Mouse pointer	Displays the position of the mouse on screen
Scroll bar	Allows you to scroll up/down or left/right to view the document
View buttons	Different ways of viewing the Word screen. The view in Figure 1.64 is Print Layout View which displays the page centrally with both scroll bars
Drawing toolbar	Includes icons for common drawing items, e.g. text box, arrow
Status bar	Displays the status of the current document, e.g. number of pages, current page, line

The Word window

Getting familiar with Word

If the **Office Assistant** icon is visible in a Word document, right-click on it. A menu is displayed. Click on **Hide** to remove the Office Assistant from the screen.

▶▶ How to... *use Word menus*

1 In your Word document, look for the **Menu bar** (Figure 1.65).

2 Click on **File**.

3 A menu (list) drops down with further choices (Figure 1.66).

4 At first, the whole menu may not display, but if you leave it open for a few seconds it displays in full.

5 Another way to display the full menu is to click on the chevrons ⬇ button at the bottom of the menu as soon as the menu drops down.

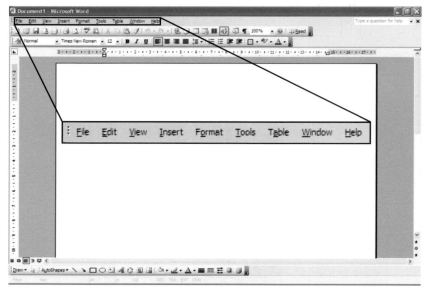

FIGURE 1.65 The **Menu** bar

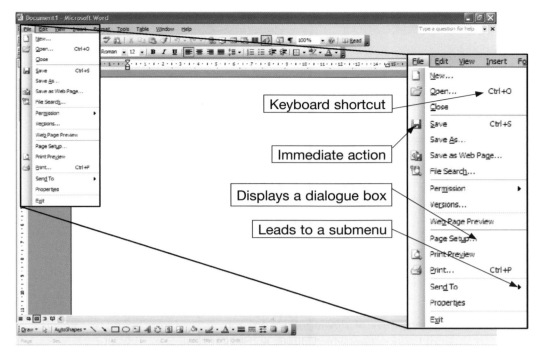

FIGURE 1.66 The File Menu

6 Click in the white area of your document (away from the menu) or click on **File** in the **Menu bar** to close the menu.

7 Click on the **Edit** menu.

8 Notice how some options are **ghosted** (paler grey) (Figure 1.67). This means that these options are not available at the moment.

9 Close the **Edit** menu.

The Toolbar buttons

In your Word document, move the mouse over each **Toolbar** button and pause; a **Tool tip** displays, showing the name of the button. In this book, we will refer to a **Toolbar** button as an icon.

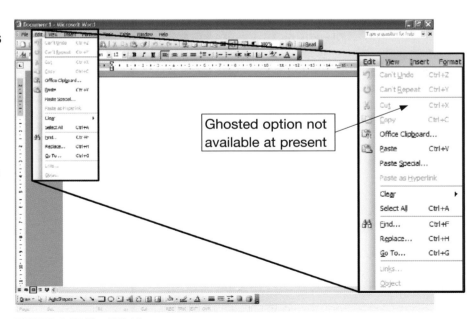

FIGURE 1.67 The Edit Menu

Making the Word window clearer

The Task Pane

Word 2003 opens with the **Task Pane** on the right of the screen (Figure 1.68). You are advised to close the **Task Pane** so that the screen is clearer (optional).

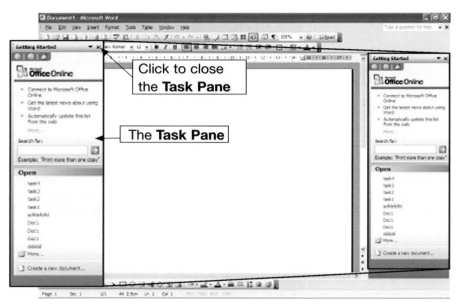

FIGURE 1.68 Closing the Task Pane

You can either click on the black cross just above the **Task Pane** to close it every time you start Word, or set the option to close the **Task Pane** so that it does not display every time you start Word.

▶▶ How to... set the option to close the Task Pane (optional)

1. In your Word document, click on **Tools** (Figure 1.69).

2. From the **Tools** menu, click on **Options**.

3. The **Options** dialogue box is displayed.

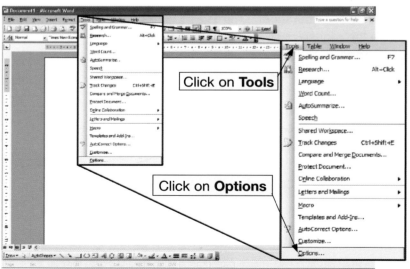

FIGURE 1.69 The Tools menu

4 Click on the **View** tab to select it (Figure 1.70).

5 Click in the **Startup Task Pane** box to remove the tick.

6 Click on **OK**.

7 The **Task Pane** will no longer display every time you start Word.

Standard and Formatting toolbars

Look at your Word document. Are the **Standard** and **Formatting toolbars** on the same row as shown in Figure 1.71?

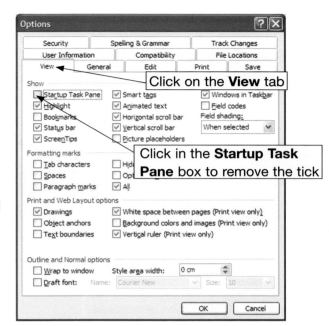

FIGURE 1.70 **Options** dialogue box with **View** option selected

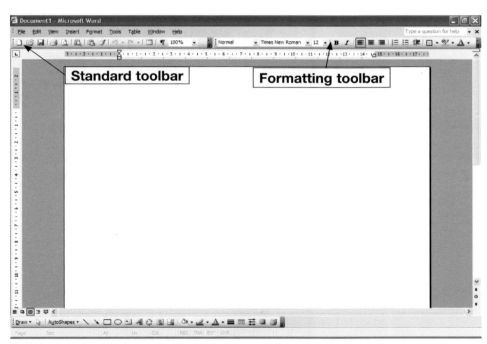

FIGURE 1.71 Standard and Formatting toolbars on the same row

If so, it is helpful to display them on two rows so that you can see all the icons on both toolbars

▶▶ How to... *display the Standard and Formatting toolbars on two rows (optional)*

1 In your Word document, click on the **Toolbar Options** symbol at the right end of the **Standard toolbar**.

2 A menu is displayed (Figure 1.72).

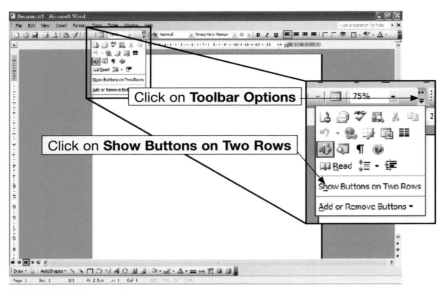

FIGURE 1.72 More buttons menu

3 Click on **Show Buttons on Two Rows**.

4 The **Standard** and **Formatting toolbars** will now display on two rows (Figure 1.73).

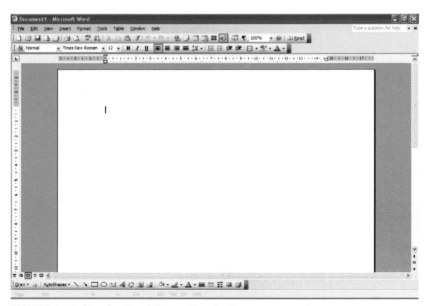

FIGURE 1.73 Standard and Formatting toolbars on separate rows

Page orientation

▶▶ How to... *set the page orientation*

1 In the **Menu bar**, click on **File**.

2 From the **File** menu, click on **Page Setup**.

3 The **Page Setup** dialogue box is displayed.

4 Select the **Margins** tab.

5 Click on **Portrait** or **Landscape** (Figure 1.74).

6 Click on **OK**.

7 The page will either be displayed portrait or landscape.

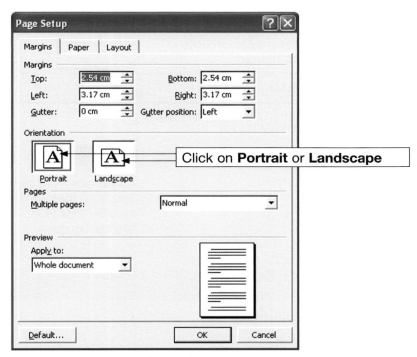

FIGURE 1.74 Page Setup dialogue box

What does it mean?

Page orientation
Page orientation refers to which way round the paper is displayed:
○ **Portrait** – an A4 sheet of paper displayed with the shortest sides at the top and bottom.
○ **Landscape** – an A4 sheet displayed with the longest sides at the top and bottom.

Check your understanding *Set the page orientation*

A blank document called Document1 should open when you start Word.

1 In Document1, set the page orientation to portrait.

Margins

Margins are the amount of white space from the edge of the paper to the text on the page. In Word you can set the top, bottom, left and right margins.

▶▶ How to... *set margins*

1 In the **Menu bar**, click on **File**.

2 From the **File** menu, click on **Page Setup**.

3 The **Page Setup** dialogue box is displayed.

4 Check that the **Margins** tab is selected.

5 Click in the box for **Top**, enter the measurements for the top margin, then do the same for the **Left**, **Right** and **Bottom** margins (Figure 1.75).

6 You can use the **up/down arrows**; however, this may not allow you to set margins to specific measurements.

7 You do not need to enter **cm** (centimetres) into the measurements box, as Word will do this automatically.

8 Click on **OK** to set the margins.

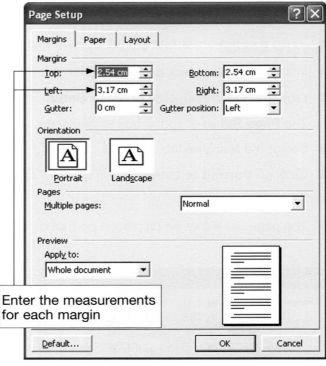

Enter the measurements for each margin

FIGURE 1.75 Setting the margins

TIP!

Double-click on the blue area of the **Ruler bar** to open the **Page Setup** dialogue box quickly.

Check your understanding *Set the margins*

1 In **Document1**, set the top, left and right margins to **3.3 cm**.

2 Do not change the bottom margin measurement.

Line spacing

Line spacing is the amount of space between each line of text. Line spacing can be set before entering text; if so, the line spacing set will be applied to all the text. Line spacing can also be set after entering text to all or part of a document.

1 Click on the **Format** menu.

2 From the menu, click on **Paragraph**.

3 The **Paragraph** dialogue box is displayed (Figure 1.76).

4 Select the **Indents and Spacing** tab.

5 Under **Line spacing** click on the **down arrow**.

6 Click on the line spacing option required, e.g. **Single**.

7 Click on **OK** to set the line spacing.

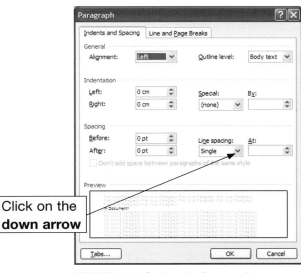

Click on the **down arrow**

FIGURE 1.76 Setting the line spacing

In **Document1**, set the line spacing to **single**.

Entering text, numbers and symbols

Entering text is also referred to as typing or keying in text. When you enter text, make sure you **enter the words exactly** as shown.

Use the **same case** as shown in the text you are copying:

- *this text is in **lower case** – there are no capital letters*
- *Each Of These Words Has An **Initial Capital** – The First Letter Of Each Word Is A Capital*
- *THIS TEXT IS IN **UPPERCASE** – ALL THE LETTERS ARE CAPITAL LETTERS.*

When you enter text, make sure you use the **correct spacing**.

WHERE	NUMBER OF SPACES
Between each word	One space
After a comma	One space
After a full stop	Two spaces (one space is also commonly used)
After a colon	One space
After a semicolon	One space
Between paragraphs	One clear line space between each paragraph

Spacing in text

To remind yourself of the keyboard and How to… Use the keyboard, see Chapter 1, page 16.

Points to remember when entering text

- *Use the same case as shown.*
- *Use the correct spacing between words and after punctuation.*
- *Do not press the **Enter** key at the end of a line within a paragraph.*
- *Press the **Enter** key twice after a heading.*
- *Press the **Enter** key twice at the end of a paragraph.*

What does it mean?

Word wrap
A word that is too long to fit on the end of a line is automatically placed on the next line. This breaks lines automatically between words, so that when the text being entered on the line reaches beyond the right-hand margin, the whole of the last word is transferred to the beginning of the next line.

Check your understanding   *Enter text*

1 In **Document1**, enter the text below.

2 Do not worry if you make any spelling or spacing errors, you will learn to correct these later.

3 Refer to the table, Using the keyboard, in Chapter 1, page 16, if you need to.

LEARNING NEW SKILLS

I am learning how to produce a document using Microsoft Word. To help with my typing skills I have been told to type the following sentence which contains all the letters of the alphabet: The quick brown fox jumps over the lazy dog.

Soon I will be able to write letters to friends, relatives and colleagues using the skills I have learned.

Saving a Word document

A document must be saved if you want to use it again. It is good practice to save your work approximately every 10 minutes so that you do not lose too much work if there is a computer problem. A new document should be given an appropriate filename when saving for the first time; after that it can be saved keeping the same filename or with a new filename.

▶▶ How to…   *save a Word document into a new folder*

1 In the **Menu bar**, click on **File**.

2 From the **File** menu, click on **Save**.

3 A **Save As** dialogue box is displayed.

4 Click on the **down arrow** to the right of the **Save in** box, then click on your user area (Figure 1.77). You may need to double-click to open any sub-folders in your user area.

5 Click on the **Create New Folder** icon.

TIP!

It is good practice to keep your saved files organised in folders.

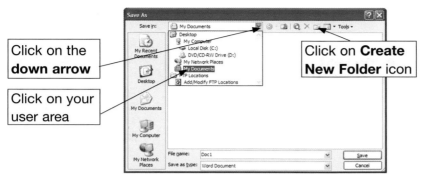

Click on the **down arrow**

Click on your user area

Click on **Create New Folder** icon

FIGURE 1.77 **Save As** dialogue box

FIGURE 1.78 **New Folder** dialogue box

6   A **New Folder** dialogue box is displayed (Figure 1.78).

7   Enter the new folder name.

8   Click on **OK.**

9   In the **Save As** dialogue box, delete any existing text in the **File name** box.

10   Enter the required filename (Figure 1.79).

11   Click on **Save**.

12   Your document is saved in a new folder within your user area.

Enter the new filename

FIGURE 1.79 Entering the required filename in the **Save As** dialogue box

Check your understanding
Save your document into a new folder

Save **Document1** into a new folder called **ocrunit1** using the filename **practice1**.

Text alignment

Before learning how to set the text alignment, you will need to know how to highlight text in a document.

TEXT	HOW TO HIGHLIGHT
A word	Position the mouse pointer over the word and **double-click.**
A phrase (a few words)	Position the mouse pointer just before the first word in the phrase and click, hold down the **Shift** key on the keyboard, position the mouse pointer just after the last word of the phrase and click.
A sentence	Hold down the **Ctrl** key on the keyboard and click anywhere in the sentence.
A paragraph	Position the mouse pointer anywhere in the paragraph and triple-click (click three times very quickly).
The whole document	Press the **Ctrl** and **A** keys at the same time.

Methods of highlighting text in a document

Left-aligned text has a neat left-hand edge and a ragged right-hand edge as displayed in the text you are reading. Words are equally spaced.

Right-aligned text has a neat right-hand edge and a ragged left-hand edge as displayed in the text you are reading. Words are equally spaced.

Justified text (also sometimes called fully justified) has straight edges on both sides as displayed in the text you are reading. Wider spaces may appear between words.

Centred text is positioned centrally between the left and right margins or within each table cell as displayed in the text you are reading.

▶▶ How to... *set the text alignment*

Text alignment can be set before or after you enter text.

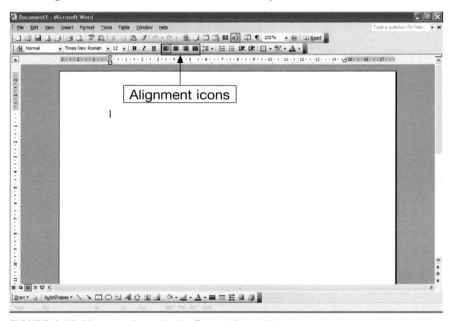

FIGURE 1.80 Alignment icons in the **Formatting** toolbar

Before you enter text

To left-align text:

○ *click on the **Align Left** 🔲 icon in the **Formatting toolbar**. All the text entered will be left-aligned.*

To right-align text:

○ *click on the **Align Right** 🔳 icon in the **Formatting toolbar**. All the text entered will be right-aligned.*

To justify text:

○ *click on the **Justify** 🔳 icon in the **Formatting toolbar**. All the text entered will be aligned to the left and to the right.*

Note: wider spaces may appear within sentences in justified text.

To centre text:

○ click the **Center** ▤ icon in the **Formatting toolbar**. *All the text entered will be centred.*

After you enter text

Highlight the text to be aligned and click the left, right, centre or justify icon.

Saving an existing document

Remember to save your document **practice1** approximately every 10 minutes. Saving an existing document that you have previously saved and named is quicker than saving a new document for the first time.

▶▶ **How to...** *save an existing document*

1 In the **Menu bar**, click on **File**.

2 From the **File** menu, click on **Save**.

TIP!

Click on the **Save** ▤ icon *OR* press **Ctrl** and **S** keys at the same time.

Check your understanding *Set the text alignment*

1 Refer to the 'Methods of highlighting text in a document' on page 55.

2 Apply the following alignments to the text in the document **practice1**:

a **Centre** the heading LEARNING NEW SKILLS.

b **Justify** all the text in the first paragraph.

c **Right-align** all the text in the second paragraph.

3 Save your document keeping the filename **practice1**.

Font size

Font size refers to the height of the characters (letters, numbers, symbols). A small font size will display small characters and a large font size displays large characters. Examples of font sizes:

Font size 10

Font size 12

Font size 14.

▶▶ **How to...** *set the font size*

Font size can be set before or after you enter text.

Before you enter text

1 In the **Formatting toolbar**, select the required font size by clicking on the **drop-down arrow** to the right of the **Font Size** box (Figure 1.81).

2 A list of sizes is displayed.

3 Click on the required size. All text that you enter will be in the font size that you selected.

After you enter text

1 Highlight the text to be changed.

2 In the **Formatting toolbar**, select the required font size by clicking on the **drop-down arrow** to the right of the **Font Size** box.

3 A list of sizes is displayed.

4 Click on the required size.

5 The font size of the highlighted text will change.

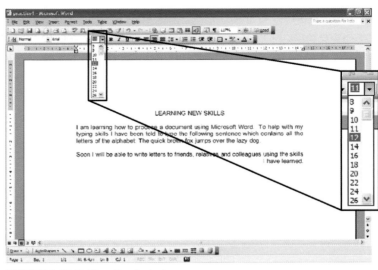

FIGURE 1.81 Setting the font size

6 Click anywhere in your document to remove the highlight from the selected text (to deselect the text).

Check your understanding

Change the font size of existing text

In the document **practice1**:

1 Highlight the heading and set it to **font size 14.**

2 Highlight the first paragraph and set it to **font size 12.**

3 Highlight the second paragraph and set it to **font size 10.**

4 Save the document keeping the filename **practice1.**

Check your understanding

Set the font size and alignment before entering new text

1 In the document **practice1**, place your cursor at the end of the second paragraph and create a new paragraph by pressing **Enter** twice.

2 Set the **font size** to **11**.

3 Set the **text alignment** to **left**.

4 Enter the following text as the third paragraph:

Another good sentence to practise keyboarding is: Now is the time for all good men to come to the aid of the party.

5 Save the document keeping the filename **practice1.**

Font type

Font type refers to the font name. It is also referred to as font or font style. Examples of font types are Arial, Times New Roman, Comic Sans MS.

▶▶ How to... *set the font type*

The font type can be set before or after you enter text.

Before you enter text

1 In the **Formatting toolbar**, click on the **drop-down arrow** to the right of the **Font** box, where the font name is displayed (Figure 1.82).

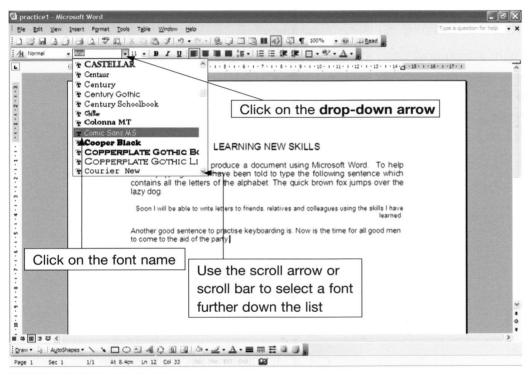

FIGURE 1.82 Setting the font type

2 A list of available fonts is displayed.

3 Click on the required font name from the list. All text that you enter will be in the font type that you selected.

After you enter text

1 Highlight the text you want to change.

2 Click on the **drop-down arrow** to the right of the **Font** box, where the font name is displayed.

3 A list of available fonts is displayed.

TIP!

The available fonts are listed in alphabetical order. To choose a font that is not visible, use the scroll bar or scroll arrow to find a font that is further down the list, or enter the first letter of the font name.

4 Click on the required font name from the list.

5 The font type of the selected text will change.

6 Click anywhere in your document to deselect the text.

Check your understanding *Set the font type*

In the document **practice1**:

1 Set the **font type** of the heading to **Times New Roman**.

2 Set the **font type** of the first paragraph to **Arial**.

3 Set the **font type** of the second paragraph to **Comic Sans MS**.

4 Set the **font type** of the third paragraph to **Lucida Handwriting**.

5 Save the document keeping the filename **practice1**.

Your document should now look similar to the one in Figure 1.83.

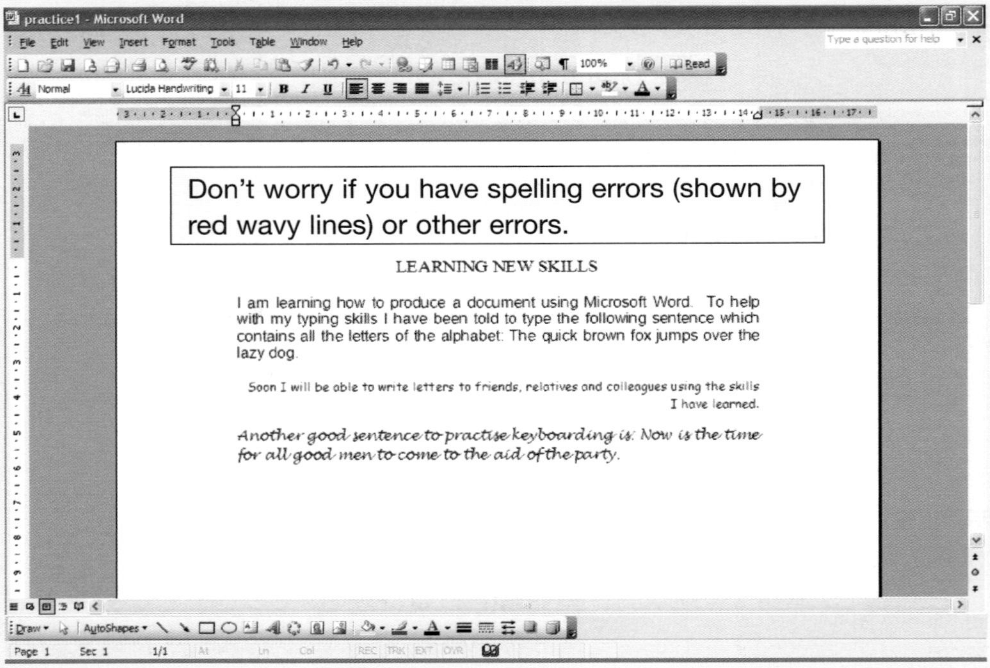
practice1 - Microsoft Word
Don't worry if you have spelling errors (shown by red wavy lines) or other errors.
LEARNING NEW SKILLS
I am learning how to produce a document using Microsoft Word. To help with my typing skills I have been told to type the following sentence which contains all the letters of the alphabet: The quick brown fox jumps over the lazy dog.
Soon I will be able to write letters to friends, relatives and colleagues using the skills I have learned.
Another good sentence to practise keyboarding is: Now is the time for all good men to come to the aid of the party.

FIGURE 1.83 The document **practice1**

Checking your document for errors

Always check your work for errors. Even though the spell checker may be set to check your spelling as you type, it cannot check for missing or incorrect words (e.g. come instead of came). Therefore, you must still check the whole document yourself.

It is very important that you spell check using a UK spell checker. Before you start checking for spelling errors, you must check that the language is set to **English (U.K.)**.

▶▶ How to... *set or check the language*

1 In the **Menu bar**, click on **Tools**.

2 From the **Tools** menu, click on **Language**.

3 From the **Language** menu click on **Set Language**.

4 The **Language** dialogue box is displayed (Figure 1.84).

5 Make sure **English (U.K.)** is highlighted. If it isn't, click on it.

6 Click on **OK**.

▶▶ How to... *spell check a document*

1 In the **Standard toolbar**, click on the **Spelling and Grammar**  icon.

2 Word checks the whole document for spelling errors.

3 If the spell checker finds an error, the **Spelling and Grammar** dialogue box is displayed (Figure 1.85).

4 The incorrect word is highlighted in red in the **Not in Dictionary** box.

5 Alternative spellings are displayed in the **Suggestions** box.

▶▶ How to... *change the spelling of an incorrect word*

If the correct spelling is displayed in the Suggestions box

1 Click on the correct spelling of the word in the **Suggestions** box.

2 Click on **Change**.

3 The spelling will be changed in your document, a dialogue box displays telling you that the spelling and grammar check is complete.

4 Click **OK**.

If the correct spelling is not displayed in the Suggestions box

You will need to know how to spell the word correctly.

1 In the **Spelling and Grammar** dialogue box, highlight the incorrectly spelt word in the **Not in the dictionary** box.

2 Enter the correct spelling of the word.

3 Click on **Change**.

FIGURE 1.84 **Language** dialogue box

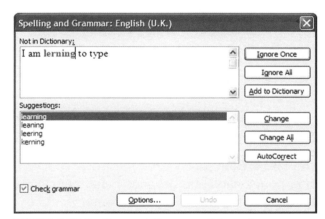

FIGURE 1.85 **Spelling and Grammar** dialogue box

What does it mean?

Spell checker
Word has a **spell checker** tool which automatically checks the spelling in a document against a large dictionary. Word shows possible spelling errors or repeated words with a red wavy line shown under the word. Green wavy lines show possible grammar errors. If you are copy-typing text, you should ignore any alternative grammar suggestions.

4 The spelling will be changed in your document.

5 Click **OK**.

Sometimes Word will highlight a word as being incorrectly spelt, even though it is correct, because that word is not in Word's UK English dictionary (e.g. your name).

▶▶ How to...   *ignore a suggested spelling*

1 Make sure that the highlighted word is spelt correctly.

2 In the **Spelling and Grammar** dialogue box, click on **Ignore Once** (if you know the word appears only once in the document) OR **Ignore All** (if you know the word appears more than once in the document).

Check your understanding   *Spell check your document*

1 In the document **practice1**, set the language to **English (U.K.)**.

2 Click on the **Spelling and Grammar** icon in the **Standard** toolbar to spell check your document.

3 Correct any spelling errors.

4 Ignore any grammar changes suggested by Word.

The Show/Hide tool

The **Show/Hide** tool is used to display spaces between words, after punctuation and between paragraphs. When you switch on the **Show/Hide** tool each space between words or after punctuation is represented by a dot. A paragraph marker ¶ shows each time that you pressed **Enter**. These dots and markers are referred to as non-printing characters.

Using the **Show/Hide tool** will help you to check a document for accuracy.

▶▶ How to...   *switch on the Show/Hide tool*

In the **Standard** toolbar, click on the **Show/Hide** ¶ icon to switch on the **Show/Hide tool**. (To switch it off, click on the icon again.)

TIP!

The dots and markers will not print whether the **Show/Hide** tool is switched on or off when you send the document to print.

Check your understanding
Use the Show/Hide tool to check your document

1 In the document **practice1**, click on the Show/Hide icon.

Your document should look similar to the one in Figure 1.86.

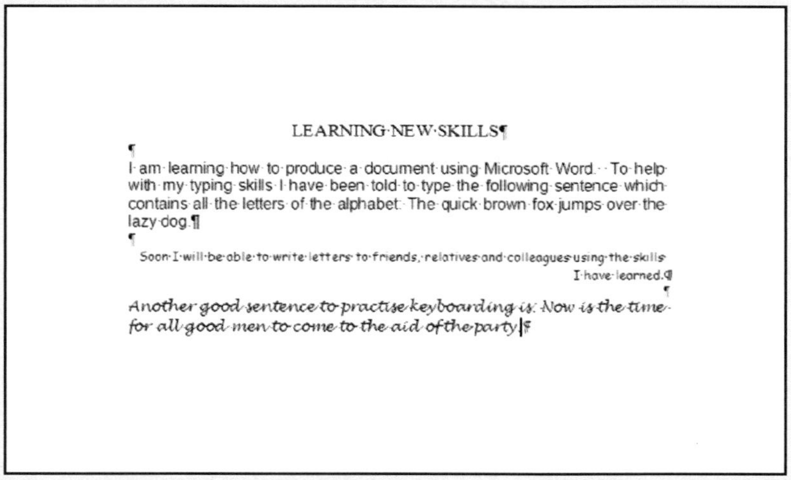
LEARNING·NEW·SKILLS¶

¶

I·am·learning·how·to·produce·a·document·using·Microsoft·Word.··To·help·with·my·typing·skills·I·have·been·told·to·type·the·following·sentence·which·contains·all·the·letters·of·the·alphabet:·The·quick·brown·fox·jumps·over·the·lazy·dog.¶

¶

Soon·I·will·be·able·to·write·letters·to·friends,·relatives·and·colleagues·using·the·skills·I·have·learned.¶

¶

Another·good·sentence·to·practise·keyboarding·is:·Now·is·the·time·for·all·good·men·to·come·to·the·aid·of·the·party.¶

FIGURE 1.86 The document **practice1** with the **Show/Hide** tool switched on

2 Check the spacing. There should be:
   a **one dot between each word**
   b **one dot after a comma**
   c **two dots after a full stop**
   d **two paragraph markers for each paragraph**, one will be at the end of the text, the second will be on a clear line.

3 Delete any additional dots or paragraph markers by pressing **Backspace** or **Delete**.

4 If required, insert space(s) between words or after punctuation by using the **Spacebar**. Insert additional paragraph markers by pressing **Enter**.

5 Now, click on the **Show/Hide** icon to switch it off and to view your document normally.

6 Save your document keeping the filename **practice1**.

Printing documents

Before printing a document, it is a good idea to check how it will look when printed by using **Print Preview**.

TIP!

Always use **Print Preview** to check your document before printing.

▶▶ *How to...* *open Print Preview*

1 In the **Standard toolbar**, click on the **Print Preview** 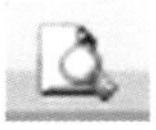 icon.

2 The **Print Preview** window is displayed. Check your document for accuracy.

3 Click on **Close** in the **Print Preview** toolbar to return to your document.

TIP!

Before you print for the first time, check the paper size.

▶▶ How to... *set paper size*

1 In the **Menu bar**, click on **File**.

2 From the **File** menu, click on **Page Setup**.

3 The **Page Setup** dialogue box is displayed.

4 Click on the **Paper** tab to select **Paper** view.

5 Check the **Paper size** box displays **A4**, (Figure 1.87).

6 If not, click on the **drop-down arrow** to the right of the box and click on **A4**, **210 x 297mm**.

7 Click on **OK** to confirm the paper size.

▶▶ How to... *print a document*

1 In the **Menu bar**, click on **File**.

2 From the **File** menu, click on **Print** (Figure 1.88).

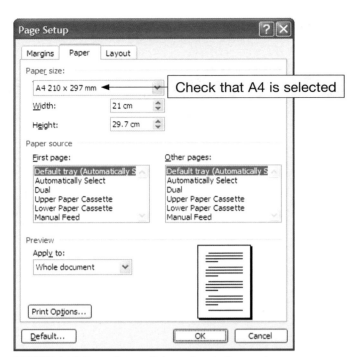

FIGURE 1.87 Page Setup dialogue box in Paper view

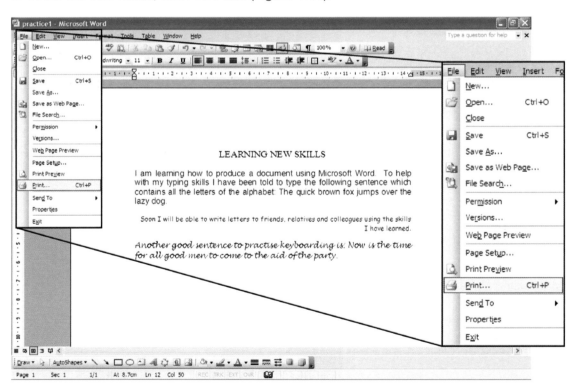

FIGURE 1.88 Click on Print in the File menu

3 A **Print** dialogue box is displayed (Figure 1.89).

Check the **Page range** is set to **All**

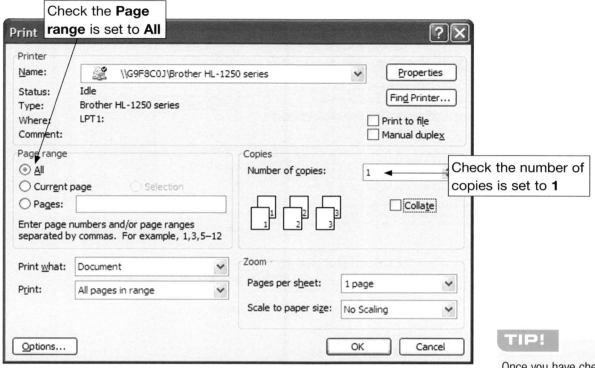

Check the number of copies is set to **1**

FIGURE 1.89 **Print** dialogue box

4 Check that the **Page Range** is set to All.

5 Check that the **Number of copies** box is set to **1**.

6 Click on **OK** to print the document.

TIP!

Once you have checked the print settings, the next time you want to print, click on the **Print** icon in the **Standard** toolbar.

Check your understanding *Set paper size and print*

1 In the document **practice1**, check the paper size is **A4**.

2 Print one copy.

Headers and footers

Headers and footers are common identifiers at the top and bottom of a page. They can be displayed on every page or on every other page. Special features such as date, filename and page numbers can be added to a header or footer.

What does it mean?

Header and footer
- A **header** is the space within the top margin.
- A **footer** is the space within the bottom margin.

1 In the **Menu bar**, click on **View**.

2 From the View menu, click on **Header and Footer** (Figure 1.90).

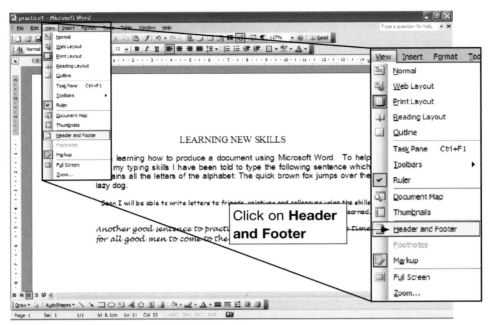

FIGURE 1.90 The **View** menu

3 The cursor is displayed in the header section of the document and the **Header and Footer toolbar** displays on the page (Figure 1.91)

FIGURE 1.91 The Header and Footer toolbar

4 Enter the required information in the header.

5 Click on the **Switch Between Header and Footer** 🔲 icon to go to the footer section.

6 The cursor is displayed in the footer section of the document.

7 Enter any required information in the footer.

8 Click on **Close** to close the **Header and Footer** toolbar and return to the document.

Automatic fields

Word can insert some information automatically into headers and footers, e.g. automatic dates and automatic filenames. The advantage of using automatic fields is that these will update automatically.

TIP!

If you need to insert several items in the header or footer, e.g. your name, centre number, automatic date and automatic filename, don't click close until you have inserted all items.

TIP!

Check that your computer is set to update fields: click the **Tools** menu, click **Options**, click the **Print** tab, make sure there is a tick in the box for **Update Fields**.

1 Open the **Header and Footer** toolbar.

2 In the header or footer section, click on the **Insert Date** 🗓 icon.

3 An automatic date is displayed on the screen.

▶▶ *How to...* add an automatic filename

1 Open the **Header and Footer** toolbar.

2 In the header or footer section, click on the **drop-down arrow** next to **Insert AutoText**.

3 A drop-down menu is displayed (Figure 1.92).

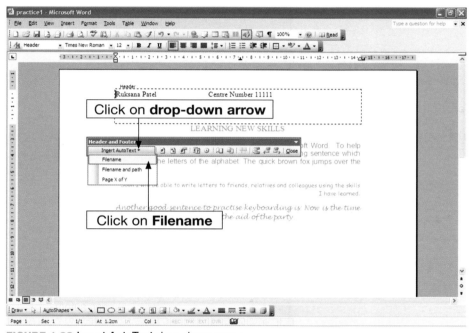

FIGURE 1.92 **Insert AutoText** drop-down menu

4 Click on **Filename** to automatically insert the document's filename in the header or footer.

5 Click on **Close** to close the **Header and Footer** toolbar and return to the document.

6 Click on the **Print Preview** 🔍 icon to check all headers and footers.

TIP!

When you insert an automatic filename, the saved name may not display immediately; **Document1** may display – this is normal. Use **Print Preview** to check all headers and footers.

TIP!

To make sure that the automatic filename updates after you have saved a document, highlight the filename in the header or footer and press F9.

TIP!

In **Print Layout** view, the headers and footers appear in a lighter shade of grey to the main body text.

TIP!

Remember to save your document again after you have added headers and footers. Click on the **Save** 🖫 icon in the **Standard** toolbar.

1 In the document **practice1**, insert the following headers and footers:

   a In the **header**, enter your **first and last name** and your **centre number**.

   b Insert at least **one space** between each item in the header *OR* press the **Tab** key.

   c In the **footer**, insert an **automatic date** and an **automatic filename**.

2 Use **Print Preview** to check your headers and footers.

3 Print one copy of your document.

Closing a document

Now that you have saved and printed your document, you should close it. It is good practice to remember to close a file before you close a program.

▶▶ How to... *close a document*

1 In the **Menu bar**, click on **File**.

2 From the **File** menu, click on **Close** (Figure 1.93).

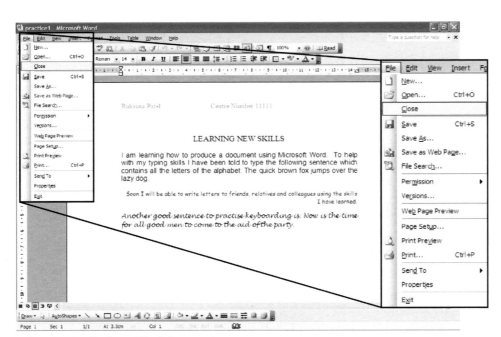

FIGURE 1.93 Closing a Word document

Exiting Word

When the document has been closed, you should exit from Word.

▶▶ How to... *exit from Word*

1 In the **Menu bar**, click on **File**.

2 From the **File** menu, click on **Exit** (Figure 1.94).

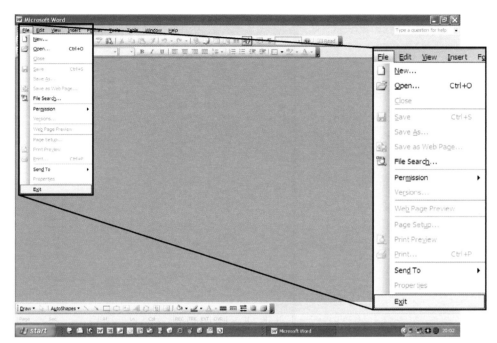

FIGURE 1.94 Exiting Word

TIP!

Once you have saved a document, click on the **Close** ☒ icon to close the document and exit Word.

Check your understanding *Close a document and exit Word*

1 Close the document **practice1**.

2 Exit Word.

ASSESS YOUR SKILLS – Create a Word document

By working through Section 1 you will have learnt the skills below. Read each item to help you decide how confident you feel about each skill.

- ○ start Word
- ○ understand the different parts of Word
- ○ create a new blank document
- ○ set the page orientation
- ○ set the top, left and right margins
- ○ set the line spacing
- ○ enter text in a blank document
- ○ set the text alignment (left, right, justify and centre)
- ○ set the font size
- ○ set the font type
- ○ use spell check
- ○ use the **Show/Hide** tool
- ○ save a new document with a specified filename
- ○ save a document into a new folder from within Word
- ○ enter text in headers and footers
- ○ insert an automatic date and an automatic filename in headers and footers
- ○ save an updated document keeping the same filename
- ○ print a document
- ○ close a document
- ○ exit Word.

If you think you need more practice on any of the skills listed above, go back and work through the skill(s) again.

If you feel confident, move on to Section 2.

LEARNING OUTCOMES

In this section you will learn how to:

- open a provided document and save it with a different filename
- emphasise text (bold, italic, underline)
- delete text
- move text
- insert text
- use **Find and Replace**
- insert paragraph break
- change line spacing
- use bullets and numbering
- use tabs and indents
- insert a table
- apply borders, gridlines and shading
- use word count.

Useful keyboard shortcuts

To use the keyboard shortcuts shown in the table (left), press both keys at the same time.

Files for this chapter

To work through the tasks in Section 2, you will need the files from the folder called **files_chapter2**, which you will find on the CD-ROM provided with this book. Copy this folder into your user area before you begin.

SHORTCUT KEYS	DESCRIPTION
Ctrl and **B**	Makes highlighted text bold
Ctrl and **I**	Makes highlighted text italic
Ctrl and **U**	Underlines highlighted text
Ctrl and **A**	Highlight the whole document
Ctrl and **C**	Copy the highlighted text
Ctrl and **X**	Cut the highlighted text
Ctrl and **V**	Paste text
Ctrl and **Z**	Undo the last action
Ctrl and **Y**	Redo the last action
Ctrl and **2**	Apply double line spacing to highlighted text
Ctrl and **1**	Apply single line spacing to highlighted text

Keyboard shortcuts

Make sure the computer is switched on and the desktop screen is displayed.

1 Insert the CD-ROM into the CD-ROM drive of your computer.

2 Close any windows that may open.

3 In the desktop, double-click on the **My Computer** icon. The **My Computer** window is displayed.

4 Under Devices with Removable Storage, double-click on the CD Drive icon to view the contents of the CD-ROM.

5 A window opens displaying the contents of the CD-ROM.

6 Double-click on the folder **L1_Unit1_FM+DP**.

7 Double-click on the folder **Source Files**.

8 Click on the folder **files_chapter2** (Figure 1.95).

9 The folder will be highlighted (usually blue).

10 In the **File and Folder Tasks** box, click on **Copy this folder**.

11 A **Copy Items** dialogue box is displayed (Figure 1.96).

12 Click on the user area where you want to copy the folder **files_chapter2**.

13 Click on **Copy**.

14 The folder **files_chapter2** is copied to your user area.

15 It is advisable to copy and paste a second copy to another folder in your user area as backup.

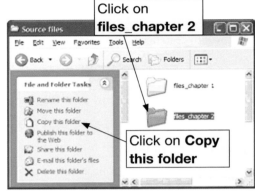

FIGURE 1.95 **Source files** window

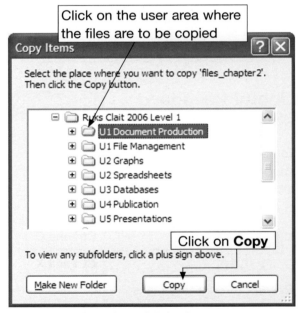

FIGURE 1.96 **Copy items** dialogue box

 **How to...** *open a provided Word file (1)*

1 In the desktop, double-click on the **My Computer** icon.

2 In the **My Computer** window, double-click on your user area to open it.

3 Double-click on the folder or subfolder containing the required file.

4 The folder contents are displayed.

5 Open the required file by double-clicking on it.

Below is another way to open a Word file.

1 Open a Word document (to remind yourself of the different ways to open Word, see page 44).

2 In the document, click on **File** in the **Menu bar**.

3 From the drop-down **File** menu, click on **Open**.

4 The **Open** dialogue box is displayed.

5 In the **Look in** box, click on the folder or subfolder where the required file is saved.

6 Click on the **down arrow** to the right of the **Look in** box to find the folder if it is not shown in the box. Double-click to open any subfolders.

7 From the files displayed, double-click on the Word file to be opened.

▶▶ **How to...** *save a file using a new filename in Word 2003 format into an existing folder*

1 In Word, click on **File** in the **Menu bar**.

2 From the **File** menu, click on **Save As**.

3 The **Save As** dialogue box opens (Figure 1.97).

4 Click on the **down arrow** to the right of the **Save in** box and click on the folder where you want to save the file.

5 In the **File name** box, delete the existing filename.

6 Enter the new filename.

7 Click on the **down arrow** to the right of the **Save as type** box.

8 Scroll up to the top of the list and click on **Word Document**.

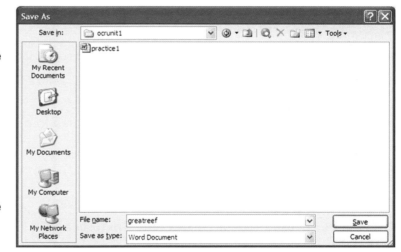

FIGURE 1.97 **Save As** dialogue box

9 Click on **Save**.

10 The file will be saved with the new filename in Word 2003 format into your folder.

Open an existing file and save it using a new filename

Before you begin, make sure you have copied the folder **files_chapter2** to your user area (see page 72).

1 In your user area, open the file **reef** from the folder **files_chapter2**.

2 Save the file **reef** as a Word 2003 file using the filename **greatreef** into the folder **ocrunit1** that you created earlier.

3 Keep the file open.

Using emphasis

Emphasis is used to make text stand out. Text can be emphasised using **bold**, *italic* or by underlining it.

▶▶ How to... *format the text to be bold*

1 In your document, highlight the text to be made bold.

2 In the **Formatting toolbar**, click on the **Bold** **B** icon. The text is made bold.

3 Click in your document outside the highlighted area to remove the highlight (to deselect the text).

▶▶ How to... *format text into italics*

1 In your document, highlight the text to be italicised.

2 In the **Formatting toolbar**, click on the **Italic** *I* icon. The text is italicised.

3 Click in your document outside the highlighted area to deselect the text.

▶▶ How to... *underline the text*

1 In your document, highlight the text to be underlined.

2 In the **Formatting toolbar**, click on the **Underline** **U** icon. The text is underlined.

3 Click in your document outside the highlighted area to deselect the text.

1 In the file **greatreef**, format the heading **The Great Barrier Reef** to be **bold**.

2 In the first paragraph, format the text *The Great Barrier Reef* to be **italic**.

3 In the first paragraph, **underline** the text 2000 km.

Deleting text

When you delete text from a document, you remove that text permanently.

▶▶ How to... *delete text*

1 In your document, highlight the text to be deleted. Make sure you also highlight any punctuation after a phrase (comma, full stop, exclamation mark).

2 In the **Formatting toolbar**, click on the **Cut** icon. The phrase is deleted from the document.

TIP!

A quick way to delete text:

Highlight the text to be deleted, then press the **Delete** key or press **Ctrl** and **X** at the same time.

TIP!

If you accidentally delete text, press **Ctrl** and **Z** at the same time to undo or click the **Undo** icon on the Standard toolbar.

Check your understanding *Delete text*

1 In the file **greatreef**, **delete** the following text from the second paragraph:

Deposits of material and growth of vegetation created them.

Make sure you delete the full stop as well.

2 Use the **Show/Hide** tool to check the spacing between the two remaining sentences of the second paragraph. There should be two spaces after the full stop.

3 Save the file keeping the filename **greatreef**.

Moving text

When text is moved in a document, it is removed from the original place and pasted in a new place.

▶▶ How to... *move text*

1 In your document, highlight the text to be moved. Make sure you also highlight any punctuation after the text.

2 In the **Formatting toolbar**, click on the **Cut** icon.

3 Click in the position that you want to paste the text.

4 Make sure you insert a space after a comma or two spaces after a full stop in the new position.

5 In the **Formatting toolbar**, click on the **Paste** icon.

6 The text is moved to the new place in the document.

1 In the file **greatreef**, **move** the following text in the third paragraph to become the **second** sentence of the **third** paragraph:

Many lagoon and ocean fish go to the reef to breed, feed on the reef plants or to catch prey.

Make sure you move the full stop as well.

2 Check the **spacing** by using the **Show/Hide** tool. There should be two spaces after a full stop.

3 Save the file keeping the filename **greatreef**.

Inserting text

You may want to add some additional words or sentences to an existing document. To do so, you will need to insert text.

Before you insert text

Before you enter any text, you will need to check that **OVR** (overwrite) in the **Status** bar is switched off (Figure 1.98). Look at the **Status bar** at the bottom of your Word screen. The OVR must be greyed out. If it is not greyed out, double-click on **OVR** to switch it off.

If the **OVR** is switched on, existing text will be deleted as you enter new text. If the **OVR** is turned off, you will simply be adding more text in between existing text.

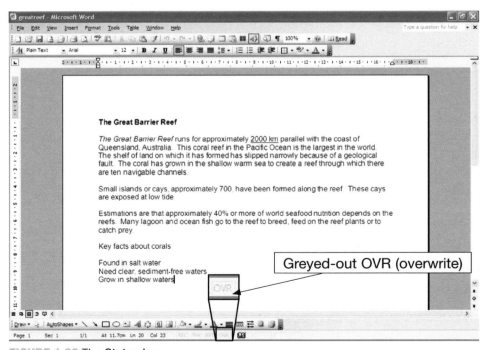

Greyed-out OVR (overwrite)

FIGURE 1.98 The Status bar

TIP!

The **OVR** button can be accidentally switched on if the **Insert (Ins)** key on the keyboard is pressed.

1 In your document, click with your mouse in the position where you want to insert text.

2 Make sure you insert a space after a comma or two spaces after a full stop in the new position.

3 Enter the required text.

4 Make sure you insert the correct spacing after the inserted text.

Check your understanding   *Insert text*

1 In the file **greatreef**, go to the third sentence of the first paragraph ('The shelf of land …') and insert the text **below sea level** after 'has slipped narrowly' and before 'because of a'.

2 Check the spacing before and after the inserted text using the **Show/Hide** tool. There should be one space before and one space after the three inserted words.

3 Save the file keeping the filename **greatreef**.

4 Check your document **greatreef**. The positioning of text should appear as shown in Figure 1.99.

The Great Barrier Reef

The Great Barrier Reef runs for approximately <u>2000 km</u> parallel with the coast of Queensland, Australia. This coral reef in the Pacific Ocean is the largest in the world. The shelf of land on which it has formed has slipped narrowly below sea level because of a geological fault. The coral has grown in the shallow warm sea to create a reef through which there are ten navigable channels.

Small islands or cays, approximately 700, have been formed along the reef. These cays are exposed at low tide.

Estimations are that approximately 40% or more of world seafood nutrition depends on the reefs. Many lagoon and ocean fish go to the reef to breed, feed on the reef plants or to catch prey.

Key facts about corals

Found in salt water
Need clear, sediment-free waters
Grow in shallow waters

FIGURE 1.99 The document **greatreef**

Find and Replace

You may want to change a word that appears more than once in your document. Using Find and Replace you can replace all instances of a particular word with a new word without having to look for it yourself. To ensure that all instances of the original word are replaced by the new word, you should let the computer carry out a **Find and Replace**.

1 In the **Menu bar**, click on **Edit**.

2 From the **Edit** menu, click on **Replace**.

3 The **Find and Replace** dialogue box is displayed.

4 If the **Replace** tab is not selected, click on it (Figure 1.100).

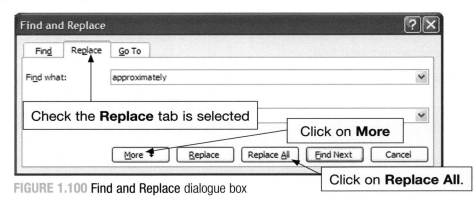

Check the **Replace** tab is selected

Click on **More**

Click on **Replace All**.

FIGURE 1.100 **Find and Replace** dialogue box

5 In the **Find what** box, enter the word to be replaced.

6 In the **Replace with** box, enter the new word.

7 Click on **More**.

8 A **Search Options** menu is displayed.

9 To select **Find whole words only**, click in the box.

10 A tick appears in the box.

11 Click on **Replace All** to replace all instances of the original word with the new word.

TIP!

Do not click on **Replace** unless you want to replace only one occurrence of the word.

12 When Word has finished, a dialogue box displays telling you that Word has completed its search and the number of replacements that have been made (Figure 1.101).

13 Click on **OK**.

14 To close the **Find and Replace** dialogue box, click on **Close**.

FIGURE 1.101 A dialogue box confirming that Word has completed Find and Replace

Check your understanding *Use Find and Replace*

1 In the file **greatreef**, replace all instances of the word 'approximately' with the word **about** (three times in all).

2 Save your file, keeping the filename **greatreef**.

TIP!

It is good practice to tick the option box **Find whole words only** whether you are replacing a short or a long word.

Paragraph breaks and line spacing

A paragraph break is used to split a long paragraph to make it into two paragraphs.

BEFORE INSERTING A PARAGRAPH BREAK	AFTER INSERTING A PARAGRAPH BREAK
Accidents can be caused in offices by carelessness or thoughtlessness. It is the duty of everyone, from management to casual employees, to help prevent accidents in the workplace. An accident book should be kept to record details of all accidents and all treatments given, both to employees and to visitors to an organisation.	Accidents can be caused in offices by carelessness or thoughtlessness. It is the duty of everyone, from management to casual employees, to help prevent accidents in the workplace. An accident book should be kept to record details of all accidents and all treatments given, both to employees and to visitors to an organisation.

Text before and after inserting a paragraph break and a linespace

▶▶ How to... *insert a paragraph break*

1 In your document, click to place the cursor just before the first word of the sentence that will start the new paragraph.

2 Press the **Enter** key **twice**.

3 You should have one clear line space between two paragraphs.

4 Make sure the first word of the new paragraph starts at the left margin and does not have an unwanted space before it.

5 Click on the **Show/Hide** tool to check the spacing.

Check your understanding *Insert paragraph break*

1 In the file **greatreef**, insert a **paragraph break** in the first paragraph and a clear **line space** after the text ending '... largest in the world'.

2 Check the spacing before the paragraph break by using the **Show/Hide** tool:

   a There should be no dots representing spaces before the text 'The shelf of land...'.

   b There should be one paragraph marker between the two paragraphs and one paragraph marker after the text '... largest in the world'.

3 Save the file keeping the filename **greatreef**.

▶▶ How to... *change line spacing*

1 In your document, highlight the text to be changed.

2 In the **Menu bar**, click on **Format**.

3 From the **Format** menu, click on **Paragraph**.

4 A **Paragraph** dialogue box is displayed (Figure 1.102).

5 Check that the **Indents and Spacing** tab is selected.

6 In the **Spacing** section, click on the **down arrow** under **Line spacing**.

7 A drop-down menu is displayed.

8 Click on the line spacing option required, e.g. **Double**.

9 Click on **OK**.

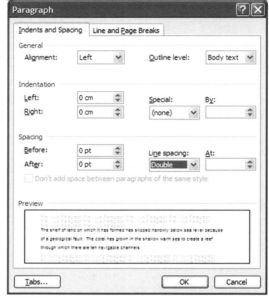

FIGURE 1.102 Paragraph dialogue box showing line spacing

TIP!

Do not highlight any blank space(s) after the text or between paragraphs.

TIP!

Press the **Ctrl** and **2** keys at the same time to apply double line spacing to highlighted text.

10 The highlighted text is displayed in double line spacing.

11 Click outside the highlighted area to deselect the text.

Check your understanding *Change line spacing*

1 In the file **greatreef**, change the line spacing of the second paragraph to be **double line spacing**.

2 Use the **Show/Hide** tool to check that there is one paragraph marker above and below the paragraph.

3 Save the file keeping the filename **greatreef**.

Lists

Bulleted list

Below are examples of bulleted lists.

- *Found in salt water*
- *Need clear, sediment-free waters*
- *Grow in shallow waters*

➤ *Found in salt water*

➤ *Need clear, sediment-free waters*

➤ *Grow in shallow waters*

▶▶ **How to...** *create a bulleted list*

1 In your document, highlight the text to be bulleted.

2 Click on the **Bullets** ≔ icon.

3 The selected text is displayed as a bulleted list. The style of the bullet character may be different on your computer.

4 Click elsewhere in your document to deselect the text.

TIP!

Word may automatically indent bullets.

Numbered list

Below are examples of numbered lists.

1. Found in salt water	1 Found in salt water
2. Need clear, sediment-free waters	2 Need clear, sediment-free waters
3. Grow in shallow waters	3 Grow in shallow waters

▶▶ **How to...** *create a numbered list*

1 In your document, highlight the text to be numbered.

2 Click on the **Numbering** ≔ icon.

3 The selected text will display as a numbered list.

4 Click elsewhere in your document to deselect the text.

TIP!

Word may automatically indent a numbered list.

Check your understanding *Create a bulleted list*

1 In the file **greatreef**, apply a bullet character to the following three lines of text:

Found in salt water

Need clear, sediment-free waters

Grow in shallow waters

2 Save the file keeping the filename **greatreef**.

Tabs and indents

Tabs are used to set the text further in from the left-hand margin.

      Indented text looks like this.

Word has preset tab positions which appear as small grey lines just under the ruler. Tabs can also be created at specific measurements.

▶▶ **How to...** *indent text to a preset tab position*

1 In your document, place the cursor before the text to be indented.

2 Make sure there are no spaces before the first letter of the text.

3 Press the Tab key.

4 The first line of text will be set further in from the left margin.

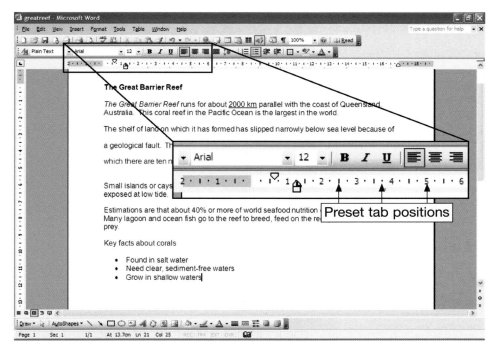

FIGURE 1.103 Ruler bar – arrows show tab positions that are already set

Another method of indenting text from the left margin is: click the **Format** menu, click **Paragraph**, in the **Indentation** section, click the up arrow to the right of Left or enter the required measurement.

▶▶ How to... *create a new tab position*

1 In the **Menu bar**, click on **Format**.

2 From the **Format** menu, click on **Tabs**.

3 A **Tabs** dialogue box is displayed (Figure 1.104).

4 In the **Tab stop position** box, enter the new measurement.

5 Click on **Set**.

6 Click on **OK** to set the tab.

7 To indent the text, place the cursor before the text to be indented.

8 Press the **Tab** key.

9 The first line of text will be set in from the left margin to the tab position that you set.

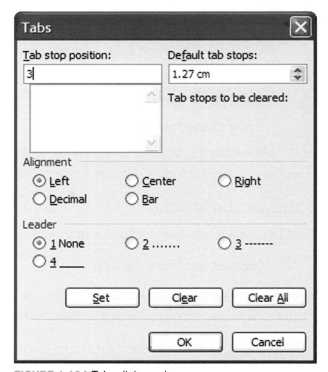

FIGURE 1.104 Tabs dialogue box

To set a tab, click on the required position on the ruler line. A tab will be set at that position (Figure 1.105).

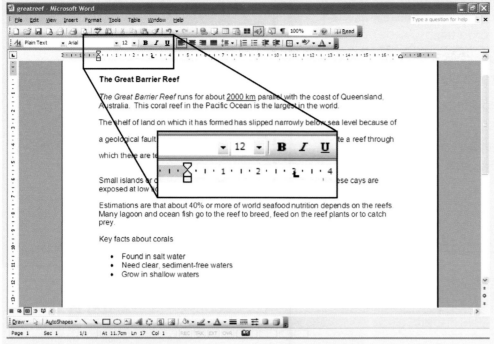

FIGURE 1.105 Tab mark on the ruler

Check your understanding · Indent text

1   In the file **greatreef**, set a tab at **3 cm** from the left-hand margin.

2   Indent the text **Key facts about corals** to the new tab position of **3 cm**.

3   Save your file, keeping the filename **greatreef**.

Tables

Tables can be used to display items in a document more clearly. Tables consist of columns and rows. Each box in the table is referred to as a cell. Tables can be displayed with or without outside borders and/or internal gridlines.

▶▶ How to... insert a table

1   In your document, place the cursor where the table is to be inserted.

2   In the **Menu bar**, click on **Table**.

3   From the **Table** menu, select **Insert** and then click on **Table**.

4 The **Insert Table** dialogue box is displayed (Figure 1.106).

5 Click in the **Number of columns** box and enter the number of columns. Alternatively, use the **up/down arrows** to do this.

6 Click in the **Number of rows** box and enter the number of rows or use the **up/down arrows**.

7 Click on **OK** to display the empty table in your document.

A table with 2 columns and 5 rows is shown below. Data is entered into the cells.

Cell	Cell
Cell	Cell
Cell	Cell
Cell	Cell
Cell	Cell

FIGURE 1.106 Insert Table dialogue box

TIP!

Click the button for **Fixed column width.** The width of each column will be the same.

▶▶ How to... enter text in a table

1 Place the cursor in the first cell (top left cell) of the table.

2 Enter the required text.

3 Press the **Tab** key or click in the next cell.

4 The cursor moves to the next column of the first row.

5 Enter the required text.

6 Press the **Tab** key again.

7 The cursor moves to the second row, first column.

8 Enter the rest of the text, pressing the Tab key to move from one cell to the next.

Displaying table borders and gridlines

Borders are the lines on the outside of the table (above, below, to the left and to the right). Gridlines are the divisions between the columns and the rows inside the table.

TIP!

Borders and gridlines may display automatically when you insert a table, but it is advisable to follow the steps on page 85 to make sure that dark borders will be clearly displayed on a printout.

▶▶ How to... *display borders and gridlines on a table*

1. To highlight the table, click in the top left cell of the table, hold down the **Shift** key, then click in the bottom right cell of the table.

2. In the **Menu bar**, click on **Format**.

3. From the **Format** menu, click on **Borders and Shading**.

4. The **Borders and Shading** dialogue box is displayed.

5. Select the **Borders** tab (Figure 1.107).

6. Under **Setting** click on **All**.

7. Under **Preview**, check that the **Apply to** option is set to **Table**.

8. Click on **OK** to display borders and gridlines on the table.

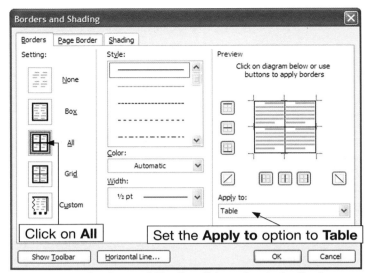

FIGURE 1.107 Borders and Shading dialogue box in the Borders tab view

TIP!

To display borders, highlight a table, click on the **drop-down arrow** next to the **Outside Border** icon on the **Standard toolbar**, and click on the **All Borders** option (Figure 1.108).

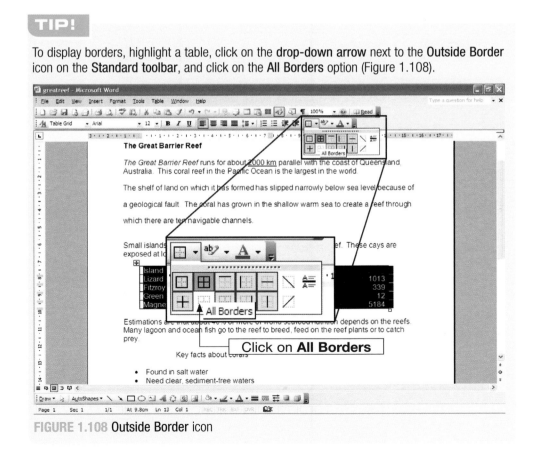

FIGURE 1.108 Outside Border icon

Applying shading to table cells

▶▶ How to... *apply shading to table cell(s)*

1 Highlight the table cells that are to be shaded by dragging your mouse over the required cells.

2 In the **Menu bar**, click on **Format**.

3 From the Format menu, click on **Borders and Shading**.

4 The **Borders and Shading** dialogue box is displayed.

5 Click on the **Shading** tab to select it (Figure 1.109).

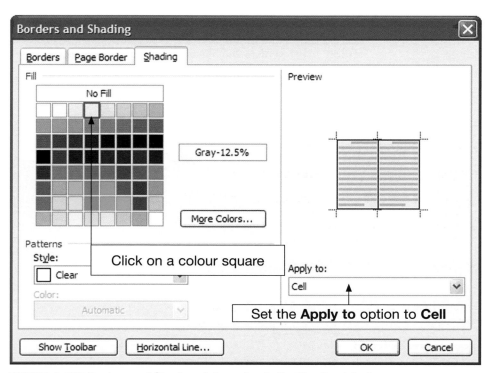

FIGURE 1.109 Borders and Shading dialogue box in the Shading tab view

6 Under **Fill**, click on a suitable colour square. Make sure you choose a colour that will allow any text in the cell to be read clearly.

7 Under **Preview**, check that the **Apply to** option is set to **Cell**.

8 Click on **OK** to apply shading to the highlighted cells.

9 Click in the document to deselect the cells.

1 In the file **greatreef**, insert a **paragraph break** and a clear **line space** at the end of the third paragraph after 'at low tide'.

2 Insert a **table** with **2 columns** and **5 rows**.

3 Enter the data below in the table:

Island	Size in hectares
Lizard Island	1013
Fitzroy Island	339
Green Island	12
Magnetic Island	5184

4 Make sure all table **borders** are displayed as shown above.

5 Format the text **Size in hectares** to be bold.

6 Right-align all the figures in the **Size in hectares** column.

7 Enter your name in the header or footer of the document.

8 Save the file keeping the filename **greatreef**.

Changing the column width of a table

When you insert a table in Word (and you choose the **Fixed Column Width** option), the table will extend from the left to the right margin. You may wish to reduce the width of the columns to improve the display. To do this you will need to have a good mouse and good mouse skills.

▶▶ How to... *change the column width of a table (optional)*

1 In the table, move the mouse pointer on to the left border of column one.

2 The mouse pointer turns into a double vertical line with arrows ◀‖▶.

3 Press and hold down the left mouse button, then drag the border to the right until the column width is reduced.

4 Release the left mouse button.

TIP!

Double-click on ◀‖▶. Word automatically adjusts the column width to fit the text within it.

Repeat this for column two as follows:

5 Move your mouse pointer on to the right border of column two.

6 The mouse pointer will turn into a double vertical line with arrows pointing both left and right.

7 Press and hold down the left mouse button, then drag the border to the left until the column width is reduced.

8 Release the left mouse button.

TIP!

Make sure the text inside both columns is fully visible.

Word count

Word count is a feature that counts the number of words in a document or in selected text.

▶▶ How to... *use word count*

1 In your document, highlight the selected text to be word counted OR, to count the number of words in the entire document, press **Ctrl** and **A** at the same time, which will highlight all the text in the document.

2 In the **Menu bar**, click on **Tools**.

3 From the **Tools** menu, click on **Word Count**.

4 The **Word Count** dialogue box is displayed (Figure 1.110).

5 The second item displays the number of words in the selected text. Make a note of this.

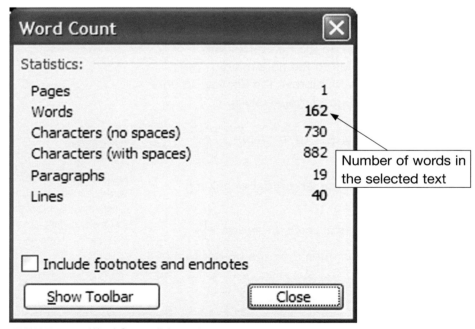

FIGURE 1.110 Word Count dialogue box

6 Click on **Close** to close the dialogue box

1 In the file **greatreef**, carry out a **word count** to count the number of words in the whole document.

2 Enter the number of words at the end of the document. (You should have 162 words.)

3 Save the file, keeping the filename **greatreef**.

4 Print one copy of the file.

5 Close the file and exit **Word**.

Now, check your document **greatreef** against the screen print in Figure 1.111. Your table width and display of the word count may be different. The **Show/Hide** has been displayed to help you check your spacing.

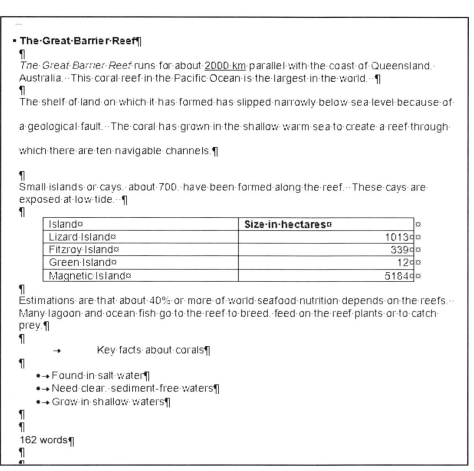

FIGURE 1.111 The final document **greatreef**, with Show/Hide tool switched on

By working through Section 2 you will have learnt the skills below. Read each item to help you decide how confident you feel about each skill.

- open an existing file and save it using a different filename
- use bold, italic and underline
- delete text
- move text
- insert text
- use **Find and Replace**
- insert paragraph break
- change line spacing
- use bullets and numbering
- use tabs and indents
- insert a table
- display borders and gridlines for a table
- apply shading to table cell(s)
- apply alignment to text in a table
- use word count
- save an updated document
- print an updated document.

If you think you need more practice on any of the skills above, go back and work through the skill(s) again.

If you feel confident, do the Build-up and Practice tasks.

Remember, you can refer to the **Quick reference** guides when doing any tasks and during an assessment.

Click means click with the left mouse button

QUICK REFERENCE – *File management*

Keep a copy of this page next to you. Refer to it when working through tasks and during any assessments.

HOW TO...	METHOD	QUICK METHOD	USING MENUS
	All file management tasks must be done in your user area through the My Computer window		
Create a folder	In the File and Folder Tasks box → Click on Make a new folder → New Folder is displayed → Press Backspace to delete the words New Folder → Type the required folder name → Press Enter	In your user area → Right-click → New → Folder → Delete 'New Folder' → Enter new name → Enter	File menu → New → Folder → Delete 'New Folder' → Enter new name → Enter
Create a subfolder	Double-click to open folder → In the File and Folder Tasks box → Click on Make a new folder → New Folder is displayed → Press Backspace to delete the words 'New Folder' → Enter the required subfolder name → Press Enter	Open relevant folder → Right click → New → Folder → Delete 'New Folder' → Enter new name → Enter	Double-click to open existing folder → File menu → New → Folder → Delete 'New Folder' → Enter new name → Enter
Rename a file	Click on the file you want to rename → In the File and Folder Tasks box → Click on Rename this file → Press Backspace to delete the existing name → Enter the new filename → Press Enter	Right-click on existing file → Click on Rename → Delete existing name → Enter new name → Enter	Click on file → File menu → Rename → Delete existing name → Enter new name → Enter
Rename a folder	Click on the folder you want to rename → In the File and Folder Tasks box → Click on Rename this folder → Press Backspace to delete the existing name → Enter the new folder name → Press Enter	Right-click on existing folder → Click on Rename → Delete existing name → Enter new name → Enter	Click on folder → File menu → Rename → Delete existing name → Enter new name → Enter
Delete a file	Click on the file you want to delete → In the File and Folder Tasks box → Click on Delete this file → A Confirm File Delete dialogue box displays → Click on Yes	Click on file → Right-click → Delete OR click on file → press Delete key → a Confirm File Delete dialogue box displays → Click on Yes	Click on file → File menu → Delete → a Confirm File Delete dialogue box displays → Click on Yes

(continued overleaf)

HOW TO...	METHOD	QUICK METHOD	USING MENUS
	All file management tasks must be done in your user area through the My Computer window		
Delete a folder	Click on the folder you want to delete → In the File and Folder Tasks box → Click on Delete this folder → A Confirm Folder Delete dialogue box displays → Click on Yes	Click on folder → Right-click → Delete OR click on folder → Press Delete key	Click on folder → File menu → Delete → a Confirm Folder Delete dialogue box displays → Click on Yes
Move a file	Click on the file you want to move → In the File and Folder Tasks box → Click on Move this file → A Move Items dialogue box displays → Select the folder that you want to move the file into → Click on Move	Right-click on file → Cut → Go to folder that you want to move file to → Right-click → Paste	Click on file → Edit menu → Cut → Go to folder that you want to move file to → Double-click to open folder → Edit menu → Paste
Move a folder	Click on the folder you want to move → In the File and Folder Tasks box → Click on Move this folder → A Move Items dialogue box displays → Select the folder that you want to move the folder into → Click on Move	Right-click on folder → Cut → Go to folder that you want to move folder to → Right-click → Paste	Click on folder → Edit menu → Cut → Go to folder that you want to move folder to → Double-click to open folder → Edit menu → Paste
Copy a file	Click on the file you want to copy → In the File and Folder Tasks box → Click on Copy this file → A Copy Items dialogue box displays → Click on the folder name in your user area that you want to copy the file to → Click on Copy	Right-click on file → Copy → Use the Back button in the toolbar to go to the folder that you want to copy file to → Right-click → Paste	Click on file → Edit menu → Copy → Go to folder that you want to copy file to → Double-click to open folder → Edit menu → Paste
Copy a folder	Click on the folder you want to copy → In the File and Folder Tasks box → Click on Copy this folder → A Copy Items dialogue box displays → Click on the folder name in your user area that you want to copy the folder to → Click on Copy	Right-click on folder → Copy → Use the Back button in the toolbar to go to the folder that you want to copy folder to → Right-click → Paste	Click on folder → Edit menu → Copy → Go to folder that you want to copy folder to → Double-click to open folder → Edit menu → Paste

| --- | --- | --- | --- |
All file management tasks must be done in your user area through the My Computer window			
Take a screen print of folder structure	Double-click to open the folder for which you want to take a screen print of the contents → Press Alt and Print Screen at the same time → Load Microsoft Word → Start → Programs → Microsoft Office → Microsoft Office Word 2003 → In blank document → Click on the Paste icon	Go to user area → Open folder that you want to screen print → Alt + Print Screen keys at the same time (or Print Screen key only) → Open Word document → Right-click in document → Menu displays → Paste	Go to user area → Open folder that you want to screen print → Alt + Print Screen keys at the same time (or Print Screen key only) → Open Word document → Edit menu → Paste
Save the screen print (Tip! Paste all your screen prints into one Word document)	In Word click on the File menu → Click on Save → Save As dialogue box displays → Click on the down arrow to the right of the Save in box, then click on your user area → In the filename row → Delete any text → Enter the required filename → Click on Save	Click on the Save icon → Save As dialogue box displays → Make sure you save into the correct folder → Enter a filename → Save OR press Ctrl + S to open Save As window	File menu → Save As → Make sure you save into the correct folder → Delete existing text, enter a filename → Save
Print your screen print	Click on the Print icon	Click on the Print icon	File menu → Print → OK
Close a document and exit Word	Click on the Close (red cross) icon at the top right of the window	Click on the Close (red cross) icon at the top right of the window	File menu → Close → File menu → Exit
Close the My Computer window	Click on the Close (red cross) icon at the top right	Click on the Close (red cross) icon at the top right	File menu → Close

Click means click with the left mouse button

QUICK REFERENCE – Create a new document

Keep a copy of this page next to you. Refer to it when working through tasks and during any assessments.

HOW TO...	METHOD	QUICK METHOD	USING MENUS
Start Word	Click on Start → All Programs → Microsoft Office → Microsoft Office Word 2003	Click on the Word icon on the Quick Launch bar *OR* double-click on the Word icon on the desktop	Start → All Programs → Microsoft Office → Microsoft Office Word 2003
Create a new document	Click on File menu → New (Note: a new blank document opens when you load Word)	Click on the New icon on the toolbar	File menu → New
Set orientation	Click on File menu → Page Setup → Margins tab → Click on Portrait or Landscape → Click on OK	Double-click on the blue part of Ruler bar → Page Setup dialogue box opens → Click on Portrait or Landscape → OK	File → Page Setup → Margins tab → Click on Portrait or Landscape → OK
Set margins	Click on File menu → Page Setup → Margins tab → Enter the measurement for each margin or use the up/down arrows → Click on OK	Double-click on the blue part of Ruler bar → Page Setup dialogue box displays → Enter required margins *OR* use up/down arrows → OK	File → Page Setup → Margins tab → Enter required margins or use up/down arrows → OK
Set line spacing	Click on Format menu → Paragraph → Indents and Spacing tab → Line spacing → Click on drop-down arrow → Select an option → Click on OK	Single line spacing is set as default. To set double line spacing, press the Ctrl and 2 keys together	Highlight text → Format menu → Paragraph → Click on down arrow next to Line spacing box → Select option → OK
Set font size before entering text	Click on drop-down arrow next to Font Size on toolbar → Click on required size	Click on the drop-down arrow next to Font Size on toolbar → Click on required size	Format menu → Font → Size → OK

HOW TO...	METHOD	QUICK METHOD	USING MENUS
Set font size after entering text	Highlight relevant text → Click on drop-down arrow next to Font Size on toolbar → Click on required size	Highlight text → Click on Ctrl and [to decrease text size by one point at a time. Click Ctrl and] to increase text size by one point at a time. [ ] are square brackets on the keyboard	Highlight text → Format menu → Font → Size → OK
Set font type before entering text	Click on drop-down arrow next to Font on toolbar → Click on required font name	Click on drop-down arrow next to Font on toolbar → Click on required font name	Format menu → Font → Font name → OK
Set font type after entering text	Highlight relevant text → Click on drop-down arrow next to Font on toolbar → Click on font name	Highlight relevant text → Click on drop-down arrow next to Font on toolbar → Click on font name	Highlight text → Format menu → Font → Font name → OK
Align text before entering text	Click on the Align Left, Align Right, Center align or Justify icon on toolbar	Left align: Ctrl + L Right align: Ctrl + R Fully justify: Ctrl + J Centre: Ctrl + E	Format menu → Paragraph → Click on drop-down arrow next to Alignment → Click on required alignment → OK
Align text after entering text	Highlight relevant text → Click on the Align Left, Align Right, Center align or Justify icon	Highlight relevant text → Left align: Ctrl + L Right align: Ctrl + R Fully justify: Ctrl + J Centre: Ctrl + E	Highlight relevant text → Format menu → Paragraph → Click on drop-down arrow next to Alignment → Click on required alignment → OK

(continued overleaf)

HOW TO...	METHOD	QUICK METHOD	USING MENUS
Set or check the language	Click on Tools menu → Language → Set Language to English (U.K.) → Click on OK	Language (English U.K.) may be displayed on Status bar (depends on your computer settings)	Tools menu → Language → Set Language → Set language to English (U.K.) → OK
Spell check	Click on Spelling and Grammar icon → If Word finds an error → Spelling and Grammar dialogue box displays → Incorrect word is highlighted in red in Not in dictionary box → Alternatives may be given in Suggestions box → Click on correct suggestion → Click on Change	Click on the Spelling and Grammar icon → Spelling and Grammar dialogue box displays → Incorrect word is highlighted in red in Not in dictionary box → Alternatives may be given in Suggestions box → Click on correct suggestion → Change	Tools menu → Spelling and Grammar → Spelling and Grammar dialogue box displays → Incorrect word is highlighted in red in Not in dictionary box → Alternatives may be given in Suggestions box → Click on correct suggestion → Change
Check spelling as you type	Right-click within word underlined in red → List of suggestions displays → Click on correct option from suggested list	Default is to check spelling as you type → Incorrect words underlined in red → Right-click within Word → Choose correct suggestion	Tools menu → Options → Spelling and Grammar tab → Make sure there is a tick in Check spelling as you type box → Incorrectly spelt words will be underlined in red
Use Show/Hide tool to check document	Click on Show/Hide icon on toolbar → Check for one dot between words, one dot after comma, two dots after full stop, one paragraph marker at the end of a paragraph and one paragraph marker between paragraphs	Click on Show/Hide icon on toolbar → Check for one dot between words, one dot after comma, two dots after full stop, one paragraph marker at the end of a paragraph and one paragraph marker between paragraphs	Click on Show/Hide icon on toolbar → Check for one dot between words, one dot after comma; two dots after full stop, one paragraph marker at the end of a paragraph and one paragraph marker between paragraphs

HOW TO...	METHOD	QUICK METHOD	USING MENUS
Save a Word document	Click on File menu → Click on Save As → Save As dialogue box displays → Click on down arrow to right of Save in box, then click on your user area → In File name box, delete any existing text → Enter required filename → Click on Save	Click on the Save icon → In Save As dialogue box → Click on down arrow to the right of the Save in box, then click on your user area → In File name box, delete any existing text → Enter required filename → Click on Save OR press Ctrl + S to open Save As dialogue box	File menu → Save As → In Save As dialogue box → Click on down arrow to the right of the Save in box, then click on your user area → In File name box, delete any existing text → Enter required filename → Save
Save a Word document into a new folder from within Word	Click on File menu → Click on Save As → Save As dialogue box displays → Click on down arrow to right of Save in box, then click on your user area → Click on the Create New Folder icon → New Folder dialogue box opens → Enter new folder name → Click on OK → In File name box delete any existing text → Enter required filename → Click on Save	Click on the Save icon → Enter a filename → Click on Create New Folder → Enter new folder name → OK → Make sure you save into the correct folder/user area → Save	File menu → Save As → Enter a filename → Click on Create New Folder → Enter new folder name → Make sure you save into the correct folder/user area → Save
Save an existing document	Click on File menu → Click on Save	Click on the Save icon OR press Ctrl + S	File menu → Save
Print a document	Click on File menu → Click on Print → Print dialogue box displays → Check Page Range is set to All → Set Number of copies to 1 → Click on OK	Click on the Print icon	File menu → Print → OK

(continued overleaf)

HOW TO...	METHOD	QUICK METHOD	USING MENUS
Add a header or footer	Click on View menu → Click on Header and Footer → Enter required information in header → Click on Switch between Header and Footer icon → Enter required information in footer → Click on Close	Click on View menu → Click on Header and Footer → Enter the required information in the header → Click on the Switch Between Header and Footer icon → Enter any required information in the footer → Don't click Close until you've added all headers and footers. In Print Layout view, if there are headers/footers entered → Double-click on header/footer to open header/footer window quickly	View menu → Header and Footer → Enter required information in the header → Click on Switch Between Header and Footer icon → Enter required information in footer → Close
Add an automatic date	Click on View menu → Click on Header and Footer → Click on Insert Date icon → Click on Close		View menu → Header and Footer → Click on Insert Date icon → Close
Add an automatic filename	Click on View menu → Click on Header and Footer → Click on the drop-down arrow next to Insert AutoText → Click on Filename → Click on Close → Use Print Preview to check		View menu → Header and Footer → Click on the drop-down arrow next to Insert AutoText → Click on Filename → Close
Close a document	Click on File menu → Click on Close	Click on the black cross to close the document	File menu → Close
Exit Word	Click on File menu → Click on Exit	Click on the red cross to exit Word	File menu → Exit
Close a document and exit Word	Click on File menu → Click on Close → Click on File menu→ Click on Exit	Click on the red cross to close any open documents and exit Word	File menu → Close → File menu → Exit

QUICK REFERENCE – *Edit a document*

Keep a copy of this page next to you. Refer to it when working through tasks and during any assessments.

HOW TO...	METHOD	QUICK METHOD	USING MENUS
Save an existing document with a new filename	Click on File menu → Save As → Save As dialogue box displays → Click on down arrow to right of Save in → Click on user area → In Filename box → Delete existing filename → Enter new filename → Click on down arrow to the right of Save as type box → Click on Word Document → Click on Save	Press Alt + F keys → File menu displays → Press A key → Save As dialogue box displays → Click on down arrow next to Save in box → Click on user area → In File name box → Delete existing filename → Enter new filename → Click on down arrow to the right of Save as type box → Click on Word Document → Save	File menu → Save As → Save As dialogue box displays → Click on down arrow to right of Save in box → Click on user area → In File name box → Delete existing filename → Enter new filename → Click on down arrow to the right of Save as type box → Click on Word Document → Save
Format text to be bold	Highlight text → Click on Bold icon → Click elsewhere in document to deselect text	Highlight text → Ctrl + B OR click on the Bold icon	Highlight text → Format menu → Font → Bold → OK
Format text to be italic	Highlight text → Click on the Italic icon → Click elsewhere in document to deselect text	Highlight text → Ctrl + I OR click on the Italic icon	Highlight text → Format menu → Font → Italic → OK
Underline text	Highlight text → Click on the Underline icon → Click elsewhere in document to deselect text	Highlight text → Ctrl + U OR click on the Underline icon	Highlight text → Format menu → Font → Click on drop-down arrow below Underline style → OK
Delete text	Highlight relevant text including any associated punctuation → Click on the Cut icon	Highlight text → Press Delete key	Highlight text → Edit menu → Cut

(continued overleaf)

HOW TO...	METHOD	QUICK METHOD	USING MENUS
Move text	Highlight relevant text including any associated punctuation → Click on the Cut icon → Click in new position → Insert correct spacing → Click on the Paste icon	Highlight text → Click and drag highlighted text to new position	Highlight text → Edit menu → Cut → Place cursor in new position → Edit menu → Paste
Insert text	Check that OVR is switched off (greyed out) in Status bar → Click in position that you want to insert text → Insert correct spacing → Enter text → Insert correct spacing after inserted text	Place cursor in required place → Enter text	N/A
Find and replace	Click on Edit menu → Click on Replace → Find and Replace dialogue box displays → In Find what box, enter word to replace → In Replace with box, enter new word → Click on More → Tick Find whole words only → Click on Replace All → Click on OK → Click on Close	Press Ctrl + H keys → In Find what box, enter word to replace → In Replace with box, enter new word → Click on More → Tick Find whole words only → Replace All → OK → Close	Edit menu → Replace → Find and Replace dialogue box displays → In Find what box, enter word to be replaced → In Replace with box, enter new word → More → Tick Find whole words only → Replace All → OK → Close
Insert a paragraph break	Place cursor just before the first word of the sentence that will start the new paragraph → Press Enter key twice → Click on the Show/Hide tool icon to check spacing is correct	Place cursor in required position → Press Enter key on the keyboard twice	N/A
Change line spacing	Highlight relevant text → Click on Format menu → Click on Paragraph → Paragraph dialogue box displays → Indents and Spacing tab → Click on down arrow below Line spacing → Click on line spacing option required → Click on OK → Click outside the highlighted area to deselect text	Highlight text → Double line spacing: Ctrl + 2 Single line spacing: Ctrl + 1	Highlight text → Format menu → Paragraph → Paragraph dialogue box displays → Indents and Spacing tab → Click on the down arrow under Line spacing → Click on line spacing required → OK → Click outside the highlighted area to remove the highlight

HOW TO...	METHOD	QUICK METHOD	USING MENUS
Create a bulleted list	Highlight relevant text → Click on Bullets icon	Highlight relevant text → Click on the Bullets icon	Highlight text → Format menu → Bullets and Numbering → Click on required bullet style → OK
Create a numbered list	Highlight relevant text → Click on Numbering icon	Highlight text → Click on Numbering icon	Highlight text → Format menu → Bullets and Numbering → Click on Numbered tab → Click on required number style → OK
Indent text to a preset tab position	Place the cursor before the text → Make sure there are no spaces before the first letter of the text → Press the Tab key	Place cursor in front of text → Press Tab key	N/A
Create a new tab position and indent text	Click on Format menu → Click on Tabs → In the Tab stop position enter new measurement → Click on Set → Click on OK → To indent the text, place the cursor before the text → Press Tab key	Click on required position on Ruler bar → Place cursor in front of text → Press Tab key	Format menu → Tabs → Enter measurement → Set → OK → To indent text, place the cursor before the text → Press Tab key
Insert a table	Place cursor in correct position → Click on the Table menu → Click on Insert → Click on Table → Insert Table dialogue box displays → Click in Number of columns box and enter number of columns required → Click in Number of rows box and enter number of rows required → Click on OK	Click on the Insert Table icon → Drag your mouse over the required number of rows and columns (option is limited to 5 columns and 4 rows) → Release mouse button	Table menu → Insert → Table → Insert Table dialogue box displays → Click in the Number of columns box and enter the number of columns → Click in the Number of rows box and enter the number of rows → OK

(continued overleaf)

HOW TO...	METHOD	QUICK METHOD	USING MENUS
Enter text in table	Place cursor in first cell of the table → Enter text → press Tab key to move from cell to cell (or click in relevant cell)	Place cursor in first table cell → Enter text → Press Tab key to move from cell to cell	N/A
Display table borders and gridlines	Highlight table as follows → Click in top left cell of table, hold down the Shift key then click in bottom right cell of table → Click on Format menu → Click on Borders and Shading → In Borders tab → Click on All → Check Apply to is set to Table → Click on OK	Highlight table → Click in top left cell, hold down Shift key, then click in bottom right cell → Click on drop-down arrow next to Borders icon on toolbar → Select All Borders option	Click in Table → Table menu → Table Properties → Borders and Shading → Borders tab → All → OK
Change the column width of a table	Move your mouse on column border → Pointer turns into a double arrow → Drag border to change column width	Move mouse pointer on border → Double arrows display on border → Drag border to change column width	Click in Table → Table menu → Table Properties → Column tab → Use up/down arrows to change measurement or enter required measurement → OK
Use word count	Highlight relevant text → Click on Tools menu → Click on Word Count → Word Count dialogue box displays → Number of words is second item → Click on Close → Click in the document to deselect the text	Highlight relevant text → Click on Tools menu → Click on Word Count → Word Count dialogue box displays → Number of words is second item → Close → Click in the document to deselect the text	Highlight relevant text → Tools menu → Word Count → Word Count dialogue box displays → Second item displays the number of words → Close → Click in the document to deselect the text

Answer the following questions:

1 What is the term for all the physical parts of a computer, e.g. monitor, keyboard, that you can see and touch?

2 How do you display the **Start** menu?

3 Why is it important to take a break from looking at the computer screen?

4 Which two keys should be used to enter the J of John?

5 Which mouse button would you press to right-click?

6 Which two keys would you press to take a screen print?

7 What is the term used to describe the action when the left mouse button is pressed quickly twice?

8 What term is used to describe the programs that allow you to use the computer?

9 What does RSI stand for?

10 You might have to use a password when logging on to a computer. When else might you need to use a password?

11 What is the term used to describe small pictures on the desktop screen?

12 What is the name of the bar that usually runs along the bottom of the computer screen?

13 Which option would you select from the **Start** menu to close down the computer?

BUILD-UP TASK ① *File management*

For this task, you will need the following folders and files from the **files_chapter1** folder:

- the folder **task1** containing three text files: **autumn, spring, summer** (Figure 1.55)

- the subfolder **t1files** containing:

  – an image file: **daffy**

  – a text file: **winter** (Figure 1.56).

FIGURE 1.55 The folder task1

1a Rename the folder **task1** to be your **name (first and last name)**.

b In this folder create a new subfolder **seasons**.

2 Copy the text file **spring** to the subfolder **seasons**.

3 Move the text file **summer** from the folder **your name** into the subfolder **seasons**.

4 Delete the folder **t1files** and its contents.

5 Take a screen print as evidence of the folder **your name** **(first and last name)** and the contents of this folder.

FIGURE 1.56 The subfolder t1files

6 Take a screen print of the subfolder **seasons** and the contents of this folder.

7 Enter your **name** and today's **date** in the document containing the screen prints.

8 Save the screen print(s) into your user area using suitable filename(s). (On your screen print, you are not expected to show the saved file(s) containing the screen print.)

9 The file(s) containing your screen prints may be saved in any folder in your user area.

10 Print the file(s) containing the screen prints. Make sure that all the contents of the folders and the subfolder are clearly visible on the printout.

11 Close any open files.

BUILD-UP TASK 2 *Create a new document*

1 Create a new word processing document.

2 Set the page orientation to **portrait**.

3 Set the **top**, **left** and **right** page margins to **3.3 cm**.

4 Set the font type to **Arial**.

5 Set the font size to **12**.

6 a Enter the following text in **single line spacing**.

   b Make sure the text is **fully justified**.

THE VICTORIA FALLS

The Zambezi River trickles to life in the highlands of north-west Zambia and meanders through the plains. Then the route becomes more hazardous, with rocky gorges, some narrow, others over a kilometre long.

The River passes through palm-fringed banks before it becomes turbulent, gathering strength for its mighty leap over the cliffs to form what is now known to the world as the Victoria Falls.

Five separate falls make up the Victoria Falls: Devil's Cataract, Main Falls, Horseshoe Falls, Rainbow Falls and Eastern Cataract. In flood season, 545 million litres of water a minute crash down the 100-metre height of the Falls along their 1688-metre width.

7 Save the file using the filename **wptask1** in a new folder called **wordpro**.

BUILD-UP TASK 3 *Create a new document*

1 Continue working in your saved file **wptask1**.

2 a In the header, enter your **name** and **centre number**.

   b In the footer, insert an **automatic date** and an **automatic filename**.

   c The headers and footers may be in any font size and style.

3 a Check the file for any errors and carry out a spell check.

   b Save the file keeping the filename **wptask1** in the folder **wordpro**.

   c Use **Print Preview** to check the automatic filename **wptask1** in the footer.

   d Print the file **wptask1**.

4 Close the file **wptask1**.

5 Exit Word.

Before you begin this task, check that you have a copy of the folder **files_chapter2** in your user area. The file called **france**, which you will need for this task, is in the folder.

1 Open the file called **france**.

2 Save the file **france** using the filename **tourism**.

3 In the first paragraph, insert a **paragraph break** and a clear **line space** after the second sentence ending '. . . Mont Saint Michel'.

4 a At the end of the third paragraph, insert a **paragraph break** and a clear **line space**.

   b Create a table with **2 columns** and **5 rows**.

   c Enter the data below in the table:

Tours	Cost in Euros
Visit with commentary	4.50
Visit with audio guide	5.00
Unaccompanied visit	5.50
Guided visit	5.50

   d Make sure all borders will be displayed for the table on the printout, as shown above.

   e Make sure there is one clear **line space** after the table.

   f Format the table heading **Tours** to be **bold**.

   g **Centre** the heading **Cost in Euros**.

   h The remaining text and numbers should be **left-aligned**.

5 Enter your **name** in the header.

6 Insert an **automatic date** and an **automatic filename** in the footer.

7 Save your file keeping the filename **tourism**.

8 Close the file.

You will make some amendments to the file **tourism** that you saved in Build-up task 4 Edit a document.

1 Open the file **tourism**.

2 In the first paragraph, insert the following text as the last sentence: **This inspired the bishop to build the original abbey**.

3 In the first paragraph, delete the text: **and the Disney Resort**
Do not delete the comma after Resort.

4 In the third paragraph, move the text: **Three million tourists go to Mont Saint Michel every year.** to be the last sentence of the third paragraph.

5 a Apply a **bullet** character to the following three lines of text:

   Paris
   Disney Resort
   Mont Saint Michel

   b Apply **double line spacing** to the bulleted text only.

   c Indent the text **Popular destinations** so that it is set in from the left margin.

6 Replace the word **visitors** with the word **tourists** wherever it occurs (three times in all).

7 Check the text for accuracy.

8 Save the file keeping the filename **tourism**.

9 a Using the software facility, carry out a **word count** in the file.

   b Enter the number of words on your printout at least two lines below the bulleted list. You may use any alignment for this.

10 Save the file keeping the filename **tourism**.

11 Print the file **tourism**.

12 Close the file.

Task 1

For this task, you will need the following folders and files from the **files_chapter1** folder:

- the folder **task2** containing:
  - two text files: **jul** and **sep**
  - an image file: **jun** (Figure 1.57)

- the subfolder **t2files** containing:
  - an image file: **may**
  - a text file: **nov** (Figure 1.58).

1 a Rename the folder **task2** to: **years**.

b In this folder create a new subfolder: **months**.

2 Copy the image file **jun** to the subfolder **months**.

3 Move the text file **jul** from the folder **years** into the subfolder **months**.

FIGURE 1.57 The folder **task2**

FIGURE 1.58 The subfolder **t2files**

4 Delete the file **sep** from the folder **years**.

a Take a screen print as evidence of the folder **years** and its contents.

b Take a screen print of the subfolder **months** and its contents.

c Enter your **name** and today's **date** in this document.

d Save the screen print(s) into your user area using suitable filename(s). (On your screen print, you are not expected to show the saved file(s) containing the screen print.)

e The file(s) containing your screen prints may be saved in any folder in your user area.

f Print the file(s) containing the screen prints. Make sure that all the contents of the folders and the subfolders are clearly visible on the printout.

5 Close any open files.

Task 2

1 Create a new word processing document.

2 Set the page orientation to **landscape**.

3 Set the **top, left** and **right** page margins to **2.5 cm**.

4 Set the font type to **Times New Roman**.

5 Set the font size to **14**.

6 a Enter the following text in **double line spacing**.

  b Make sure the text is **left-aligned**.

TIP!

When you enter **th** after 19, Word will automatically make it superscript

The World on a Plate

Volcanoes and earthquakes are more common in some parts of the world than others. Although this was known in the early 19th century, it was not until the 1960s, when the secrets of the deep ocean floor began to be revealed, that scientists found an explanation.

This became known as the theory of plate tectonics. "Tectonic" is a Greek word that means building. These tectonic plates move across the Earth's surface in response to forces and movements deep within the planet. The plate boundaries, where plates collide, rub or move, are areas of intense geological activity.

Volcanoes and earthquakes occur at these boundaries (the nature of the boundary dictates the nature of the eruption that occurs there).

7 a **Centre** the heading.

  b Format the heading to be **bold** and **italic**.

8 a In the header, insert an **automatic date** and an **automatic filename**.

  b In the footer, enter your **name** and **centre number**.

9 a Check the file for any errors and carry out a spell check.

  b Save the file with the filename **wptask2** in the folder **wordpro** that you created earlier. Use **Print Preview** to check the automatic filename **wptask2** in the footer.

10 Print the file **wptask2**.

11 Close the file **wptask2**.

12 Exit Word.

Task 3

Before you begin this task, check that you have a copy of the folder **files_chapter2** in your user area. The file called **america**, which you will need for this task, is in the folder.

1 Open the file **america.**

2 Save the file **america** using the filename **chicago**.

3 a Set a new tab at **1.5 cm**.

   b Tab the text **Chicago is recognised for its** so that this text is indented **1.5 cm** from the left margin.

4 Apply a **bullet** character to the following six lines of text:

   music and theatrical achievements
   sporting greats
   shops
   range of restaurants
   museums
   art displays.

5 In the paragraph beginning **Lake Michigan is the**… insert a **paragraph break** and a clear **line space** after the second sentence ending… **United States and Canada**.

6 Create a **table** with **2 columns** and **4 rows** below the final paragraph, leaving one clear **line space** after the paragraph.

   a Enter the data below in the table:

Attraction	Annual Visitors
Navy Pier	5325000
Adler Planetarium	458357
Sears Tower Skydeck	1363824

   b Make sure all borders will be displayed for the table on the printout, as shown above.

   c Make sure all data in the table is fully displayed.

7 **Centre** the table headings only.

8 Format the table headings to be **italic**.

9 Save the file keeping the filename **chicago**.

Task 4

Edit the file **chicago** as follows:

1 In the first paragraph, insert a paragraph break and a clear line space after the text… **the "Second City"**.

2 In the final paragraph, insert the text **pedestrians and cyclists** after the text… **with many joggers,**

3 In the paragraph beginning **Typical things**… move the text **Wrigley Field baseball,** to be after the text **…with Chicago are**…

4 Delete only the text **…and theatrical achievements** from the first bullet.

5 Apply **double line spacing** to the first paragraph only beginning **Chicago is a…**

6 Replace the word **range** with the word **variety** wherever it occurs (three times in all).

7 Using the software facility, carry out a word count in the file.

8 Enter the number of words on your printout at least two lines below the table. You may use any alignment for this.

9 Insert your **name** and **centre number** in the header.

10 Insert an **automatic date** and an **automatic filename** in the footer.

11 Check your text for accuracy.

12 Save your file, keeping the filename **chicago**.

13 Print the file **chicago**.

14 Close the file and exit Word.

> The solutions for the Build-up and Practice tasks can be found in the folder **worked_copies_unit1** on the CD-ROM.

Assessment guidelines for Unit 1

- Your tutor will provide you with all the files you need for the assessment.
- Before an assessment, you should create a new folder just for the assessment.

TIP!

Before you start, COPY the folder containing the files into another user area in case you need to open an original file again.

- There will be one folder containing one or more files, and there may be a subfolder containing one or more files.

File management task

- This task may be the first or last task.
- During the assessment, you will need to:
  - rename a folder or a file (change the existing name)
  - create a new folder and give it a name.
  - copy a file from one folder to another
  - move a file from one folder to another
  - delete a file or a folder.
- You are advised to enter file and folder names using the same case as in the assignment. However, you will not be penalised for different use of case for file or folder names.
- Your name: If you are asked to rename a folder using your name, then you should **type your own first and last name**, not the words 'your name'.
- When you have completed the file management task you will need to take a screen print to show that you have carried out all the instructions correctly.
- You may save both screen prints in one document or in separate documents.

TIP!

You must save the screen print(s). The file(s) containing the screen prints do not have to be saved in the folder/subfolder that you will be carrying out the file management tasks in.

- Check the screen printout(s) to make sure that all files and folders and the file and folder names can be clearly seen on the printout.
- If the file or folders and/or the file and folder names are not clear, or the print quality is poor, print again.

e-document production tasks

e-document production is actually word processing.

There will usually be three tasks covering word-processing skills.

- You will create a new document and enter text (approximately 100–130 words).
- You will use a word-processed file provided by OCR, and will be asked to make some changes to this file then save it with a different filename.

- In the new document or in the provided file, you will be required to:
  - create a small table
  - carry out some formatting
  - apply bullets or numbering
  - carry out a word count.

Create a new document.

- Make sure you open a new document. Do not open an existing document that may already have headers and footers or any text.

- Follow each instruction about setting the orientation, font type, font size, margins, line spacing in the correct sequence. Do not leave an instruction intending to do it later.

- Your line endings will probably be different to those on the assessment paper, this is expected. Do **NOT** press Enter at the end of lines within paragraphs!

- Do not enter the text in bold. The text is presented in bold simply to help you to see what to type.

- When asked to insert an automatic date and an automatic filename, do **NOT** type the date or the filename. You **MUST** use the automatic date and automatic filename option in Word.

Edit a provided document.

- Remember the saving tip! Save this file with the new filename before you start working through the task.

- You may be asked to apply a bullet character or numbers to a few lines of text that are already in the document:
  - You may use any style of bullet character or numbering for this.
  - In Microsoft Word, when you apply bullets or numbers the text may automatically indent – this is acceptable.

- When you replace a word, remember to use **Replace All** (not **Replace**).

Word count

Carry out the word count **twice** just to be sure that you have done this accurately. Use **CTRL + A** the first time to select all the text, and highlight with the mouse the second time. When you have completed the word count, make a note of the number of words so that you can type the number of words at the end of the document.

Creating a table

When you insert a table in Word, the table borders may extend into the margin space a little – this is acceptable. Reducing the column width is optional.

Good luck

Contents

> More general advice on preparation for the assessment and the Unit 2 Definition of terms can be found on the CD-ROM that accompanies this book.

UNIT 2: Creating spreadsheets and graphs

Chapter 1   *Creating spreadsheets*

For the first part of Unit 2, you will need to create a spreadsheet, use basic formulae and functions, and edit a spreadsheet.

You will use a software program called Microsoft Office Excel 2003, which is part of Microsoft Office 2003. Excel will help you to create spreadsheets and perform calculations on numbers quickly and easily. We will refer to it as Excel from now on. Default settings are assumed.

This chapter is divided into two sections:

- *in Section 1 you will learn how to create a new spreadsheet, use basic formulae and basic functions, and save and print a spreadsheet*
- *in Section 2 you will learn how to edit and format spreadsheets, and display and print formulae.*

A CD-ROM accompanies this book. Solutions for the spreadsheet tasks can be found in the folder **ss_worked_copies**.

> *Note:* There are many ways of performing the skills covered in this book. This book provides How to... guidelines that have proven to be easily understood by learners.

Preparing your work area

It is advisable to prepare your user area to keep your files organised.

An example of a folder structure for all units is shown in Figure 2.1 below. The main folder in **My Documents** is called **Ruks Clait 2006 Level 1**. Within this folder are subfolders for each of the units.

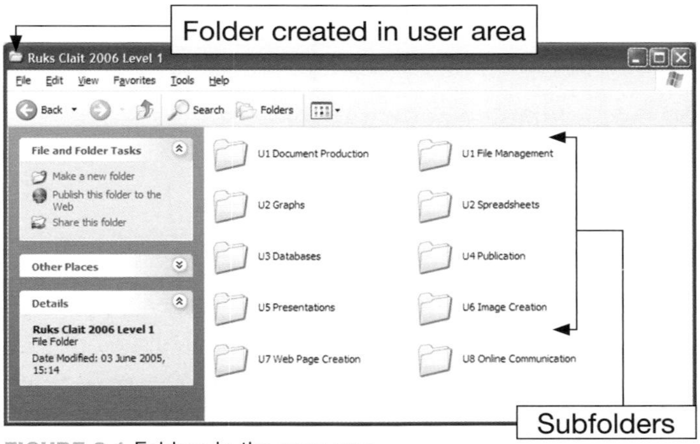

FIGURE 2.1 Folders in the user area

What does it mean?

User area
A user area is the workspace on a computer where you will save your files. One example of a user area is a folder called **My Documents**; Windows XP creates this area. In a centre, you may be given a work area on a network. This area may have a drive name, e.g. G drive. Alternatively, you may save your work on a floppy disk, which is usually the A drive. On your own personal computer, your user area may be the C drive.

You may not need to create as many folders or you may prefer to create a folder for a unit when you begin a new unit or a new chapter.

For Unit 2, two subfolders have been created, one for Spreadsheets and another for Graphs (Figure 2.1).

Within each unit subfolder, there are further subfolders.

For example, in the **U2 Spreadsheets** subfolder, the two subfolders are:

1 **U2 Chap 1 Ssheets working** – this is the working folder in which all files will be saved.

2 **ss_worked_copies** – this folder has been copied from the CD-ROM.

These subfolders are shown in Figure 2.2.

FIGURE 2.2 Subfolders in the **U2 Spreadsheets** subfolder

1: Create a new spreadsheet

LEARNING OUTCOMES

In this section you will learn how to:

- start Excel
- identify the different parts of Excel
- enter data into a spreadsheet
- widen columns to display the data in full
- set page layout (margins, orientation)
- save a spreadsheet into a new folder
- insert text in headers and footers
- insert automatic date and filename in headers and footers
- save an updated spreadsheet
- close a spreadsheet
- understand the difference between formulae and functions
- use mathematical operators * / - + in formulae
- replicate (copy) formulae and functions
- use basic functions (sum, average)
- use brackets in formulae
- use Print Preview
- print spreadsheet data.

What is a spreadsheet?

A spreadsheet is used to manipulate figures, a spreadsheet program is one created specifically to help process tabular information, usually numbers. Any task involving the use of numbers can be done on a spreadsheet. The advantage of a spreadsheet over other methods of manipulating data (e.g. tables in Microsoft Word) is its ability to constantly update (recalculate) figures automatically. Once a spreadsheet has been set up correctly, its calculations will always be correct and any changes to data will recalculate automatically.

Spreadsheet terms and actions will be explained throughout this chapter.

Mouse techniques

Unless otherwise instructed, always click using the **left** mouse button.

MOUSE ACTION	DESCRIPTION
Point	Move the mouse on the mousemat until the pointer appears at the required position on the screen.
Click	Press and release the **left** mouse button once.
Double-click	Quickly press the left mouse button **twice**, then release it.
Right-click	Press the **right** mouse button once – a menu displays.
Hover	Position the mouse pointer over an icon or menu item and pause, a **Tool tip** or a further menu item will appear.
Click and drag	Used to move items. Click with the left mouse button on any item, hold the mouse button down and move the pointer to another location. Release the mouse button.

Mouse techniques

Switch on your computer and log in.

Starting Excel

 *Start Excel*

1 On the desktop, click on **Start**.

2 From the **Windows XP Start** menu, click on **All Programs**.

3 From the **All Programs** menu, click on **Microsoft Office** (Figure 2.3).

4 From the list of Microsoft Office programs, click on **Microsoft Office Excel 2003**.

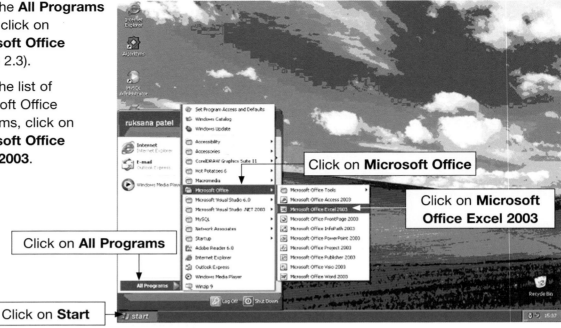

FIGURE 2.3 Starting Microsoft Office Excel 2003

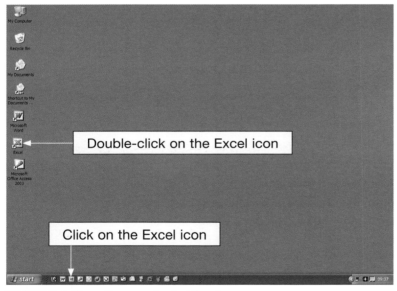

FIGURE 2.4 Alternative ways to start Excel

TIP!

A quicker way to start Excel is to double-click on the Excel icon on the desktop (if a shortcut has been created) or to click on the Excel icon on the taskbar (if a shortcut has been created) (Figure 2.4).

Check your understanding *Start Excel*

1 Start Excel, either through the **Start** menu or by using a shortcut icon.

2 A new blank workbook called **Book1** is displayed.

3 Keep this spreadsheet file open.

Getting familiar with the Excel window

Excel 2003 may open with the **task pane** on the right. Click on the black cross to close the task pane (Figure 2.5).

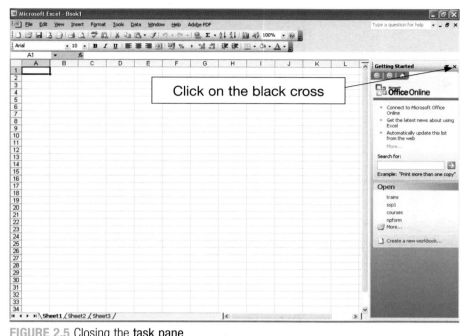

FIGURE 2.5 Closing the **task pane**

Now take a few minutes to learn about the different parts of the Excel window (Figure 2.6).

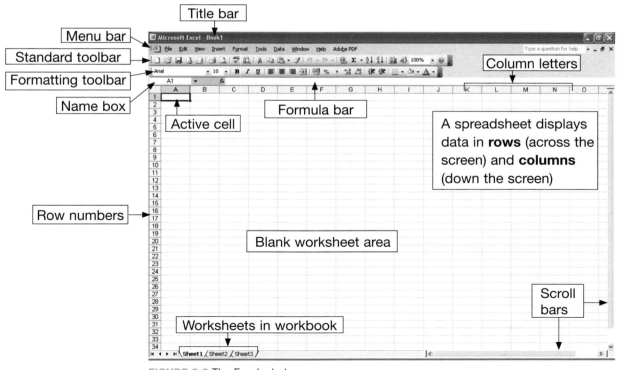

FIGURE 2.6 The Excel window

PART OF WINDOW	DESCRIPTION
Title bar	Displays the title of the current workbook (spreadsheet file).
Menu bar	A list of options, click on a menu item to see the drop-down menu.
Standard toolbar	Includes icons for commonly used tasks, e.g. save, print.
Formatting toolbar	Includes icons for commonly used formatting, e.g. bold, centre.
Blank workbook	The main window made up of cells where data and formulae are entered.
Cell	At the point where a row and column cross, a cell is formed. The cell that the user clicks in is known as the active cell (has a thick outline around it). A cell may contain text, numbers or formula.
Cell reference	Each cell has a unique cell address made up of the column letter and the row number (e.g. **A1**), this is displayed in the **Name box**.
Formula bar	Displays data or formulae being entered in a cell. When a cell is clicked, the full contents or the formula used are displayed here.
Name box	Displays the active cell reference. A cell can also be given a specific name.
Columns	Identified by letters, known as column headings. Columns go down a spreadsheet.
Rows	Identified by numbers, known as row headings. Rows go across a spreadsheet.
Workbook	A spreadsheet file – a workbook usually contains more than one worksheet.
Worksheet	Excel term for a spreadsheet – the tabs at the bottom of the screen show the number of worksheets included in a spreadsheet file (workbook).
Status bar	Displays the status of the current spreadsheet.
Scroll bar	Allows you to scroll up/down or left/right to view your spreadsheet.

The Excel window

Getting familiar with Excel

If the **Office Assistant** icon is visible in an Excel spreadsheet, right-click on it. From the menu displayed, click on **Hide** to remove the Office Assistant from the screen.

1 In your spreadsheet, look for the **Menu bar** (Figure 2.7).

2 Click on **Edit** to display the **Edit** menu. At first, the whole menu may not display, but if you leave it open for a few seconds it displays in full (Figure 2.8).

3 Another way to display the full menu is to click on the chevrons ⊗ button at the bottom of the menu as soon as the menu drops down.

4 Click on the **Edit** menu to close it.

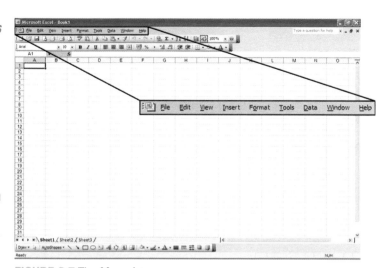

FIGURE 2.7 The **Menu** bar

The toolbar buttons

In your spreadsheet, move the mouse over each **toolbar** button and pause, a **Tool tip** displays showing the name of the button. In this book, we will refer to a toolbar button as an **icon**.

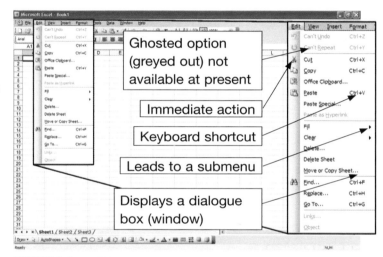

FIGURE 2.8 The **Edit** menu

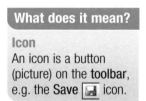

What does it mean?

Icon
An icon is a button (picture) on the **toolbar**, e.g. the **Save** 🖫 icon.

Making the Excel window clearer

The task pane

Excel 2003 opens with the **task pane** on the right of the screen (Figure 2.9). It is advisable to close the **task pane** so that the screen is clearer (optional).

Either click on the black cross just above the **task pane** to close it every time you start Excel, or set the option to close the **task pane** so that it does not display every time you start Excel.

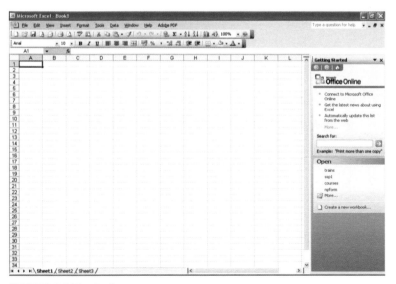

FIGURE 2.9 The **task pane**

1 In Excel, click on **Tools** (Figure 2.10).

2 From the **Tools** menu, click on **Options**.

3 The **Options** dialogue box is displayed.

4 Click on the **View** tab to select it (Figure 2.11).

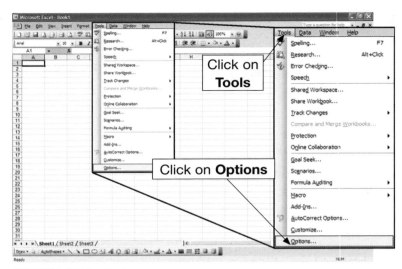

FIGURE 2.10 The Tools menu

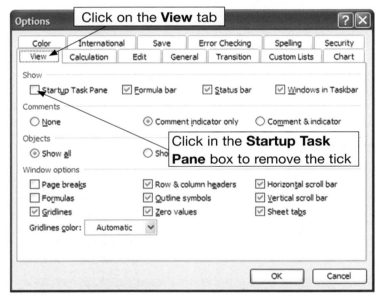

FIGURE 2.11 Options dialogue box with View tab selected

5 Click in the **Startup Task Pane** box to remove the tick.

6 Click on **OK**.

7 The **task pane** will no longer display every time you start Excel.

Standard and Formatting toolbars

Look at your spreadsheet. Are the **Standard** and **Formatting toolbars** on the same row as shown in Figure 2.12.

FIGURE 2.12 Standard and Formatting toolbars on the same row

If so, it is helpful to display them on two rows so that you can see all the icons on both toolbars.

▶▶ **How to...** *display the standard and formatting toolbars on two rows (optional)*

1 In your spreadsheet, click on the **Toolbar Options** symbol at the right end of the **Standard toolbar**.

2 A menu is displayed (Figure 2.13).

3 Click on **Show Buttons on Two Rows**.

4 The **Standard** and **Formatting toolbars** will now display on two rows (Figure 2.14).

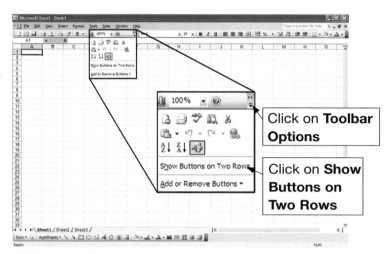

Click on **Toolbar Options**

Click on **Show Buttons on Two Rows**

FIGURE 2.13 **More buttons** menu

FIGURE 2.14 **Standard** and **Formatting toolbars** on separate rows

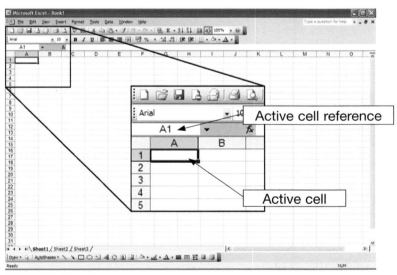

Active cell reference

Active cell

FIGURE 2.15 Cell reference

What does it mean?

Cell reference
When a cell is clicked, the cell reference is displayed in the **Name box**. This will be the column letter followed by the row number, e.g. **A1** is the active cell in the spreadsheet in Figure 2.15.

Moving around a spreadsheet

You can move from cell to cell using the cursor keys (arrow keys) on the keyboard (Figure 2.16).

FIGURE 2.16 The cursor keys

KEY	ACTION
↑ Up arrow key	Moves to the cell above the active cell.
↓ Down arrow key	Moves to the cell below the active cell.
← Left arrow key	Moves to the cell left of the active cell.
→ Right arrow key	Moves to the cell right of the active cell.

Using the cursor keys

▶▶ **How to...** *highlight cells in a spreadsheet*

HIGHLIGHT	METHOD
Cells that are next to each other	*Method 1:* Click with the mouse in the first cell. On the keyboard, hold down the **Shift** key. Click in the last cell. *Method 2:* Click in the first cell, when the white cross displays, drag the mouse across the range (block) of cells to be highlighted.
One column	Place the mouse pointer on a grey column letter and click.
One row	Place the mouse pointer on a grey row number and click.
Entire spreadsheet	*Method 1:* Click in the first cell and drag the mouse across to the last cell. *Quick method:* Click on the grey shaded cell to the left of the column letter **A** and above the row number **1** (Figure 2.17).

Highlighting cells

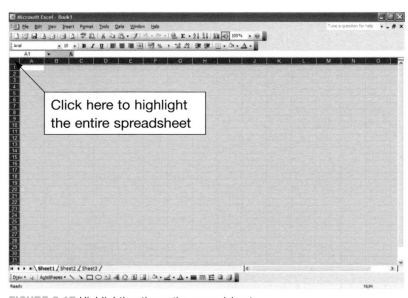

Click here to highlight the entire spreadsheet

FIGURE 2.17 Highlighting the entire spreadsheet

1 In your spreadsheet file **Book1**, look for the active cell (shown by a dark border). It should be **A1**, if not, click in **A1**.

2 Use the cursor keys to move:

a down to cell **A4**

b then to the right to cell **C4**

c then up to cell **C1**

d then to the left to cell **B1**.

3 Refer to the Highlighting cells table on page 12 and highlight cells as follows:

a from cell **B1** to **H1**

b column **C**

c row **5**

d the entire spreadsheet.

4 Practise moving around your spreadsheet until you feel confident.

Entering data

Numbers can be entered using the **Number keypad** on the right of the keyboard (check that the **Num Lock** key is switched on), or by using the number keys above the letters (Figure 2.18).

You must enter numbers in a spreadsheet with 100 per cent accuracy. One incorrect number can give incorrect information and will lead to all calculations using that number being incorrect.

When you enter text, make sure you **enter the words exactly** as shown.

Use the **same case** as shown in the text you are copying:

○ *this text is in **lower case** – there are no capital letters*

○ *Each Of These Words Has An **Initial Capital** – The First Letter Of Each Word Is A Capital*

○ *THIS TEXT IS IN **UPPER CASE** – ALL THE LETTERS ARE CAPITAL LETTERS.*

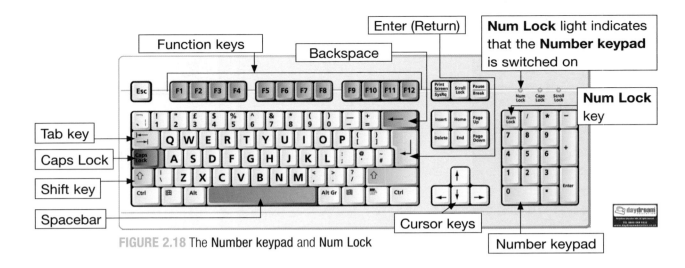

FIGURE 2.18 The Number keypad and Num Lock

▶▶ How to... *enter text and numbers*

HOW TO...	ACTION
Type one capital letter	Hold down the **Shift** key and press the required letter on the keyboard, then let go of the **Shift** key.
Type word(s) in capital letters	Press down the **Caps Lock** to switch it on (a light may indicate that **Caps Lock** is on).
Type lower case letters	Check the **Caps Lock** is switched off. If not press down the **Caps Lock** key to turn it off.
Insert a space between words	Press the **spacebar** once.
Delete a letter to the left of the cursor in an active cell	Press the **Backspace** key.
Enter numbers	Use the number keys above the QWERTY keys or press **Num Lock** and use the **Number keypad** (a light may indicate that **Num Lock** is on).
Enter a decimal point	Use the full stop key on the keyboard or the **decimal point** key on the **Number keypad**.

Using the keyboard

In Excel, data is entered into the active cell. Cells can contain:

○ *text (labels)*

○ *numbers (values)*

○ *formulae (calculations).*

To make a cell active, ready to enter data or formula into it, either click in the cell, or use the cursor keys to move to the cell.

When data is being entered into a cell, that data also appears in the **Formula bar**.

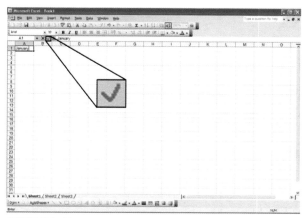

FIGURE 2.19 Clicking on the **Enter** tick in the **Formula bar** enters the data

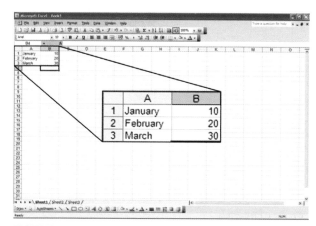

FIGURE 2.20 Text is automatically left-aligned, numbers are right-aligned

To finish entering data into a cell, either:

- *press **Enter***
- *click with your mouse in another cell*
- *use the cursor keys to move to another cell, or*
- *click on the **Enter** tick in the **Formula bar** (Figure 2.19).*

In Excel, when text is entered it is automatically left-aligned in the cell (placed to the left of the cell). Numbers are automatically right-aligned (placed to the right of the cell) (Figure 2.20).

Column labels

These are titles that identify the data in a column and are usually text. Column labels are sometimes referred to as column headings, but column headings are actually the grey column letters, **A**, **B**, **C**, etc.

Row labels

These are usually text and are generally entered in column **A**. Row labels are titles that identify the data in a row. Row numbers are the grey numbers **1**, **2**, **3**, etc. on the left of the screen.

TIP!

When you enter a long column heading or a row label, do not worry if the words extend into the second column. Columns can be widened later.

>> **How to...** *enter data*

1 In your spreadsheet, click in the cell where you want to enter data.

2 Enter the data.

3 Move to the next cell.

4 Enter the required data in the new cell.

5   Move to the next cell.

6   Enter the rest of the data into the spreadsheet by moving from cell to cell.

7   Check all data is entered in the correct cell and that numbers are entered with 100 per cent accuracy.

Check your understanding *Enter text*

1 In your spreadsheet file **Book1**, enter the text in column **A** as shown in Figure 2.21. Leave a blank cell in row **2**.

2 The text will not fit into the cells in column **A**. Some of the text will stretch across column **2**. This is normal – you will learn to widen columns later.

3 Keep the file **Book1** open.

	A	B	C
1	Popular Tourist Attractions		
2			
3	Chicago		
4	Great Barrier Reef		
5	Victoria Falls		
6	Niagara Falls		
7	Dubai		
8			

FIGURE 2.21 Text to be entered in **Book1**

Widening columns

When data is entered into an active cell in a spreadsheet, it may not fit in the cell. If the adjacent cell(s) are blank, the data is fully displayed, but if there is data in the adjacent cell(s), the data remains in the cell, but is not fully displayed. This is referred to as **truncated data**.

If cell(s) containing numbers are not wide enough, the data appears as ##### (hash signs). Once the cells are widened, the numbers will display.

Cells may be widened before or after data is entered in order to display data in full.

▶▶ How to... *widen columns*

1 Position the mouse pointer within the grey column letters over the vertical line to the right of the column to be widened.

2 The mouse pointer changes into ↔.

3 Double-click with the left mouse button.

4 Excel automatically adjusts the column width to display data in full.

5 Another method is to drag ↔ to make the column wider until all data is displayed in full.

TIP!

To adjust all columns after data has been entered, use **AutoFit**. Highlight the entire spreadsheet and double-click in the grey area between any two columns to display data in full in all columns.

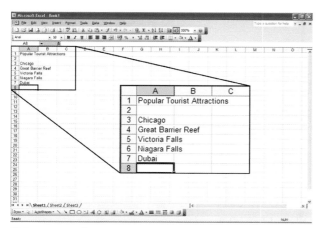

FIGURE 2.22 Column A when data is first entered

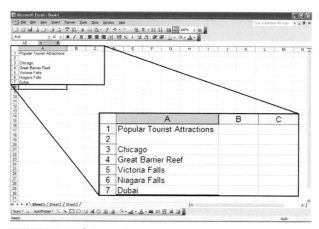

FIGURE 2.23 Column A after widening column

Check your understanding
Widen columns and enter more text and numbers

1 In your file **Book 1**, make column A wider so that all data is displayed in full.

2 Enter the data into column **B** as shown in Figure 2.24.

3 Keep the file **Book1** open.

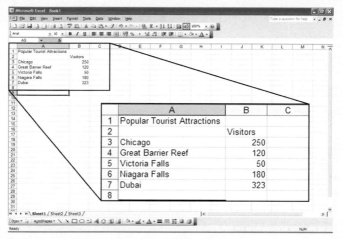

FIGURE 2.24 Data to be entered into column B

Page orientation

What does it mean?

Page orientation
Page orientation refers to which way round the paper is displayed:
Portrait – an A4 sheet of paper displayed with the shortest sides at the top and bottom.
Landscape – an A4 sheet displayed with the longest sides at the top and bottom.

▶▶ How to... *set the page orientation*

1 In the **Menu bar**, click on **File**.

2 From the **File** menu, click on **Page Setup**.

3 The **Page Setup** dialogue box is displayed (Figure 2.25).

4 Select the **Page** tab.

5 Click on **Portrait** or **Landscape**.

6 Click on **OK**.

7 The page will either be displayed portrait or landscape.

Margins

In Excel, you can set the top, bottom, left and right margins.

 **How to...** *set margins*

1 In the **Menu bar**, click on **File**.

2 From the **File** menu, click on **Page Setup**.

3 The **Page Setup** dialogue box is displayed.

4 Click on the **Margins** tab to select it (Figure 2.26).

5 Click in the box for **Top**, enter the measurements for the top margin, then do the same for the **Left**, **Right** and **Bottom** margins (Figure 2.26).

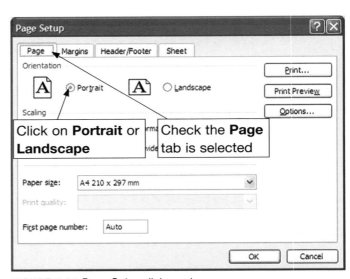

FIGURE 2.25 Page Setup dialogue box

What does it mean?

Margins
Margins are the amount of white space from the edge of the paper to the text on the page.

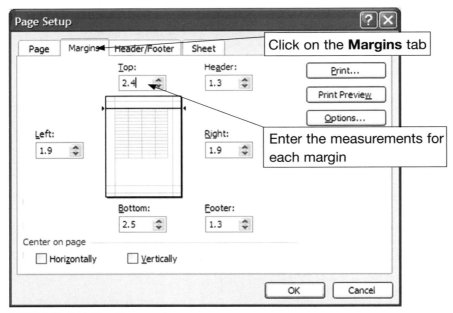

FIGURE 2.26 Setting the margins

6 You can use the **up/down arrows**, however, this may not allow you to set margins to specific measurements.

7 Click on **OK** to set the margins.

1 In your file **Book 1**, set the page orientation to **portrait**.

2 Set the top, bottom, left and right margins to **2.4 cm**.

3 Keep the file **Book1** open.

TIP!

Press the **Tab** key to move from one margin box to the next.

Saving a spreadsheet

It is good practice to save your work approximately every 10 minutes so that you do not lose too much work if there is a computer problem. Whenever you save a file, you should save it in your own user area.

TIP!

Save your files inside folders to keep your files organised, instead of saving all files into one user area.

>> How to... *save a spreadsheet into a new folder from within Excel*

1 In the **Menu bar**, click on **File**.

2 From the **File** menu, click on **Save As**.

3 The **Save As** dialogue box is displayed.

4 Click on the **down arrow** to the right of the **Save in** box.

5 A list of user areas is displayed.

6 Click on your user area, then double-click on any folders to open the required subfolder.

7 The folder name displays in the **Save in** box

8 Click on the **Create New Folder** icon (Figure 2.27).

9 A **New Folder** dialogue box appears (Figure 2.28).

10 Enter the new folder name.

11 Click on **OK** to create a new folder.

12 In the **Save As** dialogue box, in the **File name** box, delete any existing text.

13 Enter the required filename.

14 In the **Save as type** box, check **Microsoft Excel Workbook** is displayed.

15 Click on **Save**.

16 Your spreadsheet will be saved in a new folder within your user area.

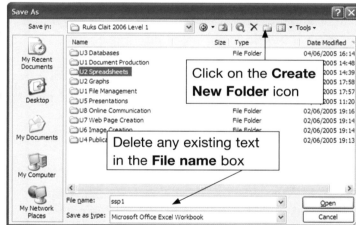

FIGURE 2.27 Creating a new folder

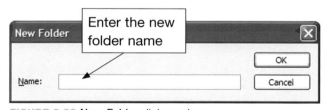

FIGURE 2.28 **New Folder** dialogue box

1 Save your file **Book1** using the filename **ssp1** into a new folder called **ssheets** in your user area.

2 Keep the file **ssp1** open.

Headers and footers

Any text entered into the header or footer of a spreadsheet will appear on every print of the same worksheet and will also appear in the header or footer if the spreadsheet is saved with a different filename. In Excel, unlike headers and footers in Word, there are three sections in the header and footer dialogue box.

What does it mean?

Headers and footers
- A header is the space within the top margin.
- A footer is the space within the bottom margin.

▶▶ How to... *add a header or footer*

1 In the **Menu bar**, click on **View**.

2 From the **View** menu, click on **Header and Footer**.

3 A **Page Setup** dialogue box is displayed (Figure 2.29).

4 Check the **Header/Footer** tab is selected.

5 Click on the **Custom Header** button.

6 A **Header** dialogue box opens (Figure 2.30).

7 Click in the **Left**, **Center** or **Right section**.

8 Enter the required information in the header.

9 Click on **OK** to close the **Header** dialogue box.

10 In the **Page Setup** dialogue box, click on the **Custom Footer** button.

11 A **Footer** dialogue box opens.

12 Click in the **Left**, **Center** or **Right section**.

13 Enter the required information in the footer.

14 Click on **OK** to close the **Footer** dialogue box.

15 Click on **OK** to close the **Page Setup** dialogue box.

FIGURE 2.29 Page Setup dialogue box

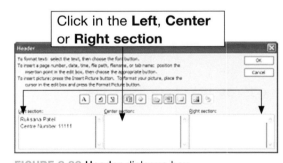

FIGURE 2.30 Header dialogue box

TIP!

The cursor is left aligned in the **Left section**, centred in the **Center section**, and right-aligned in the **Right section**.

Automatic fields

Excel can insert some information automatically into headers and footers, e.g. automatic dates and automatic filenames. The advantage of using automatic fields is that these will update automatically.

1 In the **Menu bar**, click on **View**.

2 From the **View** menu, click on **Header and Footer**.

3 Check the **Header/Footer** tab is selected.

4 Click on the **Custom Header** or **Custom Footer** button.

5 In the **Header** or **Footer** dialogue box, click in the **Left**, **Center** or **Right section** (Figure 2.31).

Click on the **Automatic Date** icon

Click on the **Automatic Filename** icon

An automatic filename is inserted in the **Left section**

An automatic date is inserted in the **Center section**

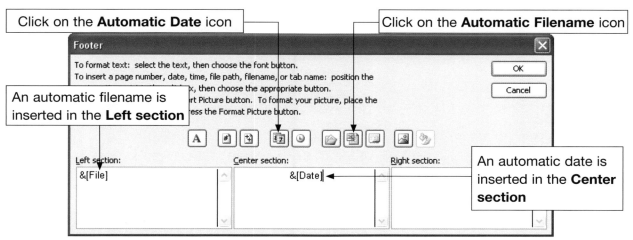

FIGURE 2.31 **Footer** dialogue box

6 Click on the 🗓 icon to insert an automatic date. **&[Date]** is displayed in the selected section.

7 Click on the 📄 icon to insert an automatic filename. **&[File]** is displayed in the selected section.

8 Click on **OK** to confirm the header or footer.

9 Click on **OK** to close the **Page Setup** dialogue box.

Remember to save your document again after you have added headers and footers.

Saving and closing an existing spreadsheet

▶▶ **How to...** save an existing spreadsheet

1 In the **Menu bar**, click on **File**.

2 From the **File menu**, click on **Save** to save the spreadsheet.

▶▶ **How to...** close a spreadsheet

1 In the **Menu bar**, click on **File**.

TIP!

In the **Header** or **Footer** window, the automatic fields do not display the actual date, filename, etc. Click on the [Print Preview] button in the **Page Setup** dialogue box to view the headers and footers. The correct automatic headers and footers will display.

TIP!

You can also preview your spreadsheet by clicking on the **Print Preview** ⬙ icon on the **Standard toolbar**.

TIP!

Alternatively click on the Save 🖫 icon.

2 From the **File menu**, click on **Close** to close the spreadsheet (Figure 2.32).

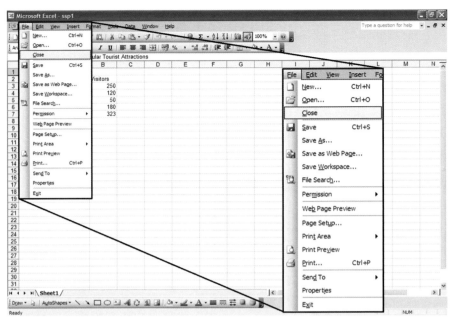

FIGURE 2.32 Click on **Close** in the **File** menu

Check your understanding

Add headers and footers including automatic fields

1 In your file **ssp1**, add the following headers and footers.

 a In the header, add your **first and last name** in the **Left section**.

 b In the header add your **centre number** in the **Center section**.

 c In the footer, insert an **automatic date** and an **automatic filename** in the **Left section**.

2 Save your spreadsheet keeping the filename **ssp1**.

3 Close your spreadsheet.

Why are formulae and functions used in spreadsheets?

In Excel, a calculation is called a **formula** (plural **formulae**) or a **function**.

Formulae

The advantage of using a formula is that when a number is changed, all calculations using that number are automatically recalculated.

Formulae are instructions to the program to perform calculations. Formulae are used to multiply, divide, add and subtract numbers in a spreadsheet.

A formula consists of:

- the **equals** (=) sign
- the **first cell reference**
- the **mathematical operator**
- the **second cell reference**.

Example of a simple formula: **=B3+C3**

A formula may also contain brackets, more than one mathematical operator and numbers instead of cell references.

What does it mean?

Mathematical operators
The mathematical operators are:
*
/
+
-

Functions

Functions are specialised formulae that make calculations easier. They are instructions to the program to carry out a particular process, and as such are pre-programmed formulae that carry out specific operations. Each function has a word that Excel recognises as an instruction, e.g. **SUM**, **AVERAGE**. The advantage of using a function is that it performs a multi-stage calculation in one step.

Functions consist of three parts:

- the **equals** (=) sign
- the **function name**
- the **range of cells**.

Example of a function: **=SUM(B3:H3)**

SUM and **AVERAGE** are two frequently used functions.

FUNCTION	CALCULATION	DISPLAYED AS	WHAT THE FUNCTION DOES
SUM	Adds all the numbers in a range of cells.	=SUM(B3:F3)	Adds all the cells starting from **B3** and ending at **F3**, i.e. adds **B3**, **C3**, **D3**, **E3**, **F3**.
AVERAGE	Calculates the average value of a range of cells.	=AVERAGE(B3:B7)	Adds all the cells starting at **B3** and ending at **B7**, then divides this figure by the number of cells in this range, i.e. adds **B3**, **B4**, **B5**, **B6**, **B7**, then divides the total by **5**.

The SUM and AVERAGE functions

The difference between formulae and functions

Look at the spreadsheet in Figure 2.33. To calculate the **Total Course Fee** for **Word Processing**, the numbers for **Jan**, **Feb**, **Mar**, **Apr**, **Jun** need to be added.

The calculation can be carried out using either a formula or a function. Both methods would give the correct result of **94**.

The **function** would be **=SUM(B3:F3)** The **formula** would be **=B3+C3+D3+E3+F3**

	A	B	C	D	E	F	G
1	Course Fees						
2		Jan	Feb	Mar	Apr	Jun	Total Course Fee
3	Word Processing	20	18	22	15	19	94
4	Spreadsheets	22	20	24	18	22	106
5	Databases	24	21	26	17	22	110
6	Web Pages	28	25	29	22	26	130
7	Desktop Publishing	28	26	26	24	28	132

FIGURE 2.33 Performing the calculation using either a formula or a function gives the same result at this stage

You may have noticed that there is no column data for **May**! If the **May** column data were to be inserted between **Apr** and **Jun**, the **function** would automatically update to:

=SUM(B3:G3)

and the new **Total Course Fee** would be automatically recalculated (Figure 2.34).

	A	B	C	D	E	F	G	H	I
1	Course Fees								
2		Jan	Feb	Mar	Apr	May	June	Total Course Fee	
3	Word Processing	20	18	22	15	17	19	111	
4	Spreadsheets	22	20	24	18	19	22	125	
5	Databases	24	21	26	17	16	22	126	
6	Web Pages	28	25	29	22	21	26	151	
7	Desktop Publishing	28	26	30	24	23	28	159	
8									

FIGURE 2.34 Where a function is used, the Total Course Fee is automatically recalculated when the May column data is added

However, the **formula** would remain the same and so would the result, which would now be incorrect, as it does not include the figures for **May**

(Figure 2.35). The user would have to remember to change the formula to:
=B3+C3+D3+E3+F3+G3.

	A	B	C	D	E	F	G	H	I
1	Course Fees								
2		Jan	Feb	Mar	Apr	May	June	Total Course Fee	
3	Word Processing	20	18	22	15	17	19	94	
4	Spreadsheets	22	20	24	18	19	22	106	
5	Databases	24	21	26	17	16	22	110	
6	Web Pages	28	25	29	22	21	26	130	
7	Desktop Publishing	28	26	30	24	23	28	136	
8									

FIGURE 2.35 Where a formula is used, the formula does not automatically recalculate, the **Total Course Fee** is now incorrect because it does not include the **May** data

In this example a function is a more appropriate choice than a formula.

Mathematical operators

Look for the **mathematical operators** on your keyboard. The symbols can be found either on the **Number keypad** or on the main part of the keyboard.

MATHEMATICAL FUNCTION	KEYBOARD SYMBOL	KEYBOARD KEY
Multiply	*	**Shift** key and number 8
Divide	/	/ key next to the full stop
Add	+	**Shift** key and = key
Subtract	-	- key above the **P**

Mathematical functions

▶▶ How to... *create a simple formula using a mathematical operator*

1 In your spreadsheet, click in the cell in which the formula is to be created.

2 Enter the = sign.

3 The = sign displays in the **Formula bar** and in the active cell (Figure 2.36).

TIP!
When **=** is entered in a cell, Excel knows that a calculation is going to be created in that cell.

= displays in the **Formula bar**   Enter = in the active cell

	A	B	C	D	E	F
	SUM					
1	Journey	Std Fare	Adv Discount	Fare	Reserve	Total
2	Birmingham	58	5	=	2	
3	Manchester	62	5		2.5	
4	Coventry	9	2		1	

FIGURE 2.36 The = sign is displayed in the **Formula bar** and in the active cell

4 Click in the cell that contains the first value (number).

5 The cell reference of that cell displays in the **Formula bar** and in the active cell (Figure 2.37).

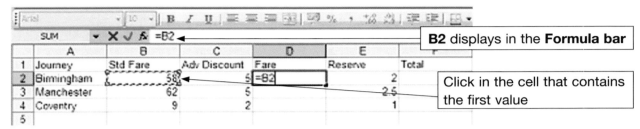

FIGURE 2.37 The cell reference is displayed in the Formula bar and in the cell

6 Use the keyboard to enter the correct mathematical operator (Figure 2.38).

	A	B	C	D	E	F
					SUM ▾ ✗ ✓ *fx* =B2-	
1	Journey	Std Fare	Adv Discount	Fare	Reserve	Total
2	Birmingham	58	5	=B2-	2	
3	Manchester	62	5		2.5	
4	Coventry	9	2		1	
5						

FIGURE 2.38 Entering the correct mathematical operator

7 Click in the cell that contains the second value.

8 The cell reference of the second cell displays after the mathematical operator in the **Formula bar** and in the cell (Figure 2.39).

C2 displays in the Formula bar

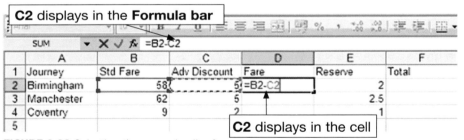

C2 displays in the cell

FIGURE 2.39 Selecting the second cell reference

9 Check the **Formula bar** to make sure that the formula is correct.

10 Press **Enter**, or click on the **Enter** tick ✓ on the **Formula bar**.

11 The calculation is made, and the result (the number) displays in the cell in which you created the formula.

12 Save the updated spreadsheet by clicking on the **Save** 🖫 icon.

TIP!

To start a formula enter the = sign. To end a formula press **Enter**.

TIP!

Although cell references can be typed into a formula, it is better to point and click in the cell to avoid the possibility of keying in errors.

1 Create a new spreadsheet.

2 Starting in cell **A1**, enter the data as shown below.

Journey	Std Fare	Adv Discount	Fare	Reserve	Total
Birmingham	58	5		2	
Manchester	62	5		2.5	
Coventry	9	2		1	

3 Widen the columns so that all data is displayed in full.

4 In cell **D2** create a formula to **subtract** the **Adv Discount** from the **Std Fare** for Birmingham.

5 Check the **Formula bar** – your formula should be **=B2-C2**.

6 In cell **F2** create a formula to **add** the **Fare** and the **Reserve** for Birmingham.

7 Check the **Formula bar** – your formula should be **=D2+E2**.

8 Insert your **name**, an **automatic date** and an **automatic filename** in the header or footer.

9 Save the spreadsheet using the filename **trains** in the folder **ssheets** you created earlier.

10 Keep the spreadsheet **trains** open.

Copying a formula

When you have created a formula for one set of data (e.g. in one row), you do not need to create the same formula again for the next set of data (e.g. for the next row) if it is to be calculated in the same way. You simply copy the formula into adjacent rows or columns.

When a formula is copied, the structure of the formula will remain the same, but Excel will automatically change the cell references. This is known as **relative cell referencing**.

In spreadsheets **copy** is referred to as **replicate**. You can replicate formulae across a row to the left or right (horizontally), or up and down a column (vertically).

▶▶ How to... *copy a formula*

Method 1: Using the fill handle

1 In your spreadsheet, click in the cell that contains the formula to be copied.

2 The bottom right-hand corner of the cell displays a black square.

3 Position the mouse pointer over the black square.

4 The mouse pointer changes to a **+** sign (Figure 2.40).

5 Drag the **+** sign over the cells where the formula is to be copied (Figure 2.41).

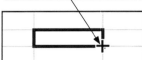

The mouse pointer changes to a **+** sign

FIGURE 2.40 Positioning the mouse pointer over the black square

	D2	▼		f_x	=B2-C2		
	A	B	C	D	E	F	
1	Journey	Std Fare	Adv Discount	Fare	Reserve	Total	
2	Birmingham	58	5	53	2	55	
3	Manchester	62	5		2.5		
4	Coventry	9	2		1		
5				Drag the **+** sign over the cells			
6							

FIGURE 2.41 Copying the formula

6 The formula is copied to the selected cells.

Method 2: Copy and paste

1 In your spreadsheet, click in the cell that contains the formula you want to copy.

2 In the **Menu bar**, click on **Edit**.

3 From the **Edit** menu, click on **Copy**.

4 A flashing border called a **marquee** will appear around the cell that you have copied.

5 Highlight the cells where the formula is to be copied to.

6 Click again on the **Edit** menu.

7 Click on **Paste** in the menu.

8 The formula is copied to the highlighted cells.

9 Press the **Enter** key and the marquee will disappear.

TIP!

Double-click on the black square, and Excel will automatically fill the formula into the appropriate cells.

When using the fill handle, a **Smart Tag** (square icon) displays. Ignore this, it will disappear.

TIP!

Remember to save the updated spreadsheet by clicking on the **Save** 🖫 icon.

Check your understanding *Copy (replicate) formulae*

1 In your spreadsheet **trains**, copy (replicate):

   a the formula in cell **D2** into cells **D3** and **D4**

   b the formula in cell **F2** into cells **F3** and **F4**.

2 Save your spreadsheet keeping the filename **trains**.

3 Your spreadsheet should look like the one in Figure 2.42.

4 Close the spreadsheet.

	A	B	C	D	E	F	G
1	Journey	Std Fare	Adv Discount	Fare	Reserve	Total	
2	Birmingham	58	5	53	2	55	
3	Manchester	62	5	57	2.5	59.5	
4	Coventry	9	2	7	1	8	
5							

FIGURE 2.42 The spreadsheet **trains**

Creating functions

If the instruction is to use a function, you must use a function rather than a formula, even though it may be possible to perform the calculation using a formula.

▶▶ How to... *use the SUM function*

There are several ways to create the **SUM** function in Excel. Read through all the instructions that follow, then complete 'Check your understanding: Create a spreadsheet and use the SUM function' on page 144 using each of the three methods. You will then be able to decide which method you prefer.

Method 1: Enter function in cell

1 In the spreadsheet, click in the cell where the calculation is to be carried out.

2 Enter the = sign.

3 Enter the word **SUM** followed by an opening bracket, i.e. **SUM(**

4 **=SUM(** displays in the **Formula bar** and in the active cell (Figure 2.43).

TIP!

The word **SUM** can be entered in upper or lower case.

FIGURE 2.43 =SUM(is displayed in the Formula bar and the cell

5 Highlight the range of cells to be added starting with the first cell and ending with the last cell.

6 **=SUM(B3:D3** displays in the **Formula bar** and in the cell (Figure 2.44). The cell references in other calculations will be the first and last cell that you highlighted with a colon between the cell references.

FIGURE 2.44 =SUM(B3:D3 is displayed in the Formula bar and in the cell

7 Enter a closing bracket **)**

8 **=SUM(B3:D3)** displays in the **Formula bar** and in the cell (Figure 2.45). Remember that the cell references in other calculations will be different.

	A	B	C	D	E	F	G	H	I
	Arial		10		B I U			%	
	SUM	▼ X √ fx	=SUM(B3:D3)						
1	Language Courses								
2		Term 1	Term 2	Term 3	Yearly Fee	Discount	Admin	Amount Due	
3	French	20	18	15	=SUM(B3:D3)		0.95		
4	German	22	20	17			0.75		
5	Spanish	24	21	18			0.5		
6	Arabic	28	26	21			0.6		
7	Average								
8									

FIGURE 2.45 =SUM(B3:D3) is displayed in the Formula bar and in the cell

9 Check the **Formula bar** to make sure the formula is correct.

10 Press **Enter**, or click on the **Enter** tick ✓ on the **Formula bar**.

11 The calculation is made, and the result (the total) will display in the cell in which you created the function.

TIP!

The cell references will be different in other spreadsheets.

TIP!

If the formula is incorrect click **Cancel** ☒ on the **Formula bar** and start again.

Method 2: Insert function

1 In the spreadsheet, click in the cell where the calculation is to be carried out.

2 Click the 𝑓𝑥 **Insert Function** icon on the **Formula Bar** (Figure 2.46).

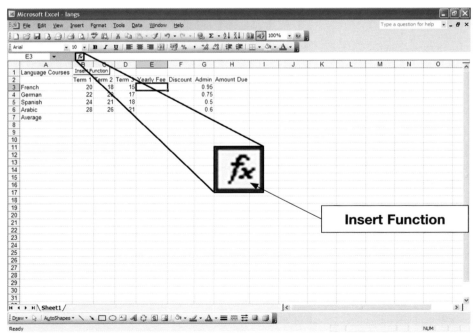

FIGURE 2.46 The *fx* Insert Function icon

3 An **Insert Function** dialogue box is displayed (Figure 2.47).

4 Click on **SUM**.

5 Click on **OK**.

6 A **Function Arguments** dialogue box appears (Figure 2.48).

7 In the **Number1** box the range of cells displays. Check this range is correct.

8 Click on **OK**.

9 The calculation is made, and the result (the total) will display in the cell in which you created the function.

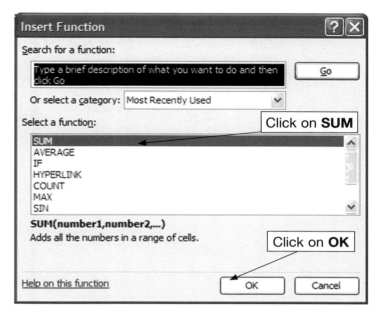

FIGURE 2.47 **Insert Function** dialogue box

TIP!

If the range of cells shown is incorrect, highlight the correct range in the spreadsheet. Click and drag the blue title bar of the dialogue box to see the spreadsheet if required.

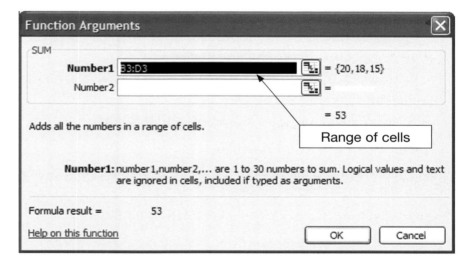

FIGURE 2.48 **Function Arguments** dialogue box

Method 3: AutoSum

Addition is the most frequently used function, so there is an **AutoSum** Σ icon on the **Standard toolbar** that creates the **SUM** function automatically. There is more than one way to use **AutoSum**, but the best way is outlined below.

1 Highlight the range of cells to be added AND the blank cell in which the result of the calculation is to be displayed.

2 Click on the **AutoSum** Σ icon.

3 The result of the calculation is displayed in what was the blank cell.

TIP!

Do not click the AutoSum icon to start every formula as this inserts **SUM** in front of every formula. The **SUM** function must only be used for adding a range of cells that are next to each other. **SUM** must not appear in any other formula.

1 Create a new spreadsheet.

2 Set the page orientation to **landscape**.

3 Starting in cell **A1**, enter the data as shown below.

Language Courses							
	Term 1	Term 2	Term 3	Yearly Fee	Discount	Admin	Amount Due
French	20	18	15			0.95	
German	22	20	17			0.75	
Spanish	24	21	18			0.5	
Arabic	28	26	21			0.6	
Average							

4 Widen all columns to display all data in full.

Using Method 1: Enter function in cell

5 In cell **E3**, use the **SUM** function to calculate the total **Yearly Fee** for the **French** row (the sum of cells **B3** to **D3**).

6 Check your function, it should be **=SUM(B3:D3)**

Using Method 2: Insert function

7 In cell **E4**, use the **SUM** function to calculate the total **Yearly Fee** for the **German** row (the sum of cells **B4** to **D4**).

8 Check your function, it should be **=SUM(B4:D4)**

Using Method 3: AutoSum

9 In cell **E5**, use the **SUM** function to calculate the total **Yearly Fee** for the **Spanish** row (the sum of cells **B5** to **D5**)

10 Check your function, it should be **=SUM(B5:D5)**

11 Copy the function from cell **E5** into cell **E6**.

12 Save your spreadsheet using the filename **langs** in the folder **ssheets**. Keep your spreadsheet open.

TIP!

From now on, when using the SUM function, use the method that you prefer.

1 In cell **F3**, create a formula to divide the **Yearly Fee** by **10**.

2 Check the **Formula bar**, your formula should be **=E3/10**

3 Copy the formula from cell **F3** into **F4**, **F5**, **F6**.

4 Insert your **name**, an **automatic date** and an **automatic filename** in the header or footer.

5 Save your spreadsheet, keeping the filename **langs**, in the folder **ssheets**.

6 Your spreadsheet should look like the one in Figure 2.49.

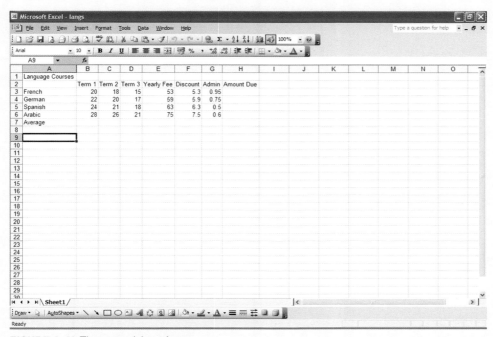

FIGURE 2.49 The spreadsheet **langs**

7 Keep the spreadsheet **langs** open.

▶▶ How to... *use the AVERAGE function*

There are several ways to create the **AVERAGE** function in Excel.

Method 1: Enter function in cell

1 In the spreadsheet, click in the cell in which the calculation is to be carried out.

2 Enter the = sign.

3 Enter the word **AVERAGE** followed by an opening bracket, i.e.
AVERAGE(

> **TIP!**
>
> The word **AVERAGE** may be entered in upper or lower case.

4 **=AVERAGE(** displays in the **Formula bar** and in the cell (Figure 2.50).

5 Highlight the range of cells to be averaged starting with the first cell and ending with the last cell.

6 **=AVERAGE(B3:B6** displays in the **Formula bar** and in the cell (Figure 2.51). The cell references in other calculations will be the first and last cell that you highlighted with a colon between the cell references.

7 Enter a closing bracket **)**

8 **=AVERAGE(B3:B6)** displays in the **Formula bar** and in the cell (Figure 2.52). Remember that the cell references in other calculations will be different.

9 Check the **Formula bar** to make sure the formula is correct.

10 Press **Enter**, or click on the **Enter** tick ✓ on the **Formula bar**.

11 The calculation is made, and the result (the average figure) will display in the cell in which you created the function.

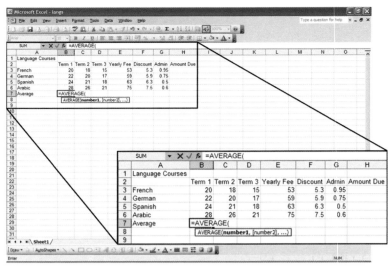

FIGURE 2.50 =AVERAGE(is displayed in the **Formula Bar** and in the cell

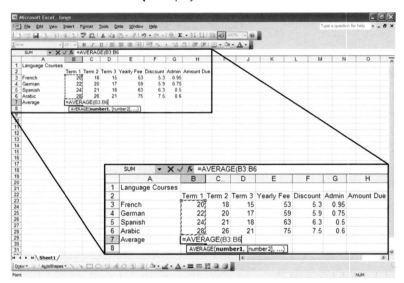

FIGURE 2.51 =AVERAGE(B3:B6 is displayed in the **Formula bar** and in the cell

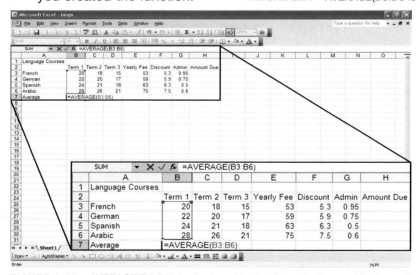

FIGURE 2.52 =AVERAGE(B3:B6) is displayed in the **Formula Bar** and in the cell

TIP!

The cell references will be different in other spreadsheets.

Method 2: Insert function

1 In the spreadsheet, click in the cell where the calculation is to be carried out.

2 Click on the *fx* **Insert Function** icon on the **Formula bar** (Figure 2.53).

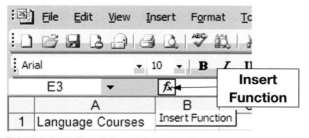

FIGURE 2.53 The *fx* Insert Function icon

3 An **Insert Function** dialogue box is displayed (Figure 2.54).

4 Click on the word **AVERAGE**.

5 Click on **OK**.

6 A **Function Arguments** dialogue box appears (Figure 2.55).

7 In the **Number1** box the range of cells displays. Check this range is correct.

8 Click on **OK**.

9 The calculation is made, and the result (the average) will display in the cell in which you created the function.

TIP!

If the range of cells shown is incorrect, highlight the correct range in the spreadsheet.

Method 3: AutoSum

1 Highlight the range of cells to be averaged AND the blank cell in which the result of the calculation is to be displayed.

2 Click on the **down arrow** next to the **AutoSum** $\boxed{\Sigma \cdot}$ icon on the **Standard toolbar**.

3 From the menu, click on **Average** (Figure 2.56).

4 The result of the calculation is displayed in what was the blank cell.

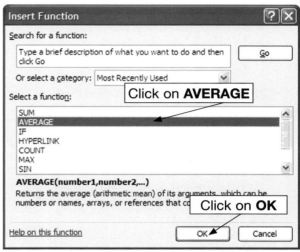

FIGURE 2.54 Insert Function dialogue box

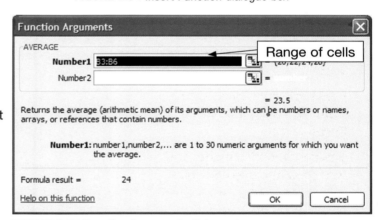

FIGURE 2.55 Function Arguments dialogue box

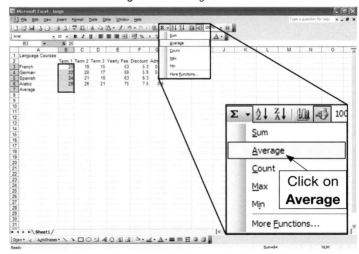

FIGURE 2.56 The AutoSum menu

1 In your spreadsheet **langs**, use each of the three methods below to create a formula using the **AVERAGE** function.

Using Method 1: Enter function in cell

2 Click in the **Average** row, in the **Term 1** column.

3 Use a function to calculate the **AVERAGE** of the **Term 1** figures for the four Language Courses.

Using Method 2: Insert function

4 Click in the **Average** row, in the **Term 2** column.

5 Use a function to calculate the **AVERAGE** of the **Term 2** figures for the four Language Courses.

Using Method 3: AutoSum (Average)

6 Click in the **Average** row, in the **Term 3** column.

7 Use a function to calculate the **AVERAGE** of the **Term 3** figures for the four Language Courses.

8 Replicate (copy) the **AVERAGE** formula into the other cells starting from **Yearly Fee** up to **Admin**.

9 Save your spreadsheet keeping the filename **langs**.

> **TIP!**
>
> From now on. when using the **AVERAGE** function, use the method you prefer.

Using brackets in a formula with more than one mathematical operator

You may need to use more than one mathematical operator * / + - in a formula. If so, you must use **brackets**.

If you need to use add or subtract and then multiply or divide, you *must* use brackets around the cells to be added or subtracted, so that Excel carries out this part of the calculation first, before carrying out the multiply or divide.

▶▶ How to... *use brackets in a formula*

1 In the spreadsheet, click in the cell where the formula is to be created.

2 Enter the = sign.

3 Enter an opening bracket (

4 Click in the cell that contains the first value (number).

5 The cell reference displays in the **Formula bar**.

6 Enter the correct mathematical operator.

7 Click in the cell that contains the second value.

8 The cell reference displays after the mathematical operator.

9 Enter a closing bracket **)**

10 Enter the correct mathematical operator after the bracket.

11 Click in the cell that contains the third value.

12 Check the **Formula bar** to make sure the formula is correct (Figure 2.57).

13 Press **Enter**, or click on the **Enter** tick ✔ on the **Formula bar**.

14 The calculation is made, and the result (the value) will be displayed in the cell in which you created the formula.

What does it mean?

Mathematical operators
The mathematical operators are:
*
/
+
-

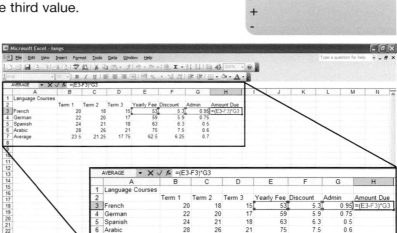

FIGURE 2.57 Using brackets in a formula

Check your understanding *Create a formula using brackets*

1 In your spreadsheet **langs**, in cell **H3** create a formula as follows:

(Yearly Fee subtract Discount) multiply by Admin.

2 Check your formula, it should be: **=(E3-F3)*G3**. If you do not use brackets, you will get an incorrect result!

3 Replicate (copy) the formula from cell **H3** into cells **H4**, **H5**, **H6**.

4 Replicate (copy) the **AVERAGE** function from cell **G7** into cell **H7**.

5 Save your spreadsheet, keeping the filename **langs**. It should look similar to one in Figure 2.58.

6 Keep the spreadsheet open.

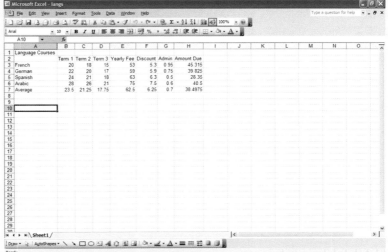

FIGURE 2.58 The spreadsheet **langs**

Spreadsheet print options

▶▶ How to... *set the spreadsheet print options*

1 In the **Menu bar**, click on **File**.

2 From the **File** menu, click on **Page Setup**.

3 The **Page Setup** dialogue box is displayed (Figure 2.59).

4 Check the **Page** tab is selected.

5 Check the orientation is set correctly.

6 In the **Scaling** section, click in the **Fit to** button.

7 In the **Fit to** boxes, check **1** is displayed in both **page(s) wide by ... tall** boxes.

8 Click on **OK** to set the print options.

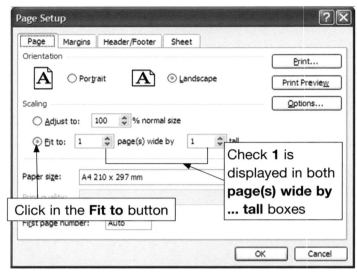

Click in the **Fit to** button

Check **1** is displayed in both **page(s) wide by ... tall** boxes

FIGURE 2.59 **Page Setup** dialogue box

Printing a spreadsheet

▶▶ How to... *print a spreadsheet*

1 In the **Menu bar**, click on **File**.

2 From the **File** menu, click on **Print** (Figure 2.60).

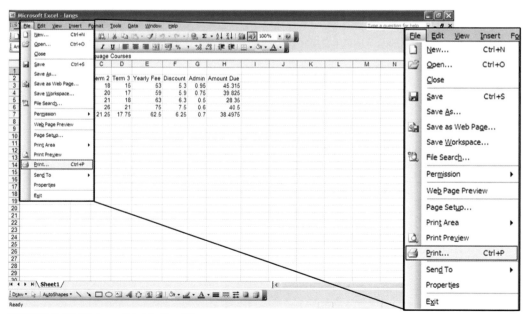

FIGURE 2.60 Click on **Print** in the **File** menu

3 The **Print** dialogue box is displayed (Figure 2.61).

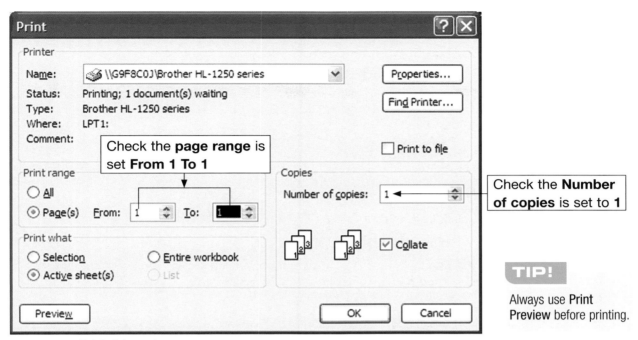

> Check the **page range** is set **From 1 To 1**

> Check the **Number of copies** is set to **1**

FIGURE 2.61 **Print** dialogue box

4 Check the **Page range** is set **From 1 To 1**.

5 Check the **Number of copies** is set to **1**.

6 Click on **OK** to print the spreadsheet.

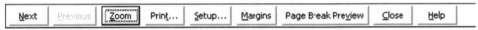

FIGURE 2.62 **Print Preview** buttons

Check your understanding *Print spreadsheets*

1 In your spreadsheet **langs**, set the spreadsheet to fit to **1** page wide and **1** page tall.

2 Use **Print Preview** to check the spreadsheet and the headers and footers.

3 Save the spreadsheet keeping the filename **langs**.

4 Print the spreadsheet.

5 Close the spreadsheet. You will continue working on this spreadsheet in Section 2.

6 Check your printout against the solutions which can be found on the CD-ROM in the folder **ss_worked_copies**.

By working through Section 1 you will have learnt the skills listed below. Read each item to help you decide how confident you feel about each skill.

- start Excel
- open a blank spreadsheet
- enter data into a spreadsheet
- widen columns to make sure that all data is fully displayed
- set the orientation
- set the margins
- save a spreadsheet with a specified filename into a folder from within Excel
- insert headers and footers
- insert an automatic date in headers and footers
- insert an automatic filename in headers and footers
- check your work for accuracy
- save an updated spreadsheet
- close a spreadsheet
- understand the difference between formulae and functions
- create basic formulae using mathematical operators
- copy (replicate) formulae
- use the **SUM** function
- use the **AVERAGE** function
- create formulae using brackets
- use **Print Preview**
- set the print options (fit to one page, orientation, number of copies)
- print a spreadsheet with all data displayed in full.

If you think you need more practice on any of the skills above, go back and work through the skill(s) again.

If you feel confident, move on to Section 2.

LEARNING OUTCOMES

In this section you will learn how to:

- open a saved spreadsheet
- save an existing spreadsheet with a new filename
- amend text and numeric data
- understand automatic recalculation of data
- insert a new column and enter data
- insert a new row and enter data
- delete a column
- delete a row
- align text and numbers
- format numeric data
- display gridlines
- display borders and shading
- display formulae in full
- display row and column headings
- print formulae
- close a spreadsheet
- exit from Excel.

Opening and saving an existing spreadsheet

▶▶ How to... *open a saved spreadsheet*

1 In the **Menu** bar, click on **File**.

2 From the **File** menu, click on **Open** (Figure 2.63).

3 The **Open** dialogue box is displayed (Figure 2.64).

4 In the **Look in** box, click on the **down arrow** to show a list of user areas. Click on your user area.

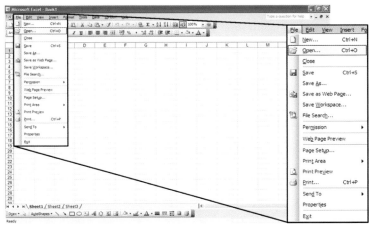

FIGURE 2.63 Click on **Open** in the **File** menu

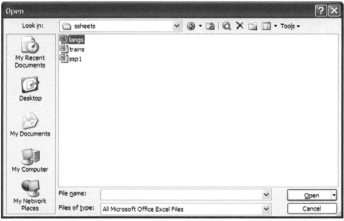

FIGURE 2.64 **Open** dialogue box

5 Click on the folder where the file is saved to open it.

6 Click on the required file.

7 Click on **Open**.

8 The selected file opens in Excel.

TIP!

Alternatively, click on the **Open** icon on the **Standard toolbar** to display the **Open** dialogue box.

Check your understanding *Open existing spreadsheets*

1 Open your saved spreadsheet **ssp1**.

2 Print the spreadsheet **ssp1**.

3 Close the file.

4 Open your saved spreadsheet **trains**.

5 Print the spreadsheet **trains**.

6 Close the file.

▶▶ How to... *save an existing spreadsheet with a new filename into an existing folder from within Excel*

1 In the **Menu** bar, click on **File**.

2 From the **File** menu, click on **Save As**.

3 The **Save As** dialogue box is displayed.

4 Click on the **down arrow** to the right of the **Save in** box, then click on your user area.

5 Double-click on the name of the folder you have already created.

TIP!

Always save your spreadsheets into folders to keep your files organised instead of saving all your files into one area.

6 The folder opens (Figure 2.65).

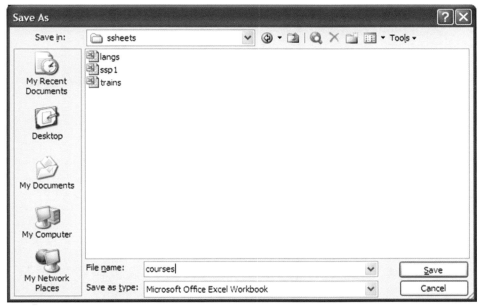

FIGURE 2.65 **Save As** dialogue box

7 In the **File name** box, enter the new filename.

8 Click on **Save** to save the file with a new filename.

Check your understanding

Open and save a spreadsheet into an existing folder

1 Open your saved spreadsheet **langs**.

2 Save it into your existing folder **ssheets** using the new filename **courses**.

Amending text and numeric data

You may be required to change (amend) the text or numbers in the cells in a spreadsheet.

▶▶ How to... *amend (change) data (1)*

Replace all the existing data in a cell

1 In the spreadsheet, click once in the cell to be amended.

2 Enter the new data (text or numbers).

3 The existing data is replaced (you type over it).

4 Move to another cell.

5 When a number is changed any calculations using that number will automatically update. Check to make sure!

1 In your file **courses**, amend the column label **Discount** to **Rebate**.

2 Amend the **Term 1** figure for **Arabic** to **18**.

3 Check your previous printout of the spreadsheet **langs** to make sure that the **Average**, **Yearly Fee**, **Rebate** and **Amount Due** figures for Arabic have recalculated.

4 Save the spreadsheet keeping the filename **courses**.

▶▶ How to... *amend (change) data (2)*

Replace part of the data in a cell

1 In the spreadsheet, double-click in the cell to be amended.

2 A cursor displays in the cell.

3 Delete only the data to be replaced.

4 Enter the new data.

5 Move to another cell.

6 If you amend part of a number, check to make sure that any calculations using that number are automatically updated.

1 In your file **courses**, amend the cell **Language Courses** to **Languages**.

2 Amend the **Term 2** figure for **French** to **16**.

3 Save your spreadsheet keeping the filename **courses**.

Inserting data

After a spreadsheet has been created, it may be necessary to add data. In Excel, rows and columns can easily be added without the need to create the spreadsheet again.

TIP!

New columns are inserted to the left of the active cell.

▶▶ How to... *insert a new column*

1 In the spreadsheet, click anywhere in the column where the new column is to be inserted.

2 This column may contain data, don't worry, you will not delete this data – Excel will automatically move this column to the right when the new column is inserted.

3 In the **Menu bar**, click on **Insert**.

4 Click on **Columns** (Figure 2.66).

5 A new blank column is inserted and the subsequent columns are automatically relabelled.

6 Enter the required data in the new column.

7 Save the updated spreadsheet.

8 Check to see that any calculations have been updated. Excel does this automatically, but it is good practice to check.

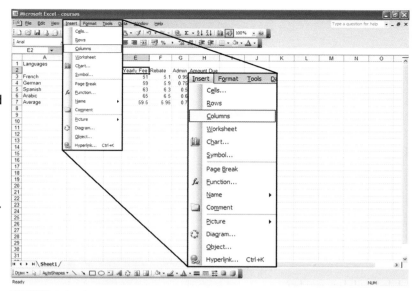

FIGURE 2.66 Click on **Columns** in the **Insert** menu

TIP!

Below is an alternative, quick way to insert a column.

1 Right-click in the grey column letter where the new column is to be inserted.

2 The entire column is highlighted and a menu is displayed.

3 From the menu, click on **Insert** (Figure 2.67).

4 The new column is inserted.

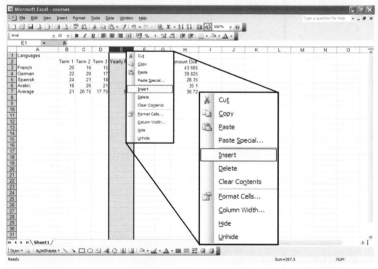

FIGURE 2.67 Inserting a new column

1 In your spreadsheet **courses**, insert a new column as column **E** between **Term 3** and **Yearly Fee**.

2 Enter the data in the new column **E** as shown below (Taster column).

Languages	Term 1	Term 2	Term 3	Taster
French	20	16	15	30
German	22	20	17	22
Spanish	24	21	18	25
Arabic	18	26	21	17
Average	21	20.75	17.75	

3 Save your spreadsheet keeping the filename **courses**.

▶▶ How to... *insert a new row*

1 In the spreadsheet, click anywhere in the row where the new row is to be inserted.

2 This row may contain data. Don't worry, you will not delete this data – Excel will automatically move this row below the inserted row.

3 In the **Menu bar**, click on **Insert** (Figure 2.68).

4 Click on **Rows**.

5 A new blank row is inserted and the subsequent rows are automatically renumbered.

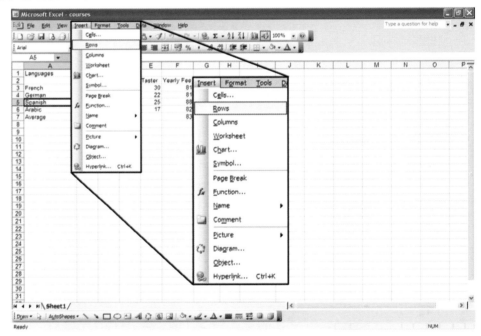

FIGURE 2.68 Click on **Rows** in the **Insert** menu

6 Enter the required data in the new row.

7 Save the updated spreadsheet.

8 Check to see that any calculations have been updated. Although Excel does this automatically, it is good practice to check.

Below is an alternative, quick way to insert a row.

1 Right-click in the grey row number where the new row is to be inserted.
2 The entire row is highlighted and a menu is displayed.
3 From the menu, click on **Insert** (Figure 2.69).
4 The new row is inserted.

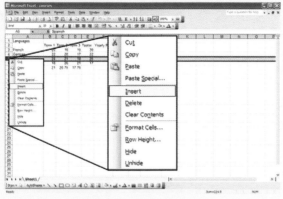

FIGURE 2.69 Inserting a new row

Check your understanding
Insert a new row and replicate formulae

1 In your spreadsheet **courses**, insert a new row between **German** and **Spanish** as new row **5**.

2 Enter the data in the new row as shown below (Italian row).

Languages	Term 1	Term 2	Term 3	Taster	Yearly Fee	Rebate	Admin	Amount Due
French	20	16	15	30	81	8.1	0.95	69.255
German	22	20	17	22	81	8.1	0.75	54.675
Italian	19	18	16	18			0.55	

3 Save your spreadsheet.

4 Replicate (copy) the formula in the **German** row for **Yearly Fee**, **Rebate** and **Amount Due** into the **Italian** row.

5 Copy the **Average** formula for **Term 3** into the **Taster** column.

6 Save your spreadsheet keeping the filename **courses**.

7 Your spreadsheet should look similar to the one in Figure 2.70. The figures in column **I** and row 8 may be formatted slightly differently.

	A	B	C	D	E	F	G	H	I	J
1	Languages									
2		Term 1	Term 2	Term 3	Taster	Yearly Fee	Rebate	Admin	Amount Due	
3	French	20	16	15	30	81	8.1	0.95	69.255	
4	German	22	20	17	22	81	8.1	0.75	54.675	
5	Italian	19	18	16	18	71	7.1	0.55	35.145	
6	Spanish	24	21	18	25	88	8.8	0.5	39.6	
7	Arabic	18	26	21	17	82	8.2	0.6	44.28	
8	Average	20.6	20.2	17.4	22.4	80.6	8.06	0.67	48.591	
9										

FIGURE 2.70 The spreadsheet **courses**

Deleting a row or a column of data

When deleting a row or a column, the entire row or column must be removed from the spreadsheet, and the subsequent row numbers or column letters will automatically readjust. Make sure that you do not delete only the contents of the cells in the row or column leaving behind a blank row or column.

▶▶ How to... *delete a column*

1 In the spreadsheet, move the mouse pointer over the grey column letter of the column to be deleted (Figure 2.71).

2 Right-click with the mouse.

3 The entire column will be highlighted.

4 A drop-down menu is displayed (Figure 2.72).

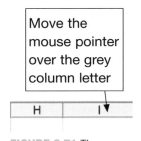

Move the mouse pointer over the grey column letter

FIGURE 2.71 The column to be deleted

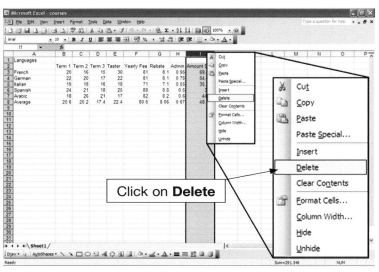

Click on **Delete**

FIGURE 2.72 Drop-down menu to delete a column

5 Click on **Delete**.

6 The column is deleted and the letters of the remaining columns are automatically relabelled.

7 When a column is deleted, any calculation using numbers in the deleted column will automatically recalculate. Check to make sure!

8 Save the updated spreadsheet.

Check your understanding *Delete a column*

1 In your file **courses**, delete the **Amount Due** column and all its contents.

2 Save your spreadsheet using the new filename **newplan** in a new folder called **sect2**.

▶▶ How to... *delete a row*

1 In your spreadsheet, move the mouse pointer over the grey row number to be deleted (Figure 2.73).

2 Right-click with the mouse.

3 The entire row will be highlighted.

4 A drop-down menu is displayed (Figure 2.74).

5 Click on **Delete**.

6 The row is deleted and the numbers of the remaining rows are automatically renumbered.

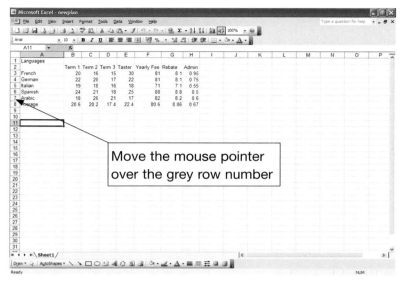

FIGURE 2.73 The row to be deleted

7 When a row is deleted, any calculation using numbers in the deleted row will automatically recalculate. Check to make sure!

8 Save the updated spreadsheet.

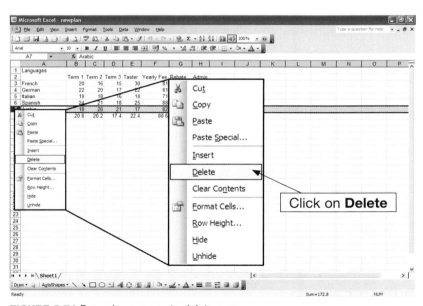

FIGURE 2.74 Drop-down menu to delete a row

Check your understanding *Delete a row*

1 In your file **newplan**, delete the row for **Arabic** and all its contents.

2 Make sure blank cells do not remain in between rows.

3 Save your spreadsheet keeping the filename **newplan**.

Alignment

Alignment is how the data lines up with the left or right edge of the cell. Data in a cell can be aligned to the left, to the right or centre. Text is usually displayed left-aligned or centred, and numbers are usually displayed right-aligned. In Excel, when text is entered into a cell, it automatically aligns to the left, while numbers are automatically right-aligned (Figure 2.75).

LEFT-ALIGNED TEXT	CENTRED TEXT AND NUMBERS	RIGHT-ALIGNED TEXT AND NUMBERS
Course fees	Term 3	Total course fee
Word processing	15.00	53.00
Spreadsheets	18.00	60.00

Examples of alignment

▶▶ How to... *left-align data*

1 In the spreadsheet, highlight the cells to be left-aligned.
2 Click on the **Align Left** icon on the **Formatting toolbar.**

▶▶ How to... *right-align data*

1 In the spreadsheet, highlight the cells to be right-aligned.
2 Click on the **Align Right** icon on the **Formatting toolbar.**

▶▶ How to... *centre data*

1 In the spreadsheet, highlight the cells to be centred.
2 Click on the **Center** icon on the **Formatting toolbar.**

TIP!

To align one cell only, click in the cell then click the required alignment icon.

TIP!

It may be difficult to see on the screen how the text is aligned. To check line alignment, click in the relevant cell(s) and look at the **Left**, **Right** or **Center** alignment icons. The icon that appears to be 'switched on' (brighter shade) shows which alignment has been set.

Check your understanding *Set the alignment*

1 In your file **newplan**, apply the following alignments:

a Right-align all the column labels from **Term 1** to **Admin** (inclusive).

b Right-align all the numbers in the spreadsheet.

2 Save the spreadsheet, keeping the filename **newplan**.

TIP!

Although numbers automatically display as right-aligned by default in Excel, it is best to highlight them and click the right-align icon.

Formatting numeric data

Numbers can be formatted so that their display changes but the actual value (number) remains the same. Common numeric formats are shown in the table opposite.

TYPE OF FORMAT	HOW FORMAT IS DISPLAYED	EXAMPLE
Integer	Whole number, no decimal places.	25
Two decimal places	A decimal point followed by two numbers without currency symbol.	25.00

>> **How to...** *format numbers to integer (no decimal places)*

1 In the spreadsheet, highlight the cells to be formatted.

2 Right-click anywhere within the highlighted cells.

3 A drop-down menu is displayed.

4 Click on **Format Cells** (Figure 2.76).

5 The **Format Cells** dialogue box is displayed (Figure 2.77).

TIP!

To format one cell only, click in the cell then right-click and select **Format Cells.**

TIP!

Below is an alternative, way to open the Format Cells dialogue box:

1 Highlight the relevant numbers.

2 In the **Menu** bar, click on **Format**.

3 From the **Format** menu, click on **Cells**.

4 The **Format Cells** dialogue box is displayed.

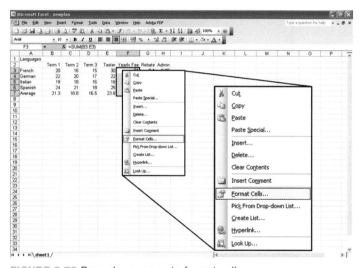

FIGURE 2.76 Drop-down menu to format cells

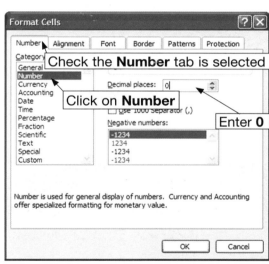

FIGURE 2.77 Format Cells dialogue box

6 Check the **Number** tab is selected.

7 In the **Category** list, click on **Number**.

8 In the **Decimal places** box, enter **0** (or use the **down arrow**).

9 Click on **OK** to format the numbers as whole numbers (integer).

What does it mean?

Decimal places
Decimal places refer to the numbers displayed after the decimal point.
○ The number 25.5 has 1 decimal place.
○ The number 25.54 has 2 decimal places.

▶▶ How to... *format numbers to a fixed number of decimal places*

1 In the spreadsheet, highlight the cells to be formatted.

2 Right-click anywhere within the highlighted cells.

3 A drop-down menu is displayed.

4 Click on **Format Cells**.

5 The **Format Cells** dialogue box is displayed (Figure 2.78).

6 Check the **Number** tab is selected.

7 In the **Category** list, click on **Number**.

8 In the **Decimal places** box, enter the required number of decimal places (or use the **up/down arrows**) (Figure 2.78).

9 Click on **OK**.

10 The numbers are displayed with decimal places.

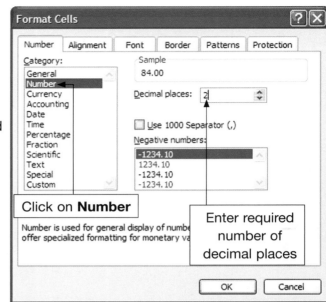

FIGURE 2.78 Format Cells dialogue box

TIP!

Use the Increase Decimal or Decrease Decimal icons on the formating toolbar.

▶▶ How to... *format numbers to currency*

1 In the spreadsheet, highlight the cells to be formatted.

2 Right-click anywhere within the highlighted cells.

3 A menu is displayed.

4 Click on **Format Cells**.

5 The Format Cells dialogue box is displayed (Figure 2.79).

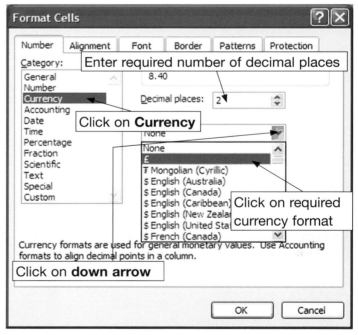

FIGURE 2.79 Format Cells dialogue box

TIP!

Do not use the **Currency** icon on the **Formatting toolbar** as this will display the cell in accounting format.

What does it mean?

Currency

Currency is the type of money that is used in a country. When currency format is applied, any currency symbol may be displayed. In the UK, the currency symbol is £. € (Euro symbol) is also used in the UK.

6 Check the **Number** tab is selected.

7 In the **Category** list, click on **Currency**.

8 In the **Decimal places** box, enter the required number of decimal places (or use the **up/down arrows**).

9 In the **Symbol** box, click on the **down arrow** and click on the required currency format, e.g. £.

10 Click on **OK**.

11 The numbers are formatted with the currency symbol.

TIP!

If hash signs ##### display in cell(s), widen the column to display the data in full.

Check your understanding *Format numeric data*

1 In your file **newplan**, format the numeric data as follows.

a Format all the figures in the **Yearly Fee** column with the £ currency symbol to **0** decimal places.

b Format all the figures in the **Rebate** and **Admin** columns with the £ currency symbol to **2** decimal places.

c Format the figures in the **Average** row for **Term 1**, **Term 2**, **Term 3** and **Taster** to **2** decimal places with **no** currency symbol.

TIP!

The currency symbol displayed should be appropriate to the country that you live in.

2 Save your spreadsheet keeping the filename **newplan**.

3 Your spreadsheet should look similar to the one in Figure 2.80.

	A	B	C	D	E	F	G	H	I
1	Languages								
2		Term 1	Term 2	Term 3	Taster	Yearly Fee	Rebate	Admin	
3	French	20	16	15	30	£81	£8.10	£0.95	
4	German	22	20	17	22	£81	£8.10	£0.75	
5	Italian	19	18	16	18	£71	£7.10	£0.55	
6	Spanish	24	21	18	25	£88	£8.80	£0.50	
7	Average	21.25	18.75	16.50	23.75	£80	£8.03	£0.69	
8									

FIGURE 2.80 The spreadsheet **newplan**

Borders, shading and gridlines

Borders give prominence to selected data in a spreadsheet. Borders are not the same as gridlines – gridlines display for all the data in the spreadsheet. However, borders can be set for selected cells to make these cells stand out. Borders can be used even if gridlines are displayed.

▶▶ How to... *add a border*

1 In the spreadsheet, highlight the cells to be framed with a border. To select one cell only click in the cell.

2 On the **Formatting toolbar**, click on the **down arrow** to the right of the **Borders** ▼ icon.

3 A drop-down selection displays the various border options (Figure 2.81).

4 Select the **Outside Border** or **Thick Box Border** option.

5 Click on the **Print Preview** ![icon] icon to check the border is displayed correctly.

TIP!

Select the Thick Box Border as this displays more clearly on a printout.

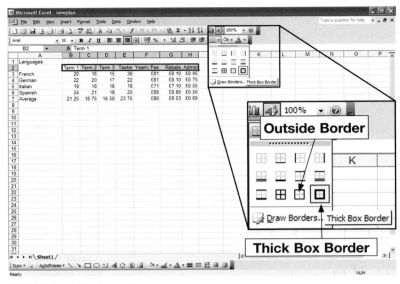

FIGURE 2.81 Border options menu

▶▶ How to... *shade cells*

1 In the spreadsheet, highlight the cells to be shaded. To shade one cell only click in the cell.

2 On the **Formatting toolbar**, click on the **down arrow** to the right of the **Fill Color** ![icon] ▾ icon.

3 A drop-down selection displays various fill colour options (Figure 2.82).

4 Click on a pale colour square.

5 The highlighted cells are filled with the selected colour.

6 Check the data in the shaded cells is still clearly readable.

7 Make sure that the shading is clearly visible on the printout.

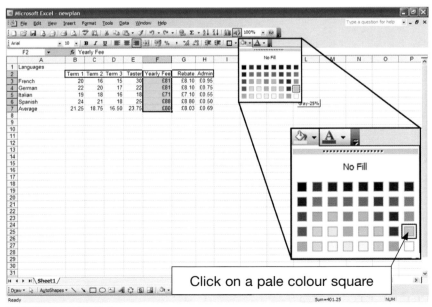

FIGURE 2.82 Fill Color menu

1 In your file **newplan**, add a single, thick outside border around all the column labels starting with **Term 1** and ending with **Admin** (inclusive).

2 Shade the column label and the numbers in the **Yearly Fee** column.

3 Save your spreadsheet keeping the filename **newplan**.

▶▶ How to... *display gridlines*

1 In the spreadsheet, click on the **File** menu.

2 From the menu, click on **Page Setup**.

3 The **Page Setup** dialogue box is displayed (Figure 2.83).

4 Click on the **Sheet** tab.

5 In the **Print** section, click in the **Gridlines** box to insert a tick.

6 Click on **OK**.

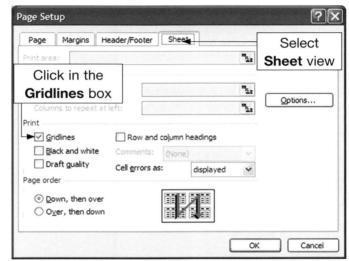

FIGURE 2.83 Page Setup dialogue box in Sheet view

TIP!

Click on the **Print Preview** icon to check gridlines are displayed.

1 In your file **newplan**, display gridlines.

2 Save the spreadsheet.

3 Print the spreadsheet.

4 Check your printout against the solution which can be found on the CD-ROM in the folder **ss_worked_copies**.

Displaying formulae

When formulae are used the actual values (numbers) display in the cell(s), and the formulae are in the background. If a cell containing a formula is clicked, the formula for that cell will display in the **Formula bar**. Printing the formulae proves that you have used formulae and functions correctly and that you have copied (replicated) the formulae and functions where instructed.

How to... *display formulae*

1 In the spreadsheet, click on the **Tools** menu (Figure 2.84).

2 From the menu, click on **Options**.

3 The **Options** dialogue box is displayed (Figure 2.85).

4 Check the **View** tab is selected.

5 In the **Window options** section, click in the **Formulas** box to insert a tick.

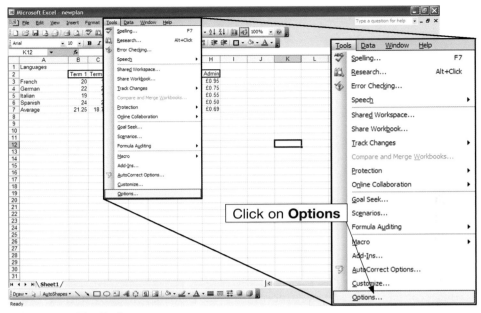

Click on **Options**

FIGURE 2.84 The **Tools** menu

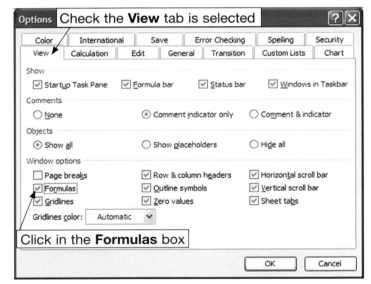

FIGURE 2.85 Options dialogue box

6 Click on **OK**.

7 The formulae are displayed on screen instead of the numbers. When formulae are displayed, columns become wider. However, you can adjust the width of all columns using **AutoFit**.

How to... *use AutoFit to adjust column widths*

1 Highlight the entire spreadsheet by clicking on the shaded cell to the left of the column letter **A** and above the row number **1** (Figure 2.86).

TIP!

To switch from spreadsheet view to formulae view and vice versa, press **Ctrl** + ` key (**Accent** key usually above the **Tab** key).

TIP!

Another method to display formulae in full is: Highlight the entire spreadsheet, click the **Format** menu, click on **Columns** and click on **AutoFit selection**.

2 In the grey area displaying the column letters, position the mouse pointer over the vertical line dividing any two columns.

3 The mouse pointer changes into ↔.

4 Double-click with the left mouse button.

5 Excel automatically adjusts all the column widths to display all data in full.

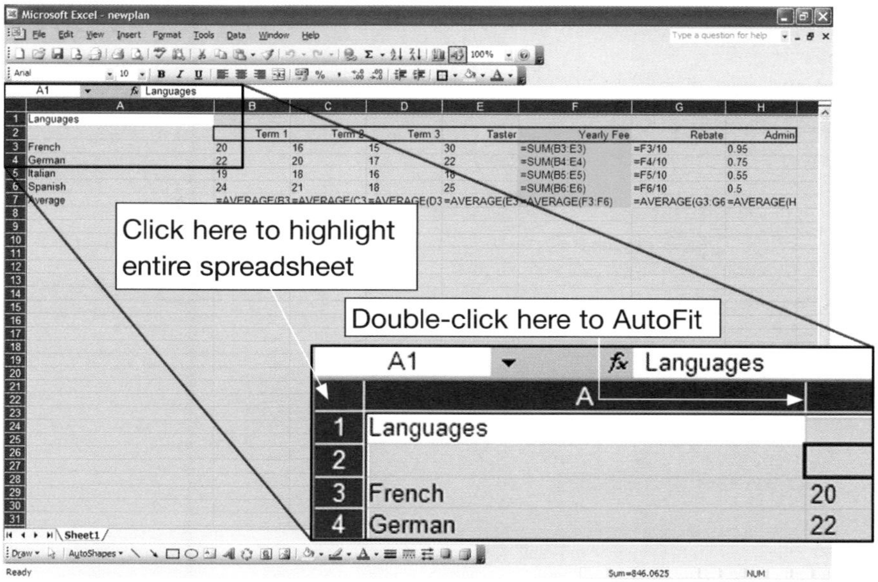

When formulae are displayed, some formatting is lost, e.g. left and right alignment, decimal places, currency format, date format. This is normal. When you return to the spreadsheet view, all the formatting you had set will display again.

FIGURE 2.86 Highlight the spreadsheet

TIP!

Click on the **Print Preview** icon to check all formulae are fully displayed (Figure 2.87).

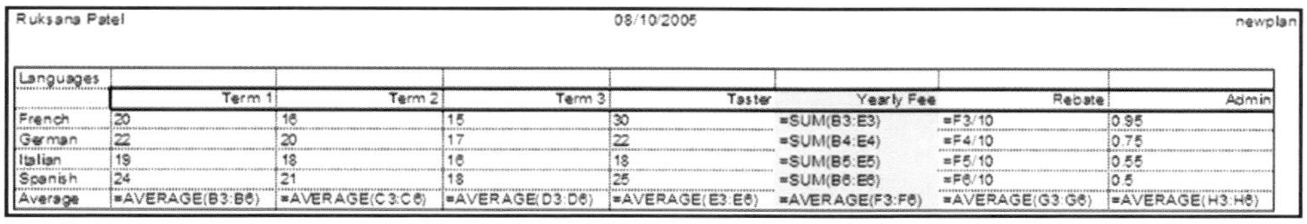

FIGURE 2.87 All formulae are fully displayed

Row and column headings

Row and column headings are the column letters **A**, **B**, **C**, etc. and the row numbers **1**, **2**, **3**, etc. Do not confuse row and column headings with the row and column labels (titles) that you enter in the cells of the spreadsheet. Displaying row and column headings is normally required on a formula printout.

▶▶ How to... *display row and column headings on the printout*

1 In the spreadsheet, click on the **File** menu.

2 From the menu, click on **Page Setup**.

3 The **Page Setup** dialogue box is displayed (Figure 2.88).

4 Click on the **Sheet** tab.

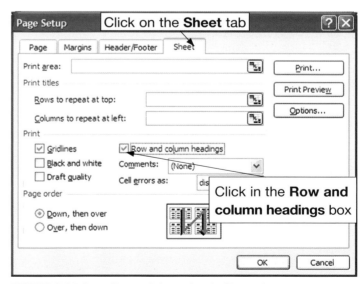

FIGURE 2.88 Page Setup dialogue box in Sheet view

5 In the Print section, click in the **Row and column headings** box to insert a tick.

6 Click on **OK**.

Formula print options

▶▶ How to... *set/check the formula print options*

1 In the spreadsheet, click on the **File** menu.

2 From the menu, click on **Page Setup**.

3 The **Page Setup** dialogue box is displayed (Figure 2.89).

4 Check the **Page** tab is selected.

5 Check the orientation is set correctly.

6 In the **Scaling** section, click in the **Fit to** button.

7 In the **Fit to** boxes, check **1** is displayed in both **page(s) wide by ... tall** boxes.

8 Click on **OK** to set the print options.

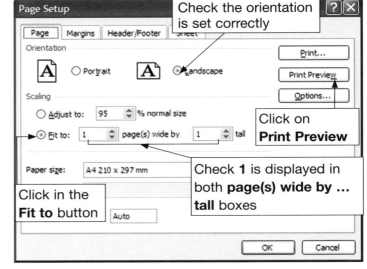

FIGURE 2.89 **Page Setup** dialogue box in **Page** view

Printing formulae

▶▶ How to... *print formulae*

1 In the spreadsheet, click on the **File** menu.

2 From the menu, click on **Print**.

3 The **Print** dialogue box is displayed.

4 Check the **Page Range** is set **From 1 To 1**.

5 Check the **Number of copies** is set to **1**.

6 Click on **OK** to print out the formulae.

Check your understanding
Display formulae, row and column headings and print formulae

1 In your file **newplan**, display the formulae.

2 Adjust the column widths to make sure all formulae are fully displayed.

3 Set the formulae to print on **one page** in **landscape** orientation.

4 Display **row and column headings**.

5 Use **Print Preview** to check that you have carried out the instructions above.

6 Print the formulae on one page.

7 Save the formulae print using the new filename **npform** into the folder you created earlier called **sect2**.

8 Check your formulae printout against the solution which can be found on the CD-ROM in the folder **ss_worked_copies**.

Formula and spreadsheet views

▶▶ How to... *change from formula view to spreadsheet view*

TIP!

To switch from spreadsheet view to formulae view and vice versa, press **Ctrl** + `` ` `` key (**Accent** key usually above the **Tab** key).

1 In the spreadsheet, click on the **Tools** menu.

2 From the menu, click on **Options**.

3 An **Options** dialogue box is displayed.

4 Check the **View** tab is selected.

5 Click in the **Formulas** box to remove the tick.

6 Click on **OK** to return to spreadsheet view.

▶▶ How to... *display all spreadsheet data in full*

TIP!

Another method is: Highlight the entire spreadsheet, click the **Format** menu, click on **Columns** and click on **AutoFit selection**.

1 When the spreadsheet is displayed again after displaying formula, the columns may not be wide enough to display the data in full.

2 Highlight the entire spreadsheet by clicking on the shaded cell to the left of the column letter **A** and above the row number **1** (Figure 2.90).

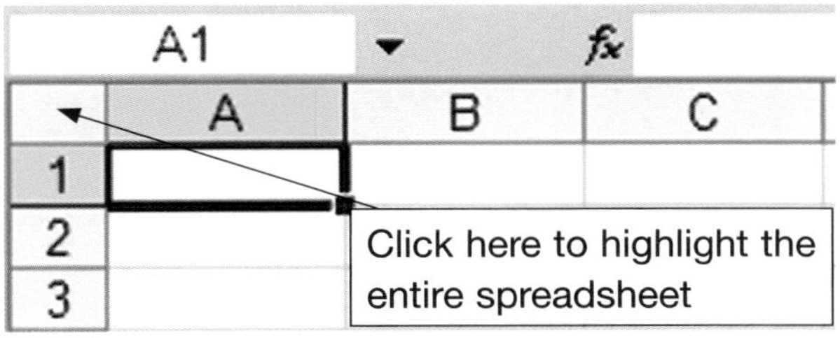

FIGURE 2.90 Highlighting the entire spreadsheet

3 Position the mouse pointer over the vertical line dividing any two columns in the grey area displaying the column letters.

4 The mouse pointer changes into ↔.

5 Double-click with the left mouse button.

6 Excel automatically adjusts all the column widths to display the data in full.

Closing a spreadsheet

When you have saved and printed your document, you should close it. It is good practice to remember to close a file before you close a program.

▶▶ How to... *close a spreadsheet*

1 In the spreadsheet, click on the **File** menu.

2 From the menu, click on **Close**.

Exiting from Excel

When the spreadsheet has been closed you should exit from Excel.

▶▶ How to... *exit from Excel*

1 In the spreadsheet, click on the **File** menu.

2 From the menu, click on **Exit**.

TIP!

Alternatively, at the top right corner of the Excel window, click on the black cross to close the spreadsheet and the red cross to close Excel (Figure 2.91).

FIGURE 2.91 Closing the spreadsheet and exiting Excel

Check your understanding
Change from formula view to spreadsheet view and exit Excel

1 In your file **npform**.

2 Change the view from formulae back to the spreadsheet view.

3 Adjust the column widths using AutoFit to display all data in full.

4 Close the spreadsheet, do not save it again (you have previously saved **newplan** and **npform**).

5 Exit Excel.

By working through Section 2 you will have learnt the skills below. Read each item to help you decide how confident you feel about each skill.

- open an existing spreadsheet
- save an existing spreadsheet with a new filename into an existing folder from within Excel
- amend text and numeric data
- check that formulae automatically recalculate when data is amended
- insert a new column and enter data
- insert a new row and enter data
- delete a column
- delete a row
- align text and numbers
- format numeric data as integer (no decimal places) with a currency symbol, as integer with no currency symbol
- display gridlines
- display borders
- shade cells
- display formulae
- check that all formulae are displayed in full
- display row and column headings
- print formulae with all formulae displayed in full
- change the view to display the spreadsheet data
- use **AutoFit** to display all spreadsheet data in full
- close a spreadsheet
- exit from Excel.

If you think you need more practice on any of the skills above, go back and work through the skill(s) again.

If you feel confident, move on to Chapter 2.

UNIT 2: Creating spreadsheets and graphs

In this chapter, you will learn how to create three types of graphs:

○ *pie charts*

○ *bar charts*

○ *line graphs.*

You will use Microsoft Office Excel 2003, which you have become familiar with in Chapter 1. We will refer to the program as Excel from now on. Default settings are assumed.

This chapter is divided into three sections:

○ *in Section 1, you will learn how to create pie charts*

○ *in Section 2, you will learn how to create bar charts including comparative bar charts*

○ *in Section 3, you will learn how to create line graphs including comparative line graphs.*

A CD-ROM accompanies this book. On it are the files required to create the graphs, which can be found in the folder **files_graphs**. The solutions for the creating graphs tasks can be found in the folder **graphs_worked_copies**.

> *Note:* There are many ways of performing the skills covered in this book. This book provides How to… guidelines that have proven to be easily understood by learners.

Files for this chapter

To work through the tasks in this chapter, you will need the files from the folder *files_graphs*, which you will find on the CD-ROM provided with this book. Copy this folder into your user area before you begin.

▶▶ How to...   *copy the folder files_graphs from the CD-ROM*

1 Make sure the computer is switched on and the desktop screen is displayed. Insert the CD-ROM into the CD-ROM drive of your computer.

2 Close any windows that may open.

3 On the desktop, double-click on the **My Computer** icon to display the **My Computer** window. The **My Computer** window is displayed.

4 Under **Devices with Removable Storage**, double-click on the **CD-ROM Drive** icon to view the contents of the CD-ROM.

5 Double-click on the **L1_Unit2_SS+GR** folder. Double-click on the **Source files** folder.

6 The **Source files** window displays (Figure 2.92).

7 Click on the folder **files_graphs**.

8 The folder will be highlighted (usually blue).

9 In the **File and Folder Tasks box**, click on **Copy this folder**.

10 The **Copy Items** dialogue box is displayed (Figure 2.93).

11 Click on the user area that you want to copy the folder **files_graphs** to.

12 Click on **Copy**.

13 The folder **files_graphs** is copied to your user area.

14 It is advisable to copy and paste a second copy of the file to another folder in your user area as backup.

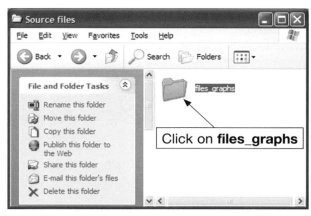

Click on files_graphs

FIGURE 2.92 The **Source files** window

FIGURE 2.93 **Copy Items** dialogue box

1: Create a pie chart

LEARNING OUTCOMES

In this section you will learn how to:

- understand the types and purpose of graphs
- open a datafile from within Excel
- open a datafile from **My Computer**
- save a datafile with a new name
- view a datafile and identify data for a chart
- identify the parts of a pie chart
- select the data for a pie chart
- use the Chart Wizard to create a pie chart
- save an updated file
- print a chart
- understand legends
- understand the importance of distinctive data
- make sure that chart data is clearly distinctive (set the print options and fill sectors with patterns).

What are graphs?

Graphs are an effective way of presenting numeric data in a visual (graphical) form. By creating a graph, you can see particular trends or patterns, sale of products, differences in performances, etc. Sometimes it can be difficult to identify important information from a spreadsheet. A visual picture of the numbers often makes it easier to identify trends or changes in data.

TIP!

Graphs are also referred to as charts.

Excel offers a wide range of graph styles and options to present data for different types of information. There are three common chart types.

- **Pie charts**. *Data is displayed as slices of a round pie. Each slice represents a proportion of the total.*
- **Bar charts**. *Data is displayed as vertical bars. The bars show comparisons between categories.*
- **Line graphs**. *Data is displayed as individual points joined by a line. The line shows trends over time or for categories.*

Charts make **comparison of data** much simpler and clearer and can make the data easier to understand.

Another advantage of graphs in Excel is that a graph is not a static (unchanging) picture. When the data in a spreadsheet is changed, the graph automatically updates. This is referred to as **live data modelling**.

Using the Chart Wizard makes creating graphs very simple as it guides you step-by-step, with a preview of the chart at each step. Once the graph has been created, changes can also be made to any part of the graph.

Now, using the skills that you learned in Unit 1 Chapter 1, switch on your computer and log in. Start Excel (to remind you how to do this, turn to pages 117–118 of this Unit).

Opening datafiles

A datafile can be opened from within Excel or from the **My Computer** window. Both methods are described below.

What does it mean?

Datafile
A file that contains data. You will be supplied with a datafile which will contain the data needed to create the graph.

1 In Excel, click on **File** in the **Menu bar.**

2 From the **File** menu, click on **Open** (Figure 2.94).

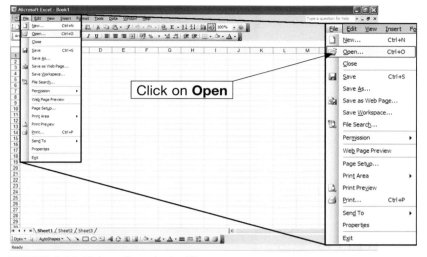

FIGURE 2.94 Click on Open in the File menu

3 The **Open** dialogue box displays (Figure 2.95).

4 Click on the **down arrow** next to the **Look in** box.

5 A list of user areas is displayed.

6 Find your user area and double-click on it.

7 Double-click on the folder in your user area where the file is saved.

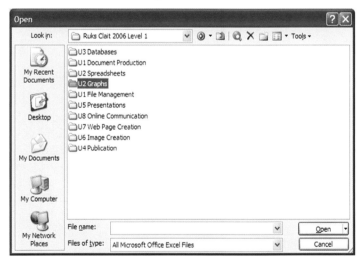

FIGURE 2.95 Open dialogue box

8 The folder opens and a list of files is displayed (Figure 2.96).

9 Click on the required file.

10 Click on **Open**.

11 The selected file opens in Excel.

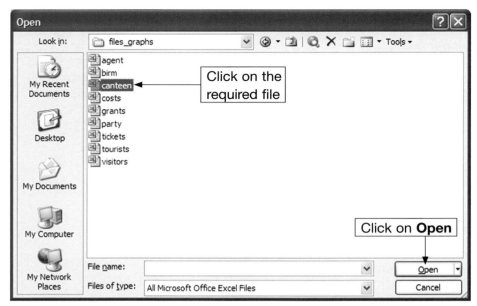

FIGURE 2.96 List of files in Open dialogue box

▶▶ How to... *open the datafile from My Computer*

1 On the desktop, double-click on the **My Computer** icon.

2 The **My Computer** window is displayed.

3 Go to your user area and double-click on it.

4 Double-click on the folder icon containing the files, e.g. **files_graphs**.

5 The list of files is displayed (Figure 2.97).

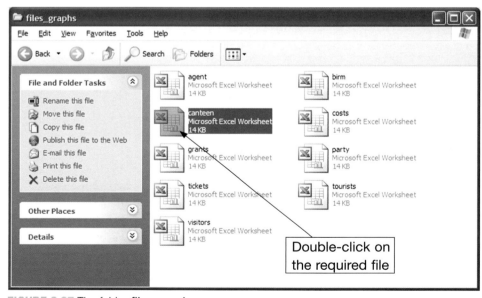

FIGURE 2.97 The folder files_graphs

6 Double-click on the required Excel file.

7 The file opens in Excel.

Saving datafiles

▶▶ How to... *save a datafile with a new filename into a new folder from within Excel*

1 In the **Menu bar**, click on **File**.

2 From the **File** menu, click on **Save As** (Figure 2.98).

TIP!

Save a datafile with a new filename as soon as you open it, so if you incorrectly make changes to it you can go back to the original.

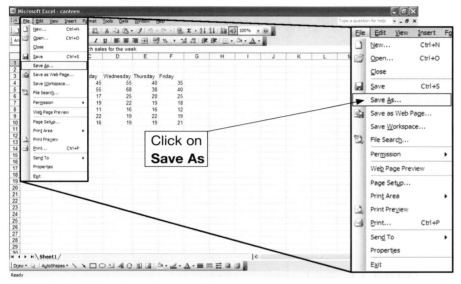

FIGURE 2.98 Click on **Save As** in the **File** menu

3 The **Save As** dialogue box is displayed (Figure 2.99).

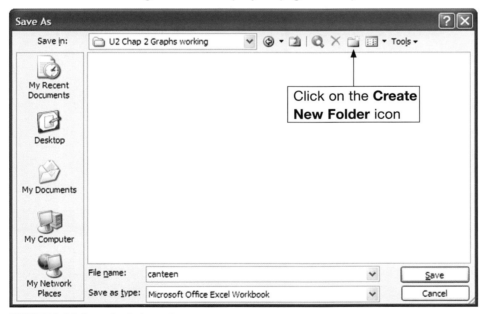

FIGURE 2.99 **Save As** dialogue box

TIP!

Save all files for one topic/section in a separate folder to keep your files organised.

4 Click on the **down arrow** to the right of the **Save in** box, then click on your user area.

5 Double-click to open the required subfolder(s).

6 The folder name displays in the **Save in** box.

7 Click on the **Create New Folder** icon.

8 A **New Folder** dialogue box is displayed (Figure 2.100).

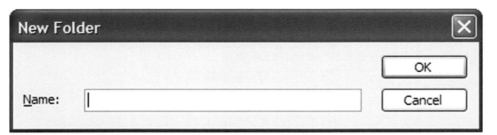

FIGURE 2.100 New Folder dialogue box

9 Enter the new folder name in the **Name** box.

10 Click on **OK** to create a new folder.

11 In the **Save As** dialogue box, in the **File name** box, delete the existing filename.

12 Enter the new filename.

13 Click on **Save**.

14 The file is saved with a new filename in a new folder within Excel.

Check your understanding
Open a datafile and save into a new folder

1 Open the datafile **canteen** from the folder **files_graphs** and save it into a new folder called **grc** using the filename **sales**.

2 Keep the file open.

Viewing a datafile and identifying data for a chart

Before you create a chart, you should look at the data in the datafile. Check to see:

○ which cells you will need to select for the chart

○ if the data is presented in columns or rows

○ if the data to be plotted on the x-axis is numeric (this will affect how you define the data series for bar charts and line graphs).

What does it mean?

Data series
The range of values that make up one set of data on a chart.

Look at the datafile **Lunch sales** in Figure 2.101.

	A	B	C	D	E	F	G
1	Lunch sales for the week						
2							
3	Item	Monday	Tuesday	Wednesday	Thursday	Friday	
4	Sandwiches	40	45	55	40	35	
5	Crisps	55	55	68	38	40	
6	Salads	21	17	25	20	25	
7	Soups	15	19	22	19	18	
8	Hot Drinks	9	11	16	16	12	
9	Cold Drinks	15	22	19	22	19	
10	Desserts	11	16	19	19	21	
11							

FIGURE 2.101 The datafile Lunch sales

- *To create a **chart** to show the week's sandwich sales you would select data in **rows**.*

- *To create a **pie chart**, the range of cells would be **B3** to **F4**.*

- *To create a **bar chart** or **line graph**, the row labels in column **A** should also be selected, as Excel will use these for the titles and labels. The range of cells would be **A3** to **F4**.*

- *The **data labels** would be taken from row **3: Monday, Tuesday, Wednesday,** etc., and the values would be taken from row **4: 40, 45, 55**, etc.*

- *To create a **comparative bar** or **line graph** to show the week's sandwich and crisps sales, the range of cells would be **A3** to **F5**.*

Look at the datafile **Lunch sales** in Figure 2.102.

	A	B	C	D	E	F	G
1	Lunch sales for the week						
2							
3	Item	Monday	Tuesday	Wednesday	Thursday	Friday	
4	Sandwiches	40	45	55	40	35	
5	Crisps	55	55	68	38	40	
6	Salads	21	17	25	20	25	
7	Soups	15	19	22	19	18	
8	Hot Drinks	9	11	16	16	12	
9	Cold Drinks	15	22	19	22	19	
10	Desserts	11	16	19	19	21	
11							

FIGURE 2.102 The datafile Lunch sales

- *To create a **chart** to show the sales of each Item for Monday, you would select data in **columns**.*

- *To create a **pie chart**, the range of cells would be **A4** to **B10**. However, selecting cells **A3** to **B10** would also enable the creation of the chart.*

- To create a **bar chart** or **line graph**, the column labels in row **3** should also be selected, as Excel will use these for the titles and labels. The range of cells would be **A3** to **B10**.

- The **data labels** would be taken from column **A: Sandwiches**, **Crisps**, **Salads**, etc., and the **values** would be taken from column **B**: **40, 55, 21**, etc.

- To create a **comparative bar or line graph** to show the Item sales for **Monday** and **Tuesday**, the range of cells would be **A3** to **C10**.

▶▶ **How to...** highlight a range of adjacent cells (select data)

Method 1

1 In your datafile, click in the first cell. When the white cross displays in the cell, drag the mouse across the range (block) of cells to be highlighted.

2 A block of cells will be highlighted.

Method 2

1 Click with the mouse in the first cell.

2 Hold down the **Shift** key.

3 Click in the last cell.

4 A range (block) of cells will be highlighted.

Check your understanding
View the data in a datafile and select data

1 In your file **sales**, view the data in the rows and columns so that you are familiar with the data.

2 Highlight the data in rows from cells **B3** to **F4**.

3 Click in a blank cell to remove the highlight (to deselect the range).

4 Highlight the data in rows from cells **A3** to **F5**.

5 Click in a blank cell to remove the highlight (to deselect the range).

6 Highlight the data in columns from cells **A3** to **C10**.

7 Click in a blank cell to remove the highlight (to deselect the range).

8 Highlight the data in columns from cells **A4** to **B10**.

9 Keep this range of cells highlighted, do not deselect the range.

Using the Chart Wizard

There are several ways to create graphs in Excel. Using the Chart Wizard makes creating graphs easier because it helps you create a graph using a step-by-step approach as follows.

Step 1: Select the chart type and sub-type.

Step 2: Select or check the range of cells, preview the chart.

Step 3: Select and enter or display the chart options, e.g. Titles, Legends, Data labels.

Step 4: Select the chart location e.g. **As a new sheet**.

Pie charts

A pie chart shows data as slices of a pie. The size of each slice represents the value (number) from the data on which the chart is based – a slice shows each item of data in proportion to the whole set of data. Pie charts always show only one data series and are useful if you want to emphasise a significant element. Each slice is called a **sector**.

In Excel, there are many different pie chart sub-types. Some examples are shown in Figures 2.103, 2.104 and 2.105.

It is recommended that you always use 2-dimensional (2D) pie charts.

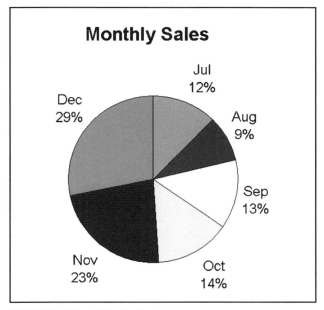

FIGURE 2.103 A 2D pie chart

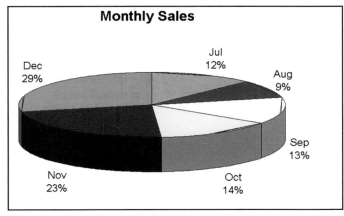

FIGURE 2.104 A 3D pie chart

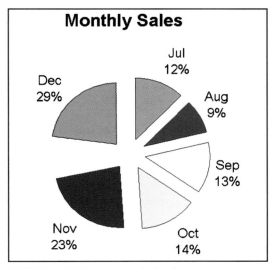

FIGURE 2.105 An exploded pie chart

The parts of a pie chart are shown in Figure 2.106.

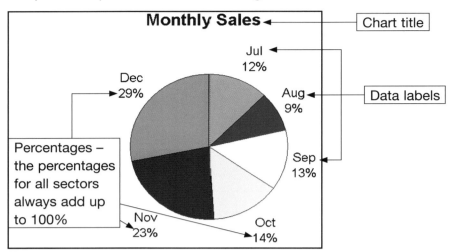

FIGURE 2.106 The parts of a pie chart

▶▶ How to... *create a pie chart*

1 In your datafile, highlight only the relevant range of cells.

2 Click on the **Chart Wizard** 📊 icon in the Standard toolbar.

3 The **Chart Wizard – Step 1 of 4** dialogue box opens.

4 In the **Standard Types** tab, in the **Chart type** section, click on **Pie**.

5 In the **Chart sub-type** section, check that **Pie** is selected (darker) (Figure 2.107). (The box below the **Chart sub-type** describes the type of chart.)

6 Click on **Next**.

7 The **Chart Wizard – Step 2 of 4** dialogue box opens (Figure 2.108).

8 A preview of the chart is displayed.

TIP!

Numbers may be displayed for each sector instead of percentages.

TIP!

Do not highlight any extra cells or blank cells.

TIP!

If the preview of data range is incorrect, click on **Cancel** and start again.

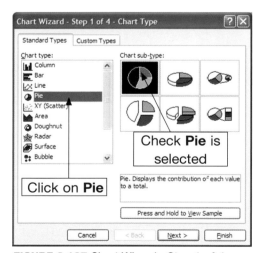

FIGURE 2.107 Chart Wizard – Step 1 of 4

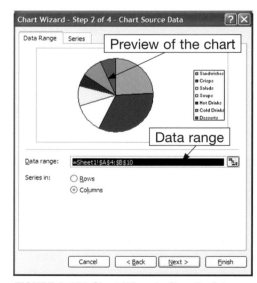

FIGURE 2.108 Chart Wizard – Step 2 of 4

9 The data range displays the selected range with the Sheet name and a $ sign before the column letter and row number.

10 You do not need to make any changes at Step 2.

11 Click on **Next**.

12 The **Chart Wizard–Step 3 of 4** dialogue box opens.

13 You will need to set options in each of the three tabs **Titles, Legend, Data Labels**.

14 Click on the **Titles** tab (Figure 2.109).

15 In the **Chart title** box, enter the title.

16 Click on the **Legend** tab (Figure 2.110).

17 Click to remove the tick in the **Show legend** box (unless required for your chart).

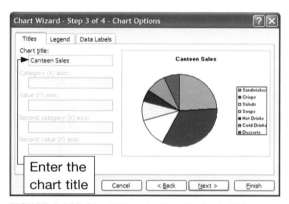

FIGURE 2.109 Chart Wizard–Step 3 of 4 in Titles view

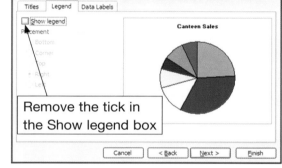

FIGURE 2.110 Chart Wizard–Step 3 of 4 in Legend view

18 Click on the **Data Labels** tab (Figure 2.111).

   a Click to insert a tick in the **Category name** box (for data labels).

   b Click to insert a tick in the **Value** or **Percentage** box (as required for your chart).

   c Click to remove the tick for **Show leader lines** (optional).

19 Click on **Next**.

TIP!

Notice how the chart preview updates as you make changes.

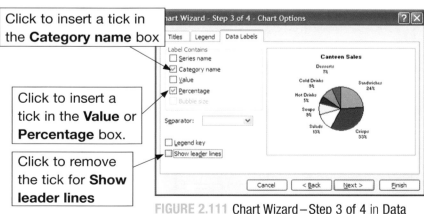

FIGURE 2.111 Chart Wizard–Step 3 of 4 in Data Labels view

20 The **Chart Wizard–Step 4 of 4** dialogue box opens (Figure 2.112).

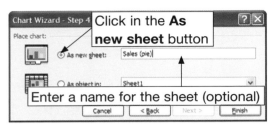

FIGURE 2.112 Chart Wizard–Step 4 of 4

21 Click in the button for **As new sheet**.

22 Enter a name for the sheet (optional).

23 Click on **Finish**.

24 The pie chart is displayed on a full page.

25 Hover with the mouse on the different parts of the chart: title, data labels, chart area, sectors. When you hover over the different areas a **Tool tip** displays showing the name of each part.

▶▶ How to... *save the updated file*

1 Click on **File** in the **Menu bar**.

2 From the menu, click on **Save**.

TIP!

If you have mistakenly created the chart on the spreadsheet move it to a separate sheet. Right-click within the chart in the worksheet, a menu displays, select **Location** from the menu, a **Chart Location** dialogue box displays, click the button for **As new sheet** and click **OK**.

TIP!

If you have made an error in the title, click on the title once you have created the chart, then click again to display the cursor and amend the title.

TIP!

Click on the **Save** icon on the Standard toolbar.

Check your understanding *Create a pie chart*

1 In your file **sales**, check that cells **A4** to **B10** are still highlighted.

2 Use the Chart Wizard to create a pie chart.

3 Enter the chart title **Canteen Sales**.

4 Do not display a legend.

5 Display **data labels** (category name) and **percentages** for each sector.

6 Make sure that you create the chart as a new sheet.

7 In the footer, add your **name**, **centre number**, an **automatic date** and an **automatic filename**.

8 Save your chart keeping the filename **sales**.

TIP!

'How to... add a header or footer' and 'How to... add an automatic date and an automatic filename' were covered in Unit 2 Chapter 1 Creating Spreadsheets. If you need to revise these skills, refer to pages 132–133.

▶▶ How to... *print a chart*

Click on the **Print Preview** icon in the Standard toolbar.

Method 1

1 The **Print Preview** window opens.

2   Click on [Print...].

3   The **Print** dialogue box is displayed.

4   Click on **OK**.

Method 2

1   The **Print Preview** window opens.

2   Close **Print Preview**.

3   The **Chart** view is displayed.

4   Click on the **Print** 🖨 icon in the **Standard toolbar**.

TIP!

Always use Print Preview to check the chart, including headers and footers, before you print.

Check your understanding *Print a pie chart*

1   Print the pie chart in your file **sales**.

2   Check your printout against the solution which can be found on the CD-ROM in the folder **graphs_worked_copies**.

Legends

A legend acts as a key for the data on a chart. It is a box that identifies the colours or patterns for each item of data. Legends are mainly used on comparative charts.

A legend should only be displayed on a pie chart if the data labels are not displayed next to each sector.

What is distinctive data?

If a chart displays a legend instead of data labels, it is very important that the legend identifies the data clearly. On the screen all the sectors are different colours, so by referring to the different colour squares in the legend, the label of each sector can be identified.

If the chart is printed in colour, the legend will still identify each sector clearly. However, if it is printed in black and white, then the sector shades are grey and the corresponding shades in the legend will be shades of grey. This can often mean that some of the grey shades are not clearly different on the printout, so that it is not possible to identify the label for each sector by referring to the legend. The chart is unusable as it does not identify the data clearly.

Using patterns in pie charts

▶▶ How to... *fill pie chart sectors with patterns*

Note: This is not necessary for pie charts with data labels next to the sectors.

1 In your pie chart, click on a sector. All the sectors become selected, a dot is displayed on each sector.

2 Click again to select a single sector only.

3 Make sure square handles display on one sector only.

4 Right-click to display a menu.

5 From this menu, click on **Format Data Point**.

6 A **Format Data Point** dialogue box is displayed.

7 Click on **Fill Effects**.

8 A **Fill Effects** dialogue box appears.

9 Click on the **Pattern** tab and then select a pattern.

10 To change the colour, click on the **drop-down arrow** for Foreground or Background colour, and then select a colour.

11 Click on **OK**.

12 Click on **OK** again.

▶▶ How to... *set the option to print in black and white (to make a legend distinctive)*

1 From the **Chart** view, click on the **Print Preview** icon to open the **Print Preview** window.

2 From **Print Preview**, click on the Setup... button in the toolbar.

3 A **Page Setup** dialogue box is displayed.

4 Click on the **Chart** tab (Figure 2.113).

5 In **Chart** view, in the **Printing quality** section, click in the **Print in black and white** box to insert a tick.

6 Click on **OK**.

7 The sectors are filled with different patterns.

8 Click on **Close** to close the **Print Preview** window.

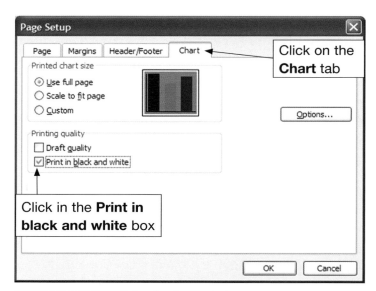

FIGURE 2.113 Page Setup box in Chart view

TIP!

Alternatively, double-click in the selected sector to open the **Format Data Point** dialogue box.

TIP!

Normally, for pie charts with no legend, you do not need to set the option to print in black and white.

TIP!

In the Chart view, the black and white patterns that were set will not display on-screen, but they will show on the printout.

1 In the file **sales**, set the chart to **Print in black and white**.

2 Print the chart.

3 Compare this printout to the previous one of the pie chart.

You do not need to save the updated chart.

ASSESS YOUR SKILLS – Create a pie chart

By working through Section 1 you will have learnt the skills below. Read each item to help you decide how confident you feel about each skill.

- understand pie charts
- open a provided datafile
- save the datafile using a different filename
- view the datafile and identify the data for the chart
- identify the parts of a pie chart
- select the data for a pie chart
- use the Chart Wizard to create a pie chart
- add the chart title
- show/remove the legend
- display data labels, values, percentages
- select the chart location
- save the updated file
- print the chart
- understand legends
- understand what distinctive data is and its importance
- set the chart to print in black and white to make sure that data is clearly distinctive
- fill pie chart sectors with patterns
- make sure the data is clearly distinctive on the print.

If you think you need more practice on any of the skills above, go back and work through the skill(s) again.

If you feel confident, move on to Section 2.

Bar charts

A bar chart is used to show data changes over a period of time, comparisons between individual items or comparisons between data. A comparative bar chart displays comparisons for two or more sets of data. Data can be displayed as vertical or horizontal bars. Excel refers to a horizontal bar chart as a bar chart and a vertical (upright) bar chart as a column chart. In the UK, bar charts are usually vertical with upright bars, so the column chart option in Excel should always be selected.

In Excel, there are many different bar chart sub-types. Some examples are shown in Figures 2.114 and 2.115.

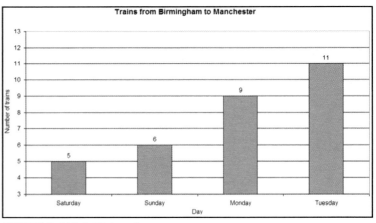

FIGURE 2.114 A 2D bar chart

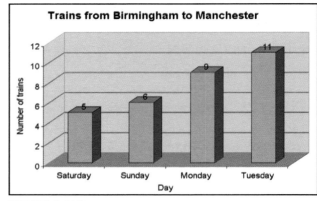

FIGURE 2.115 A 3D bar chart

It is recommended that you always use 2-dimensional vertical bar charts.

The parts of a bar chart are shown in Figure 2.116.

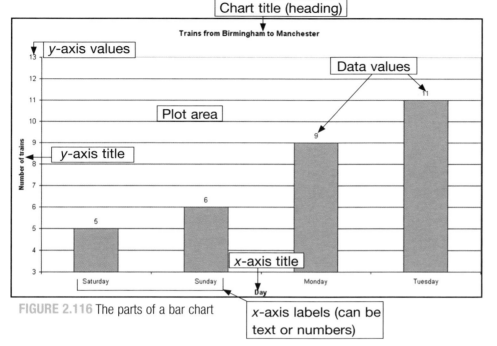

FIGURE 2.116 The parts of a bar chart

What does it mean?

x-axis labels
The *x*-axis labels are the category labels. They describe what each bar represents.
y-axis labels
The *y*-axis is the value axis. It shows the numeric value (quantity) for each bar.
Data values
Data values are the actual numbers for each data item (bar).

Before you create a bar chart, look at the data in the datafile. If the data series is numeric, at **Step 2 of 4** the **Chart** preview will be incorrect. Refer to 'How to... define the data series' on pages 202–204.

When selecting data for a bar chart, you should select the row/column labels, as Excel will use these for titles or legends.

TIP!

Do not highlight a single blank or additional cell. If you do, click in a blank cell and select the data again.

▶▶ How to... *create a bar chart*

1 In your datafile, highlight only the relevant range of cells.

2 Click on the Chart Wizard icon on the **Standard toolbar**.

3 The Chart Wizard – **Step 1 of 4** dialogue box opens (Figure 2.117).

4 In the Standard Types tab, in the Chart type section, click on **Column**.

5 In the Chart sub-type section, check that **Clustered Column** is selected (darker) (Figure 2.117). (The box below the Chart sub-type describes the type of chart.)

6 Click on Next.

TIP!

Do NOT click on **Bar**.

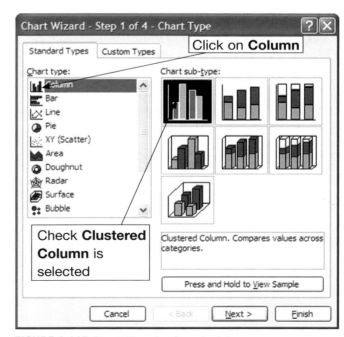

FIGURE 2.117 Chart Wizard – Step 1 of 4

7 The Chart Wizard – Step 2 of 4 dialogue box opens (Figure 2.118).

8 A preview of the chart is displayed. Check the preview.

9 Click on **Next**.

10 The **Chart Wizard – Step 3 of 4** dialogue box opens (Figure 2.119).

TIP!

If the selected data is numeric, refer to 'How to... define the data series' on pages 202–204.

11 You will need to set options in three tabs: **Titles, Legend, Data Labels**.

12 Click on the **Titles** tab (Figure 2.119).

   a In the **Chart title** box, enter the title.

   b In the **Category (X) axis** box, enter the *x*-axis title.

   c In the **Value (Y) axis** box, enter the *y*-axis title.

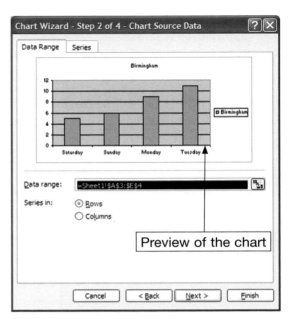

FIGURE 2.118 Chart Wizard – Step 2 of 4

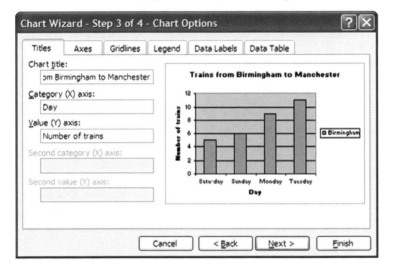

FIGURE 2.119 Chart Wizard – Step 3 of 4 in Titles view

TIP!

Notice how the chart preview updates as you make changes.

13 Click on the **Legend** tab (Figure 2.120).

14 Click to remove the tick in the **Show legend** box if your chart is not comparative.

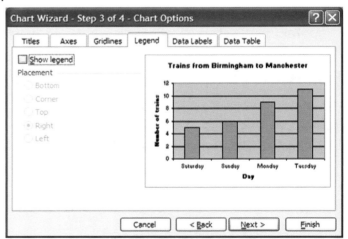

FIGURE 2.120 Chart Wizard – Step 3 of 4 in Legend view

15 Click on the **Data Labels** tab (Figure 2.121).

16 Click to insert a tick in the **Value** box if required (to display numbers above the bars).

17 Click on **Next**.

18 The **Chart Wizard – Step 4 of 4** dialogue box opens (Figure 2.122).

19 Click in the button for **As new sheet**.

20 Enter a name for the sheet (optional).

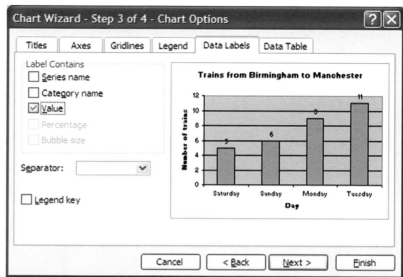

FIGURE 2.121 Chart Wizard – Step 3 of 4 in Data Labels view

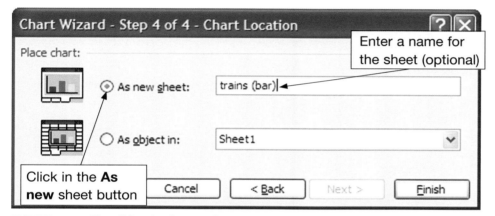

FIGURE 2.122 Chart Wizard – Step 4 of 4

21 Click on **Finish**.

22 The bar chart is displayed on a full page.

23 Hover with the mouse on the different parts of the chart: title, data labels, y-axis, y-axis title, x-axis, x-axis title, chart area, plot area, bars. A **Tool tip** displays showing the name of each part when you hover over each area of the chart.

The y-axis scale

The scale is the minimum (lowest) value and the maximum (largest) value displayed on the y-axis. Excel sets the scale that it thinks is the most appropriate for the data, however, you can change these.

▶▶ How to... *set the scale on the y-axis*

1 In your chart, hover with the mouse on any of the y-axis values (numbers).

2 A Value Axis **Tool tip** is displayed.

TIP!

If you have mistakenly created the chart on the spreadsheet, to move it to a separate sheet: right-click within the chart in the worksheet, a menu displays, select **Location** from the menu, a **Chart Location** window displays, click the button for **As new sheet** and click **OK**.

TIP!

If you have made an error in the title, x-axis label or y-axis label, click twice in the title or label and amend the data.

TIP!

Changes to the axis are made once the chart is created.

3 Double-click with the mouse.

4 A **Format Axis** dialogue box is displayed.

5 Click on the **Scale** tab (Figure 2.123).

6 In the **Auto** section, click in **Minimum** box.

7 Delete any numbers, then enter the required minimum value.

8 Click in the **Maximum** box.

9 Delete any numbers, then enter the required maximum value.

10 Click on **OK**.

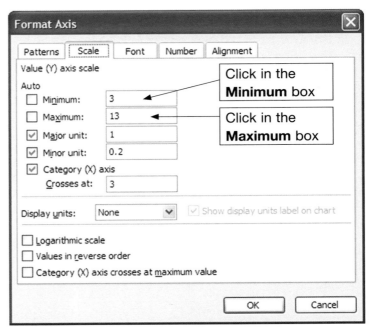

FIGURE 2.123 **Format Axis** dialogue box in **Scale** view

TIP!

When you enter minimum and maximum values, the tick in each (left-hand) box is removed, which ensures that the values remain set. If the values you are required to set are already displayed, you must click to remove the tick in the minimum/maximum box or Excel may change the value(s).

Changing the fill of the plot area

Excel displays the background of the chart (the plot area) as grey. To make the chart clearer and to save printer ink, the grey shade can be removed.

TIP!

Alternatively, double-click in the plot area to open the **Format Plot Area** dialogue box.

▶▶ How to... *change the fill of the plot area (optional)*

1 Hover with the mouse anywhere in the grey plot area.

2 A Plot Area **Tool tip** is displayed.

3 Right-click with the mouse in the plot area.

4 A menu is displayed.

5 Click on **Format Plot Area** (Figure 2.124).

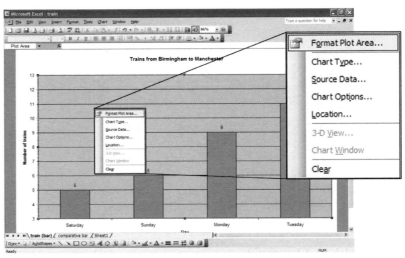

FIGURE 2.124 Drop-down menu showing **Format Plot Areas**

6 The **Format Plot Area** dialogue box displays (Figure 2.125).

7 In the **Area** section, click on **None**.

8 Click on **OK**.

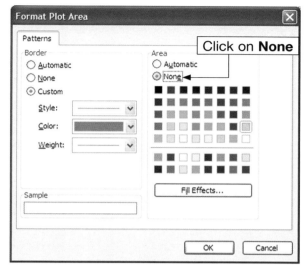

FIGURE 2.125 Format Plot Area dialogue box

TIP!

If you wish, you could select white instead of **None**.

Check your understanding   *Create a bar chart*

1 Open the datafile **birm**.

2 Save the file using the new filename **train** into the folder you created earlier called **grc**.

3 Create a bar chart to show the Trains to Manchester for **Birmingham** from **Saturday to Tuesday** only.

4 Display the day along the *x*-axis.

5 Title the chart **Trains from Birmingham to Manchester**.

6 Give the *x*-axis the title **Day**.

7 Give the *y*-axis the title **Number of trains**.

8 Do not display a legend.

9 Display data values (numbers) for each bar.

10 Make sure that the chart is created on a separate sheet.

11 Set the *y*-axis range from **3** to **13**.

12 In the footer, enter your **name**, **centre number**, an **automatic date** and an **automatic filename**.

13 Save the file keeping the filename **train.**

14 Print one copy of the bar chart.

15 Check your printout against the solution which can be found on the CD-ROM in the folder **graphs_worked_copies**.

Understanding comparative charts

Comparative charts are a simple and effective way to show a direct comparison between data in visual form.

Selecting data for comparative charts

Comparative bar charts are created in exactly the same way as simple bar charts, except that more than one data series is selected. Remember to select the row/column labels, as Excel will use these for the legend.

Legends in comparative charts

Any comparative chart MUST display a legend which should identify the data clearly on a printout. The small boxes in the legend are used to identify each set of bars.

One way of making sure that the legend identifies the data clearly is to set the option to print in black and white (described on page 188). Another method is to use a pattern fill (for the bars on bar charts or sectors on pie charts).

▶▶ How to... *use a pattern fill for bars*

1 In your chart, click on one of the bars.

2 A square dot displays in all the bars for that series (Figure 2.126).

3 Right-click in any of the bars with the dot.

4 A menu is displayed.

5 Click on **Format Data Series** (Figure 2.127).

TIP!

In the Chart Wizard – Step 2 of 4, if the preview shows the legend as Series1, Series2, this means that you have not selected the row/column labels. Refer to page 205 for How to... select the name to be displayed on the legend.

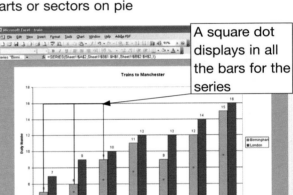

A square dot displays in all the bars for the series

FIGURE 2.126 Comparative bar chart

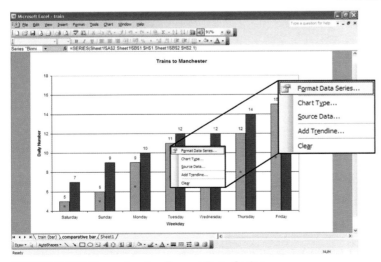

FIGURE 2.127 Menu showing **Format Data Series**

TIP!

Fill effects are applied after the chart is created.

TIP!

Alternatively, double-click on a bar to open the **Format Data Series** dialogue box.

6   The **Format Data Series** dialogue box appears.

7   Click on the **Patterns** tab (Figure 2.128).

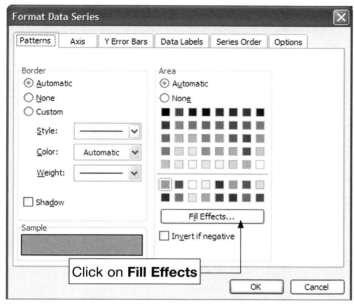

8   Click on **Fill Effects**.

9   The **Fill Effects** dialogue box is displayed.

10 Click on the **Pattern** tab (Figure 2.129).

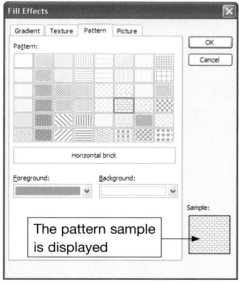

TIP!

Click on the drop-down arrow next to the Foreground and/or Background box to choose another colour.

FIGURE 2.129 Fill effects dialogue box in Pattern view

11 Click on one of the patterns in the **Pattern** section.

12 The pattern sample is displayed.

13 Click on **OK**.

14 Click on **OK** to close the **Format Data Series** dialogue box.

Viewing the spreadsheet

 **How to...** *view the spreadsheet*

1 At the bottom left of the screen, click on the sheet tab, e.g. **Sheet1** (Figure 2.130).

2 To view the chart, click on the chart tab.

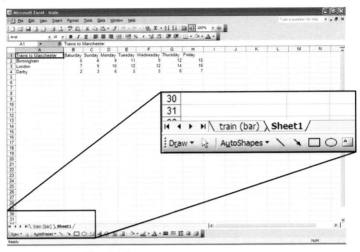

FIGURE 2.130 Sheet tab

TIP!

The chart tab in your file may be named **Chart1**.

Check your understanding *Create a comparative bar chart*

1 In your file **train**, click on the **Sheet1** tab to see the spreadsheet.

2 Create a comparative bar chart to show the Trains to Manchester for **Birmingham** and **London** from **Saturday to Friday**.

3 Display the days along the *x*-axis.

4 Title the chart **Trains to Manchester**

5 Give the *x*-axis the title **Weekday**

6 Give the *y*-axis the title **Daily Number**

7 Use a legend to identify the bars. Make sure that the bars are distinctive and can be clearly identified when printed.

8 Display data values (numbers) for each bar.

9 Make sure that the chart is created on a separate sheet.

10 Set the *y*-axis range from **4** to **18**

11 Use a pattern fill for one data series (set of bars).

12 Enter your **name**, **centre number**, an **automatic date** and an **automatic filename** in the header or footer.

13 Save the file keeping the filename **train**.

14 Print one copy of the comparative bar chart.

15 Make sure that the legend identifies the data clearly on the printout.

16 Close the file.

ASSESS YOUR SKILLS – Create bar a chart and a comparative bar chart

By working through Section 2 you will have learnt the skill listed below. Read each item to help you decide how confident you feel about each skill.

- understand bar charts including comparative bar charts
- identify the parts of a bar chart
- select the data for the chart
- use the Chart Wizard to create a bar chart
- add the chart title
- add the *x*-axis and *y*-axis titles
- show/remove the legend
- display data values (numbers) for the bars
- select the chart location
- set the *y*-axis minimum and maximum values
- change the fill of the plot area
- create a comparative bar chart
- use a pattern fill for the bars
- save the updated file
- print the chart
- close an updated file
- make sure the legend identifies the data clearly on the printout.

If you think you need more practice on any of the skills above, go back and work through the skill(s) again.

If you feel confident, move on to Section 3.

LEARNING OUTCOMES

In this section you will learn how to:

- understand line graphs
- identify the parts of a line graph
- understand the selection of data for line graphs
- select data for the graph
- use the Chart Wizard to create a line graph
- create a comparative line graph
- define the data series for numeric data
- format lines and markers.

Line graphs

Line graphs are used to show trends in data at intervals. They display a set of related values plotted as a line. A marker is usually displayed for each value (data point). Comparative line graphs show trends for more than one data series.

In Excel, there are many different line graph sub-types. Some examples are shown in Figures 2.131 and 2.132.

It is recommended that you always use 2-dimensional line graphs.

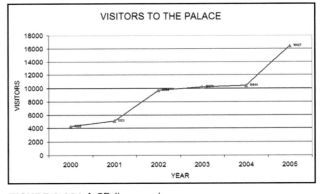

FIGURE 2.131 A 2D line graph

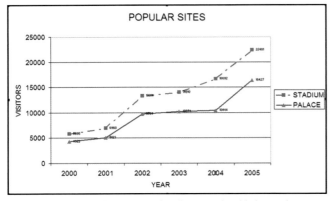

FIGURE 2.132 A 2D comparative line graph with legend

The parts of a line graph are shown in Figure 2.133.

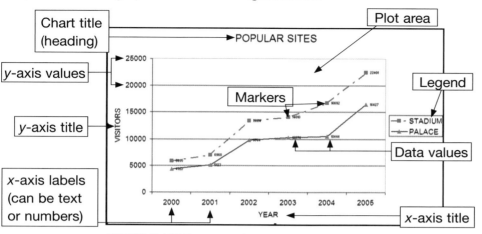

FIGURE 2.133 The parts of a line graph

Before you create a line graph, look at the data in the datafile. If the data to be plotted on the x-axis is numeric, at Step 2 of 4 the Chart preview will be incorrect. Refer to 'How to... define the data series' on page 202.

Remember, when selecting data for a line graph, you should select the row/column labels as Excel will use these for titles or legends.

▶▶ **How to...** *create a line graph*

1 In your datafile, highlight only the relevant range of cells.

2 Click on the **Chart Wizard** icon.

3 The **Chart Wizard – Step 1 of 4** dialogue box opens.

4 In the **Standard Types** tab, in the **Chart type** section, click on **Line**.

5 In the **Chart sub-type** section, check that the **Line with markers** ... type is selected (darker) (Figure 2.134). (The box below the **Chart sub-type** describes the type of chart.)

6 Click on **Next**.

7 The **Chart Wizard – Step 2 of 4** dialogue box opens.

8 A preview of the chart is displayed. Check the preview.

9 If the preview is correct, click on **Next** and follow the **Chart Wizard – Step 3 of 4**.

TIP!

Do not highlight any blank or additional cells. If you do, click on a blank cell to deselect the data and select the correct range of cells.

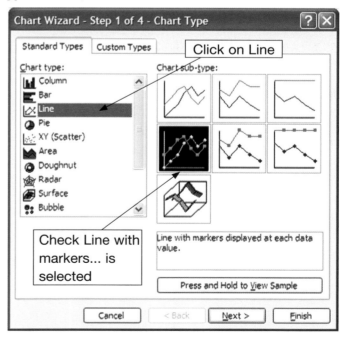

FIGURE 2.134 Chart Wizard – Step 1 of 4

10 If the preview is incorrect (e.g. it shows two lines instead of one for a simple line graph, or three lines instead of two for a comparative line graph), you MUST define the data series before continuing. Refer to 'How to... define the data series' below before going to the **Chart Wizard – Step 3 of 4**.

11 **The Chart Wizard – Step 3 of 4** dialogue box opens:

a Enter the chart title, x-axis title and y-axis title.

b Display/remove the legend as required.

c Display data labels as required.

12 Click on **Next.**

13 The **Chart Wizard – Step 4 of 4** dialogue box opens.

14 Click in the button for **As new sheet.**

15 Enter a name for the sheet (optional).

16 Click on **Finish**.

17 The line graph is displayed on a full page.

TIP!

If the data selected for the x-axis is numeric, Excel displays it as an additional line.

TIP!

If you have mistakenly created the chart on the spreadsheet, to move it to a separate sheet: right-click within the chart in the worksheet, a menu displays, select **Location** from the menu, a **Chart Location** window displays, click the button for **As new sheet** and click **OK**.

Defining the data series

It may be necessary to define the data series for bar charts and line graphs. If the data to be plotted on the x-axis is numeric, you must check the preview of the chart in the **Chart Wizard – Step 2 of 4**. You will need to define each data series so that Excel knows which row/column of data is to be used for the x-axis and which should be used for the y-axis.

▶▶ How to... *define the data series (Chart Wizard – Step 2 of 4)*

1 In the **Chart Wizard – Step 2 of 4**, click on the **Series** tab.

2 In the **Series** section, click on the name of the series that should not be plotted on the x-axis (Figure 2.135).

3 Click on **Remove**.

4 The chart preview will change – the incorrect data set will be removed from the preview.

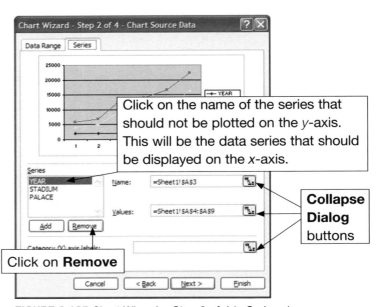

FIGURE 2.135 Chart Wizard – Step 2 of 4 in Series view

5 Click on the **Collapse Dialog** button next to **Category (X) axis labels** box.

6 You will see the spreadsheet and a small (collapsed) window (Figure 2.136)

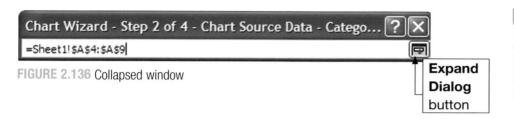

FIGURE 2.136 Collapsed window

TIP!

Click and drag the title bar (usually blue) of the collapsed window to move it out of the way if required.

7 In the spreadsheet, highlight only the cells that should display as the *x*-axis labels. Do not include the row/column label.

8 A marquee (dotted line) displays around the selected cells (Figure 2.137).

9 The range of cells is displayed in the **Category (X) axis labels** collapsed box.

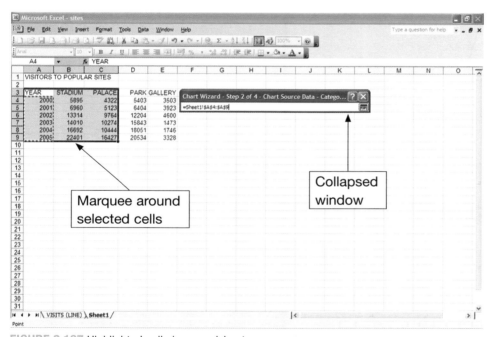

FIGURE 2.137 Highlighted cells in spreadsheet

10 In the collapsed window, click on the **Expand Dialog** button.

11 You will be returned to the **Source Data** dialogue box.

12 Click on the **Collapse Dialog** button next to the **Values** box.

13 Highlight the correct range of cells to be plotted on the *y*-axis (do NOT include the row/column label). This may have a marquee, but it is best to define the range again.

14 In the collapsed window, click on the **Expand Dialog** button.

15 You will be returned to the **Source Data** dialogue box.

16 If you are creating a comparative chart:

   a Click on the name on the second data series (Figure 2.138).

   b Click on the **Collapse Dialog** button next to the **Values** box.

   c Highlight the correct range of cells to be plotted on the *y*-axis.

   d Click on the **Expand Dialog** button.

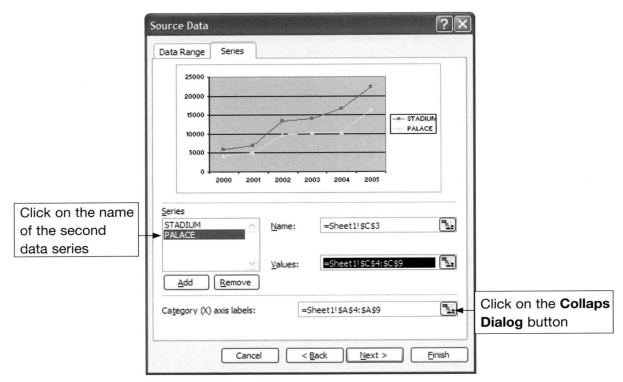

FIGURE 2.138 Second data series

17 You will be returned to the **Source Data** dialogue box.

18 In the **Source Data** dialogue box, check that the chart preview is correct. If the legend displays Series1, Series2, refer to the section Legend labels.

19 Click on **Next.**

20 Continue setting the options in Steps 3 and 4 of the Chart Wizard.

Legend labels

If the chart preview displays the legend items as Series1 and Series2, the chart is unusable. You must ensure that the legend labels identify the lines/bars in the chart correctly.

1 In the **Series** section, click on the name displayed (e.g. this may be displayed as **Series1**).

2 In the Name section, click on the **Collapse Dialog** button.

3 You will see the worksheet and a small (collapsed) window.

4 Click in the cell to be used as the name of the legend item.

5 Click the **Expand Dialog** button.

6 Repeat this process for the next legend item.

Formatting lines and markers on a line graph

On a comparative line graph, it is important that the data will be clearly distinctive on the printout if printed on a black and white printer. To make the data distinctive, the line and/or marker style may be changed.

How to... *format a line on a line graph*

1 Hover the mouse pointer over the first line on the graph.

2 Right-click with the mouse on the line.

3 A menu is displayed.

4 From the menu, select **Format Data Series**.

5 The **Format Data Series** dialogue box is displayed.

6 Click on the **Patterns** tab (Figure 2.139).

7 In the **Line** section, click in the **Custom** button.

8 To select a line style, click on the **down arrow** next to the **Style** box.

What does it mean?

Markers
A marker is the symbol, e.g. diamond, square, etc. that shows each data point.

TIP!

Move the mouse over any part of the line and double-click to open the **Format Data Series** dialogue box.

TIP!

If **Format Data Point** displays instead of **Format Data Series**, you have clicked on a marker. Left-click in the graph to deselect the marker, then hover the mouse pointer over the line and double-click to open the **Format Data Series** dialogue box.

TIP!

For comparative line graphs, choose one dotted line and one solid line.

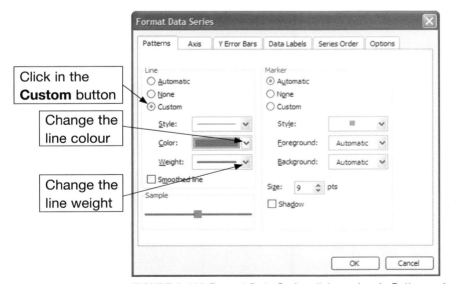

FIGURE 2.139 **Format Data Series** dialogue box in **Patterns** view.

9 To select a line weight, click on the **down arrow** next to the **Weight** box. Choose a thick line as this will be clearer on the printout.

10 Change the line colour by clicking on the down arrow next to the **Color** box (optional).

11 Click on **OK** to format the line (to format the markers, see below).

▶▶ How to... *format the markers on a line*

1 Follow steps 1–6 of 'How to... format a line on a line graph' (see above).

2 In the **Marker** section, click in the **Custom** button.

3 Click on the **down arrow** next to the **Style** box.

4 Choose one of the marker styles.

5 To change the marker colour, click on the **down arrow** next to the **Foreground** and/or **Background** box (optional).

6 Click on **OK** to format the markers.

Check your understanding *Create a comparative line graph*

1 Open the datafile **tourists**.

2 Save the file using the new filename **sites** into the folder **grc**.

3 Create a comparative line graph to show the visitors to popular sites for the **YEAR** from **2000 to 2005** for **STADIUM** and **PALACE**.

4 Display the years along the *x*-axis.

5 Title the graph **POPULAR SITES**.

6 Give the *x*-axis the title **YEAR**.

7 Give the *y*-axis the title **VISITORS**.

8 Use a legend to identify each line. Make sure that the lines and/or data points are distinctive and can be clearly identified when printed.

9 Display the values (numbers) for each data point on both lines.

10 Make sure that the chart is created on a separate sheet.

11 In the footer, enter your **name**, **centre number**, an **automatic date** and an **automatic filename**.

12 Save the file keeping the filename **sites**.

13 Print one copy of the line graph.

14 Make sure that the legend clearly identifies the data on the printout.

15 Close the file.

16 Check your printout against the solution which can be found on the CD-ROM in the folder **graphs_worked_copies**.

ASSESS YOUR SKILLS – Create a line graph and a comparative line graph

By working through Section 3 you will have learnt the skills listed below. Read each item to help you decide how confident you feel about each skill.

- ○ understand line graphs including comparative line graphs
- ○ identify the parts of a line graph
- ○ select the data for the graph
- ○ use the Chart Wizard to create a line graph
- ○ define the data series
- ○ add the chart title
- ○ add the x-axis and y-axis titles
- ○ show/remove the legend
- ○ display data values (numbers) for the lines
- ○ select the chart location
- ○ create a comparative line graph
- ○ format the line(s)
- ○ format the markers
- ○ save the updated file
- ○ print the chart
- ○ close an updated file
- ○ make sure that the legend identifies the data clearly on the printout.

If you think you need more practice on any of the skills above, go back and work through the skill(s) again.

If you feel confident, do the Build-up and Practice tasks.

Remember, you can refer to the Quick reference guides on pages 208–217 when doing any tasks and during an assessment.

Click means click with the left mouse button

QUICK REFERENCE – Create a new spreadsheet

Keep a copy of this page next to you. Refer to it when working through tasks and during any assessments.

HOW TO...	METHOD	QUICK METHOD
Start Excel	Click on Start → All Programs → Microsoft Office → Microsoft Office Excel 2003.	Single-click on the Excel icon on the Quick Launch bar OR double-click on the Excel icon on the desktop.
Create a new spreadsheet	Click on File menu → New (note: a new blank spreadsheet opens when you load Excel).	Click on the New icon on the toolbar.
Set orientation	Click on File menu → Page Setup → Page tab → click on Portrait or Landscape → click on OK.	
Enter data	Click in cell where data is to be entered → enter data → to move to next cell, use a Cursor key OR click with the mouse in the cell OR use the Tab key.	
Widen columns	Double-click between grey column dividers or drag ↔ to widen individual columns, OR highlight cells → click on Format menu → click on Column → click on AutoFit Selection.	Highlight the entire spreadsheet (click in top left grey cell) → double-click on ↔ in between any of the grey column letters.
Save a spreadsheet	Click on File menu → click on Save → Save As dialogue box displays → click on down arrow to right of Save in box, then click on your user area → in File name box → delete any existing text → enter required filename → click on Save.	Click on the Save icon → enter a filename → make sure you save into the correct folder → click on Save OR press Ctrl + S.
Save a spreadsheet into a new folder from within Excel	Click on File menu → click on Save → Save As dialogue box displays → click on down arrow to right of Save in box, then click on your user area → click on the Create New Folder icon → New Folder dialogue box opens → enter new folder name → click on OK → in File name box → delete any existing text → enter required filename → click on Save.	Click on the Save icon → Save As dialogue box displays → click on down arrow to right of Save in box, then click on your user area → click on the Create New Folder icon → New Folder dialogue box opens → enter new folder name → click on OK → in File name box → delete any existing text → enter required filename → click on Save. To save an existing spreadsheet with a new filename, use Save As not Save.

HOW TO...	METHOD	QUICK METHOD
Add a header or footer	Click on View menu → click on Header and Footer → Page Setup dialogue box displays → click in Left, Center or Right section → click on Custom Footer → Footer dialogue box displays → enter required information in Left, Center or Right section → click on OK → click on OK in Page Setup dialogue box.	Click on View menu → click on Header and Footer → Page Setup dialogue box displays → click on Custom Header → Header dialogue box displays → click in Left, Center or Right section → enter required information → click on OK → click on OK → click on OK in Page Setup dialogue box.
Add an automatic date	Click on View menu → click on Header and Footer → Page Setup dialogue box displays → click in Left, Center or Right section → click on Insert Date icon → click on OK → click on OK in Page Setup dialogue box.	Click on View menu → click on Header and Footer → Page Setup dialogue box displays → click on Custom Header → click in Left, Center or Right section → click on Insert Date icon → click on OK → click on OK in Page Setup dialogue box.
Add an automatic filename	Click on View menu → click on Header and Footer → Page Setup dialogue box displays → click in Left, Center or Right section → click on Insert Filename icon → click on OK → click on OK in Page Setup dialogue box.	Click on View menu → click on Header and Footer → Page Setup dialogue box displays → click on Custom Header → click in Left, Center or Right section → click on Insert Filename icon → click on OK → click on OK in Page Setup dialogue box.
Save an existing spreadsheet	Click on File menu → click on Save. To save with a new filename, use Save As.	Click on the Save icon OR press Ctrl + S.
Fit to one page	Click on File menu → click on Page Setup → Page Setup dialogue box displays → click on Fit to button → check display is 1 in page(s) wide by box and 1 in tall box.	Click on File menu → click on Page Setup → Page Setup dialogue box displays → click on Page tab → in Scaling section → click on Fit to button → check display is 1 in page(s) wide by box and 1 in tall box.
Print a document	Click on File menu → click on Print → Print dialogue box displays → check Page Range is set to All → set Number of copies to 1 → click on OK.	Once you have set the Print settings (e.g. orientation, fit to one page, etc.) → click on the Print icon.

QUICK REFERENCE – Edit a spreadsheet

Keep a copy of this page next to you. Refer to it when working through tasks and during any assessments.

Click means click with the left mouse button

HOW TO...	METHOD	QUICK METHOD
Edit data	Click in the relevant cell → click in Formula bar → delete existing data → enter the new data → press Enter or click in another cell.	Double-click in the relevant cell → delete unwanted content → enter new data.
Insert a column	Click anywhere in the column where the new column is to be inserted → click on Insert menu → click on Columns → a new blank column is inserted and subsequent columns are automatically relabelled.	Right-click in the column letter where the new column is to be inserted → the entire column is highlighted and a menu displays → click on Insert.
Insert a row	Click anywhere in the row where the new row is to be inserted → click on Insert menu → click on Rows → a new blank row is inserted and subsequent rows are automatically renumbered.	Right-click in the row letter where the new row is to be inserted → the entire row is highlighted and a menu displays → click on Insert.
Delete a column	Move mouse pointer over grey column letter to be deleted and click → entire column is highlighted → right-click in highlighted column → a menu displays → click on Delete → column is deleted and remaining columns are automatically relabelled.	Move mouse pointer over grey column letter to be deleted and right-click → a menu displays → click on Delete → column is deleted and remaining columns are automatically relabelled.
Delete a row	Move mouse pointer over grey row number to be deleted and click → entire row is highlighted → right-click in highlighted row → a menu displays → click on Delete → row is deleted and remaining rows are automatically renumbered. OR, click anywhere in the row to be deleted → click on the Edit menu → click on Delete → Delete dialogue box displays → click in the button for Entire Row → click on OK.	Move mouse pointer over grey row number to be deleted and right-click → a menu displays → click on Delete → row is deleted and remaining rows are automatically renumbered.
Display formulae	Click on Tools menu → click on Options → Options dialogue box displays → click on View tab → click in Formulas box to insert tick → click on OK.	Press Ctrl + ` (Accent key above the Tab key).
Adjust column widths	Double-click with left mouse button on the vertical line in the grey area displaying the column letters dividing two columns OR drag the vertical line to make column wider until all data is displayed in full. OR, highlight the cells → click on Format menu → click on Column → click on AutoFit Selection.	Use AutoFit to adjust the column widths of all columns → click on shaded cell to left of column letter and above row number → double-click in between any of the grey column letters.

HOW TO...	METHOD	QUICK METHOD
Display gridlines	Click on File menu → click on Page Setup → Page Setup dialogue box displays → click on Sheet tab → click in Gridlines box to insert tick → click on OK.	
Display row and column headings	Click on File menu → Page Setup dialogue box displays → click on Sheet tab → click in Row and column headings box to insert tick → click on OK.	
Format with currency symbol and set decimal places	Highlight relevant cells → right-click within highlighted cells → a menu displays → click on Format Cells → Format Cells dialogue box displays → click on Number tab → click on Currency → in Decimal places box → use up/down arrows to display required number of decimal places → in Symbol box → click on down arrow and click on required currency format, e.g. £ → click on OK.	
Format decimal places	Highlight relevant cells → right-click within highlighted cells → a menu displays → click on Format Cells → Format Cells dialogue box displays → click on Number tab → in Decimal places box → use up/down arrow to display required number of decimal places → click on OK.	
Align data	Highlight relevant cells → click on Align Left, Align Right or Center icon. OR, highlight cells → click on Format menu → click on Cells → Format Cells dialogue box displays → click on Alignment tab → click on drop-down arrow next to Horizontal → click on required alignment → click on OK.	
Add a border	Highlight relevant cells → on the toolbar → click on down arrow next to Borders icon → drop-down selection displays → click on Outside Borders or Thick Box Border option. OR, highlight cells → click on Format menu → click on Cells → Format Cells dialogue box displays → click on Border tab → click on Outline → in the Line section → click on the thick line style option → click on drop-down arrow next to Color → select black → click on OK.	
Use shading	Highlight relevant cells → on the toolbar → click on down arrow next to Fill Color icon → drop-down menu displays → select suitable colour. OR, highlight cells → click on Format menu → click on Cells → Format Cells dialogue box displays → click on Patterns tab → click on required shade (not too dark as text cannot be read and not too light as shade must show on the printout) → click on OK.	
Close a spreadsheet	Click on File menu → click on Close.	Click on black cross.
Exit from Excel	Click File menu → click on Exit.	Click on red cross.
Close a spreadsheet and exit Excel	Click on File menu → click on Close → click on File menu → click on Exit.	Click on black cross → click on red cross.

QUICK REFERENCE – Use formulae and functions in spreadsheets

Keep a copy of this page next to you. Refer to it when working through tasks and during any assessments.

HOW TO...	METHOD
Create a simple formula with + (add)	Click in cell → enter an = sign → click in cell that contains first value (number) → cell reference displays in Formula bar → enter the + sign → click in cell that contains second value → cell reference of second cell displays after + sign → check Formula bar to make sure formula is correct → press Enter key OR click on Enter tick in Formula bar.
Create a simple formula with – (subtract)	Click in cell → enter an = sign → click in cell that contains first value (number) → cell reference displays in Formula bar → enter the – sign → click in cell that contains second value → cell reference of second cell displays after – sign → check Formula bar to make sure formula is correct → press Enter key OR click on Enter tick in Formula bar.
Create a simple formula with * (multiply)	Click in cell → enter an = sign → click in cell that contains first value (number) → cell reference displays in Formula bar → enter the * sign → click in cell that contains second value → cell reference of second cell displays after * sign → check Formula bar to make sure formula is correct → press Enter key OR click on Enter tick in Formula bar.
Create a simple formula with / (divide)	Click in cell → enter an = sign → click in cell that contains first value (number) → cell reference displays in Formula bar → enter the / sign → click in cell that contains second value → cell reference of second cell displays after / sign → check Formula bar to make sure formula is correct → press Enter key OR click on Enter tick in Formula bar.
Replicate (copy) a formula	*Method 1:* Click in the cell containing the formula to be copied → click on fill handle (black square on the bottom right of the cell) → drag fill handle over the cells that formula is to be copied into. *Method 2:* Click in the cell containing the formula to be copied → click on the Edit menu → click on Copy → a marquee displays around the copied cell → highlight the cells that you want to copy the formula to → click on the Edit menu → click on Paste → press the Enter key to stop the marquee.

HOW TO...	METHOD
Use brackets in a formula	Click in the relevant cell → enter an = sign → enter an opening bracket (→ click in cell that contains the first number → the bracket and cell reference display in the Formula bar → enter a + or - or * or / sign → click in cell that contains the second value → the cell reference of the second cell displays in the Formula bar after the mathematical operator → enter a closing bracket → enter a + or - or * or / sign → click in the cell that contains the third value → check the Formula bar to make sure the formula is correct → press the Enter key on keyboard OR click on the Enter tick in the Formula bar.
Use AUTOSUM	Use only for cells that are next to each other: Highlight the cells to be added and the cell in which to display the result → Click on the AutoSum icon.
Use the SUM function	Method 1: Click in the relevant cell → enter an = sign → enter the word SUM and an opening bracket (→ highlight the range of cells to be added → enter a closing bracket) → press the Enter key OR click on the Enter tick in the Formula bar.
	Method 2: Click in the relevant cell → click on the fx Insert Function icon on the Formula bar → Insert Function dialogue box displays → click on the word SUM → click on OK → Function Arguments dialogue box displays → check the range of cells in the Number 1 row → click on OK.
Use the AVERAGE function	Method 1: Click in the relevant cell → enter an = sign → enter the word AVERAGE and an opening bracket (→ highlight the range of cells to be averaged → enter a closing bracket) → press the Enter key OR click on the Enter tick in the Formula bar.
	Method 2: Click in the relevant cell → click on the fx Insert Function icon on the Formula bar → Insert Function dialogue box displays → click on the word AVERAGE → click on OK → Function Arguments dialogue box displays → check the range of cells in the Number 1 row → click on OK.

Click means click with the left mouse button

QUICK REFERENCE – Creating graphs

Keep a copy of this page next to you. Refer to it when working through tasks and during any assessments.

HOW TO...	METHOD
Start Excel	Click on Start → All Programs → Microsoft Office → Microsoft Office Excel 2003.
Open a datafile from Excel	Click on File menu → click on Open → Open dialogue box displays → click on drop-down arrow next to Look in box → find your user area and double-click on it to open → double-click on folder containing files → list of files displays → double-click on file (instead of double-click, you can single-click, then click on Open).
Open a datafile from My Computer	From desktop → double-click on My Computer icon → My Computer window opens → go to your user area → double-click to open → find folder containing files → double-click on folder to open → look for required file → double-click on file → file opens in Excel.
Save a datafile into a new folder from within Excel	Click on File menu → click on Save As → Save As dialogue box displays → click on down arrow next to Save in box, then click on your user area → click on Create New Folder icon (or, to save in existing folder, double-click on folder name) → New Folder dialogue box displays → enter new folder name → click on OK → in File name box → delete any existing text → enter required filename → click on Save.
Highlight a range of cells	*Method 1:* Click in the first cell, a white cross displays, and drag the mouse across the range (block) of cells to be highlighted. *Method 2:* Click with the mouse in the first cell → hold down the Shift key → click in the last cell.
Create a pie chart	Highlight only the relevant range of cells → click on the Chart Wizard icon → in Step 1 of 4, in Standard Types tab, in Chart type section → click on Pie → in Chart sub-type section, check that Pie is selected → click on Next → in Step 2 of 4 → check the chart preview → if preview is correct, click on Next (if incorrect, click on Cancel and start again) → in Step 3 of 4 → click on Titles tab → in Chart title box, enter the title → click on Legend tab → click to remove tick in Show legend box (unless required) → click on Data Labels tab → click in Category name box (for data labels) → click in Value or Percentage box → click to deselect Show leader lines → click on Next → In Step 4 of 4 → click button for As new sheet → click on Finish.
Set a chart to print in black and white	From chart view, click on Print Preview icon → click on Setup → in Page Setup dialogue box → click on Chart tab → click on button for Print in black and white → click on OK → click on Close (patterns will not display in chart view but will print).
Fill pie chart sectors with patterns	Click on a sector, then click again to select it → make sure square handles display on one sector only → right-click → a menu displays → click on Format Data Point → Format Data Point dialogue box displays → click on Fill Effects button → Fill Effects dialogue box displays → click on Pattern tab → select a pattern → click on OK.

HOW TO...	METHOD
Create a bar chart	Highlight only the relevant range of cells (include row or column labels) → click on the Chart Wizard icon → in Step 1 of 4, in Standard Types tab, in Chart type section → click on Column → in Chart sub-type section, check that Clustered Column is selected → click on Next → in Step 2 of 4 → check the chart preview → if preview is correct, click on Next (if incorrect, refer to 'Define the data series (bar charts or line graphs')). → In Step 3 of 4 → click on Titles tab → in Chart Title box, enter the title → click in Category (X) axis box → enter x-axis title → click in Value (Y) axis box → enter y-axis title → click on Legend tab → click to remove tick in Show legend box → click on Data Labels tab → click in Value box (to display numbers on bars) → click on Next → in Step 4 of 4 → click in button for As new sheet → click on Finish.
Create a comparative bar chart	Highlight only the relevant range of cells (include row or column labels) → click on the Chart Wizard icon → in Step 1 of 4, in Standard Types tab, in Chart type section → click on Column → in Chart sub-type section, check that Clustered Column is selected → click on Next → in Step 2 of 4 → check the chart preview → if preview is correct, click on Next (if incorrect, refer to 'Define the data series (for comparative charts')). → In Step 3 of 4 → click on Titles tab → in Chart Title box, enter the title → click in Category (X) axis box → enter x-axis title → click in Value (Y) axis box → enter y-axis title → click on Legend tab → check for tick in Show legend box (should be ticked) → click on Data Labels tab → click in Value box (to display numbers on bars) → click on Next → in Step 4 of 4 → click in button for As new sheet → click on Finish → refer to 'How to... fill bars with pattern' (below).
Set the y-axis scale (bar charts or line graphs)	Hover with mouse pointer on any number on y-axis scale → Value Axis Tool tip displays → double-click with mouse → Format Axis dialogue box displays → click on Scale tab → click in Minimum box → delete existing number → enter value (number) → click in Maximum box → delete existing number → enter value → click on OK.
Format plot area (bar charts and line graphs)	Hover with mouse in grey plot area → Plot Area Tool tip displays → right-click → a menu displays → click on Format Plot Area → Format Plot Area dialogue box displays → in Area section on the right → click on None → click on OK.
Fill bars with pattern	Click on one bar → square dot displays for that series (all bars with same colour) → right-click in any bar → a menu displays → click on Format Data Series → Format Data Series dialogue box displays → click on the Patterns tab → click on Fill Effects button → Fill Effects dialogue box displays → click on Pattern tab → click on a pattern → to change colour, click on drop-down arrow next to Foreground or Background box → select colour → click on OK → click on OK to close Format Data Series dialogue box.

(continued overleaf)

HOW TO...	METHOD
Create a line graph	Highlight only the relevant range of cells (include row or column labels) → click on the Chart Wizard icon → in Step 1 of 4, in Standard Types tab, in Chart type section → click on Line → in Chart sub-type section, check that Line with markers ... is selected → click on Next → in Step 2 of 4 → check the chart preview → if preview is correct, click on Next (if incorrect, refer to 'Define the data series (bar charts or line graphs')). → In Step 3 of 4 → click on Titles tab → in Chart Title box, enter the title → click in Category (X) axis box → enter x-axis title → click in Value (Y) axis box → enter y-axis title → click on Legend tab → click to remove tick in Show legend box → click on Data Labels tab → click in Value box (to display numbers on data points) → click on Next → in Step 4 of 4 → click in button for As new sheet → click on Finish.
Create a comparative line graph	Highlight only the relevant range of cells (include row or column labels) → click on the Chart Wizard icon → in Step 1 of 4, in Standard Types tab, in Chart type section → click on Line → in Chart sub-type section, check that Line with markers ... is selected → click on Next → in Step 2 of 4 → check the chart preview → if preview is correct, click on Next (if incorrect, refer to 'Define the data series (for comparative charts')). → In Step 3 of 4 → click on Titles tab → in Chart Title box, enter the title → click in Category (X) axis box → enter x-axis title → click in Value (Y) axis box → enter y-axis title → click on Data Labels tab → check for tick in Show legend box (should be ticked) → click on Next → in Step 4 of 4 → click in button for As new sheet → click on Finish.
Define the data series (bar charts or line graphs)	In Chart Wizard – Step 2 of 4 → click on Series tab → under chart preview in Series section → click on name of series → click on Remove → next to Category (X) axis labels box, click on Collapse Dialog button → the spreadsheet displays → highlight only the cells to be plotted on the x-axis (do not include the row/column label) → dotted line (marquee) surrounds cells → click on Expand Dialog button from collapsed window → Source Data dialogue box displays → next to Values box, click on Collapse Dialog button → the spreadsheet displays → highlight only the cells to be plotted on the y-axis (do not include the row/column label) → dotted line (marquee) surrounds cells → click on Expand Dialog button from collapsed window → check that chart preview is correct → click on Next.
Define the data series for comparative charts (bar charts or line graphs)	In Chart Wizard – Step 2 of 4 → click on Series tab → under chart preview in Series section → click on name of series → click on Remove → next to Category (X) axis labels box, click on Collapse Dialog button → the spreadsheet displays → highlight only the cells to be plotted on the x-axis (do not include the row/column label) → dotted line (marquee) surrounds cells → click on Expand Dialog button from collapsed window → Source Data dialogue box displays. → *For first data series:* Next to Values box, click on Collapse Dialog button → the spreadsheet displays → highlight only the cells to be plotted on the y-axis (do not include the row/column label) → dotted line (marquee) surrounds cells → click on Expand Dialog button from collapsed window → Source Data dialogue box displays. → *For second data series:* Under chart preview in series section → click on name of second series → next to Values box, click on Collapse Dialog button → the spreadsheet displays → highlight only the cells that should be displayed on the y-axis (do not include the row/column label) → dotted line (marquee) surrounds cells → click on Expand Dialog button from collapsed window → Source Data dialogue box displays → check that chart preview is correct → click on Next.

HOW TO...	METHOD
Select the name for legend items	In Chart Wizard – Step 2 of 4 → click on Series tab → in Series section, click on name of first series (may be displayed as Series1) → in the Name section, delete any existing text then click on the Collapse Dialog button → the spreadsheet displays → click in the cell to be used as the name of the legend item → click on Expand Dialog → click on the name of the second series (may be displayed as Series2) → repeat this process.
Format lines on a line graph	Hover with mouse on a line → right-click → a menu displays → click on Format Data Series → Format Data Series dialogue box displays → click on Patterns tab → in Line section → click on Custom button → click on down arrow next to Style box → select a style → click on down arrow next to Weight box → select a thick line → to change colour, click on drop-down arrow next to Color box* → click on OK. *To format markers, move to right section of Format Data Series dialogue box.
Format markers on a line graph	Hover with mouse pointer on a line → right-click → a menu displays → click on Format Data Series → Format Data Series dialogue box displays → click on Patterns tab → in Marker section → click on drop-down arrow next to Style box → select a style → to change marker colour, click on drop-down arrow next to Foreground and/or Background box(es) → select colour → click on OK.
Add a header or footer	Click on View menu → click on Header and Footer → Page Setup dialogue box displays → click on Custom Header → Header dialogue box displays → click in Left, Center or Right section → enter required information → click on OK → click on Custom Footer → Footer dialogue box displays → enter required information in Left, Center or Right section → click on OK → click on OK in Page Setup dialogue box.
Add an automatic date	Click on View menu → click on Header and Footer → Page Setup dialogue box displays → click on Custom Header → click in Left, Center or Right section → click on Insert Date icon → click on OK → click on OK in Page Setup dialogue box.
Add an automatic filename	Click on View menu → click on Header and Footer → Page Setup dialogue box displays → click on Custom Header → click in Left, Center or Right section → click on Insert Filename icon → click on OK → click on OK in Page Setup dialogue box.
Save an existing datafile	Click on the Save icon.
Close a datafile	Click on File menu → click on Close.
Exit from Excel	Click on File menu → click on Exit.

Scenario

You are working in the ticket office of a local cinema. You are required to produce a spreadsheet to analyse sales of the cinema's revenue.

1 a Create a new spreadsheet.

   b Set the page orientation to **landscape**.

2 Enter the following data, leaving the **Takings** and **Total** columns blank as shown.

Cinema Takings						
Day	Five Ways	Ticket Price	Takings	Expenses	Refreshments	Total
Monday	200	3.5		54	35	
Wednesday	250	3.75		66	42	
Friday	400	4.2		76	88	
Saturday	450	4.75		85	92	
Sunday	175	4.5		65	78	
Week Total						

You need to make some calculations in your spreadsheet.

3 a In the **Takings** column use a formula to calculate the Takings for Monday by multiplying the **Five Ways** figure by the **Ticket Price**.

   b Replicate (copy) this formula to show the **Takings** for all other Days.

4 a In the **Total** column use a formula to calculate the Total for Monday as follows: (**Takings** subtract **Expenses**) plus **Refreshments**.

   b Replicate (copy) this formula for all other Days.

5 Save the spreadsheet using the filename **cinema1**.

In your saved file **cinema1**:

6 a In the **Week Total** row, use the **SUM** function to calculate the total for **Five Ways** from **Monday** to **Sunday**.

   b Replicate this function for all remaining columns

7 a In the footer:

   i Enter your **name** and **centre number**.

   ii Insert an **automatic date** and an **automatic filename**.

   b Set the spreadsheet to fit on **one page**.

8 Make sure that all data is displayed in full.

9 Save the spreadsheet, keeping the filename **cinema1**.

10 Print one copy of the spreadsheet on **one page** in **landscape** orientation, showing the figures, not the formulae.

11 Close the spreadsheet.

You will need to make some amendments in your saved spreadsheet **cinema1** and apply some formatting. (Alternatively, you may use the file **cinema1** from the worked copies folder.)

Open your saved spreadsheet **cinema1**.

1 The cinema will no longer be opening on Mondays.
   a Delete the **Monday** row.
   b Make sure blank cells do not remain where the data was deleted.

2 a Insert a new row with the label **Thursday** between Wednesday and Friday.
   b Enter data into the Thursday row as follows:

Day	Five Ways	Ticket Price	Takings	Expenses	Refreshments	Total
Thursday	100	2.55		44	25	

3 Copy the formula for **Takings** and **Total** from the Wednesday row into the Thursday row.

4 Make sure that the formulae in the Week Total row have updated after the Monday row was deleted and the Thursday row added.

5 Save your spreadsheet using the new filename **cinema2**.

6 Apply the following alignments:
   a Centre the column label **Day**.
   b **All** other text in the first column should be displayed as left-aligned.
   c Display all numeric data as right-aligned.

7 Format the numbers as follows:
   a Display the figures in the **Ticket Price** column with a **currency symbol** and **2** decimal places.
   b Display the figures in the **Total** column with a **currency symbol** and in **integer** format (zero decimal places).
   c Display the figures in all the other columns in **integer** format (zero decimal places).

8 Add a single outside border around all the column labels starting with **Day** and ending with **Total**.

9 Save the spreadsheet keeping the filename **cinema2**.

10 Print one copy of the spreadsheet on one page.

BUILD-UP TASK 3 · Edit a spreadsheet

You need to update your saved spreadsheet **cinema2**. (You may use the file **cinema2** from the worked copies folder.)

1 Make the following changes to the spreadsheet file **cinema2**.

    a Change the label Week Total to **Weekly Total**.
    b Change the Expenses figure for Friday to **85**.
    c Change the Ticket Price for Wednesday to **£3.25**. (The currency symbol should remain displayed.)
    d Make sure that all the figures have recalculated as a result of these changes.

2 a Save the spreadsheet using the new filename **cinema3**.
    b Make sure **gridlines** will be displayed on the printout.
    c Print one copy of the spreadsheet on **one page** in **landscape** orientation showing the **figures**, not the formulae.

3 a Display the formulae. Make sure they are displayed in full.
    b Make sure that the page orientation is **landscape** and that the spreadsheet fits on one page.
    c Make sure that **gridlines** and **row and column headings** (1, 2, 3, etc. and A, B, C, etc.) will be displayed when printed.
    d Save the spreadsheet formulae using the new filename **cinform**.
    e Print the entire spreadsheet on **one page** in **landscape** orientation showing the **formulae.**
    f Make sure that all formulae are displayed in full and are readable on your printout.
    g Close the file **cinform**.

4 Close all open files.

5 Check your printouts for accuracy.

BUILD-UP TASK 4 · Create a pie chart

For this task, you will need the file **agent** from the folder **files_graphs**.

Scenario

You work for a letting agent who has asked you to produce a pie chart to show the flats available for rent in August 2006.

1 Using suitable software for creating graphs, open the datafile **agent** which contains data about properties available for rent.

2 a Create a pie chart to show the **Number** for all **Flat Types**.

    b Title the chart **Flats Available August 2006**.

    c Do not display a legend.

    d Display data labels and percentages for each sector.

e Make sure that the chart is created on a full page on a sheet that is separate from the source data.

3 In the **header**, enter your **name**, **centre number**, an **automatic date** and an **automatic filename**.

4 Save the file using the filename **rent**.

5 Print one copy of the pie chart.

6 Close the file.

7 Check your printout for accuracy.

BUILD-UP TASK ⑤ *Create a bar chart*

For this task, you will need the file **tickets** from the folder **files_graphs**.

Scenario

You work in a school music department which holds several concerts in an academic year. Concert tickets are sold at full or reduced price (concession tickets are available for children and senior citizens). You have been asked to produce a graph to show the concert ticket sales.

1 Using suitable software for creating graphs, open the datafile **tickets** which gives figures for the tickets sold.

2a Create a comparative bar chart to show the **Concert** tickets sold for **Full Price** and **Concession.**

b Display the **Concert** along the *x*-axis.

c Title the chart **Attendance at Concerts**.

d Give the *x*-axis the title **Concert**.

e Give the *y*-axis the title **Tickets Sold**.

f Use a legend to identify the bars. Make sure that the bars are distinctive and can be clearly identified when printed.

TIP!
You may use pattern fills.

g Display the values (numbers) for each bar.

h Make sure that the chart is created on a full page on a sheet that is separate from the source data.

i Set the *y*-axis range from **50 to 450**.

3 In the footer, enter your **name, centre number,** an **automatic date** and an **automatic filename**.

4 Save the file using the filename **concerts**.

5 Print one copy of the bar chart.

6 Close the file.

7 Check your printout for accuracy.

For this task, you will need the file **visitors** from the folder **files_graphs**.

Scenario

You work in an events organising team. You need to produce a graph to show the number of visitors to an annual exhibition.

1 Using suitable software for creating graphs, open the datafile **visitors**, which gives figures for the number of visitors to the exhibition each year.

2a Create a line graph to show the **Visitors** from **2006 to 2002** only. Do not include the data for 2001.

 b Display the **Year** along the *x*-axis.

 c Title the graph **Art in Action**.

 d Give the *x*-axis the title **Year**.

 e Give the *y*-axis the title **Visitors**.

 f Do not display a legend.

 g Display the values (numbers) for each data point on the line.

 h Make sure that the chart is created on a full page on a sheet that is separate from the source data.

 i Set the *y*-axis range from **8300 to 9100**.

3 In the **footer**, enter your **name**, **centre number**, an **automatic date** and an **automatic filename.**

4 Save the file using the filename **artvisits.**

5 Print one copy of the line graph.

6 Close the file.

7 Check your printout for accuracy.

For this task, you will need the file **party** from the folder **files_graphs**.

Scenario

You work as a conference organiser. A national event has been organised to which representatives of the five main political parties have been invited.

1. Using suitable software for creating graphs, open the datafile **party** which contains data about the number of candidates representing the political parties.

2a Create a pie chart to show the **Representative** for each **Party**.

  b Title the chart **Political Party Representatives**.

  c Display a legend to identify the data.

  d Display the actual value (number, not percentages) for each sector.

  e Make sure that the chart is created on a full page on a sheet that is separate from the source data.

  f Make sure that the legend will clearly identify each sector on the printout.

3. In the **footer**, enter your **name**, **centre number**, an **automatic date** and an **automatic filename**.

4. Save the file using the filename **politics**.

5. Print one copy of the pie chart.

6. Close the file.

7. Check your printout for accuracy.

For this task, you will need the file **costs** from the folder **files_graphs**.

Scenario

You work in a housing development office. You have been asked to produce charts to display information for tenants.

1 Using suitable software for creating graphs, open the datafile **costs**, which shows the electricity costs for different apartment types.

2a Create a comparative bar chart to show the electricity costs for every **Season** for **Penthouse** and **Studio** apartments.

  b Display the **Season** along the x-axis.

  c Title the chart **Seasonal Electricity Costs**.

  d Give the x-axis the title **Season**.

  e Give the y-axis the title **Cost £**.

  f Use a legend to identify the bars. Make sure that the bars are distinctive and can be clearly identified when printed.

  g Display the values (numbers) for each bar.

  h Make sure that the chart is created on a full page on a sheet that is separate from the source data.

  i Set the y-axis range from **15 to 85**.

3 In the **header**, enter your **name**, **centre number**, an **automatic date** and an **automatic filename**.

4 Save the file using the filename **electric**.

5 Print one copy of the bar chart.

6 Close the file.

7 Check your printout for accuracy.

Task 1

Scenario

You are working in the London office of a company that employs sales people in various cities. The manager has asked you to create a spreadsheet to show the regional sales.

1 a Create a new spreadsheet.

   b Set the page orientation to **landscape**.

2 Enter the following data, leaving the **TOTAL** and **SALES** columns blank as shown.

REGIONAL SALES							
CITY	SEP	OCT	NOV	TOTAL	MINIMUM	WEIGHTING	SALES
LONDON	203	360	314		19	1.31	
BIRMINGHAM	231	369	538		22	1.49	
MANCHESTER	478	222	554		18	1.21	
CARDIFF	582	453	453		15	1.12	
NEWCASTLE	489	342	695		22	1.59	
CARLISLE	762	526	397		27	1.96	
OVERALL SALES							

You need to make some calculations in your spreadsheet.

3 a In the **TOTAL** column use the **SUM** function to calculate the total for **LONDON** by adding the **SEP**, **OCT** and **NOV** figures.

   b Replicate (copy) this formula to show the **TOTAL** for all other cities.

4 a Calculate the **SALES** for **LONDON** by multiplying the **TOTAL** by the **WEIGHTING**, then multiplying this figure by **1.15**.

   (TOTAL*WEIGHTING)*1.15

   b Replicate (copy) this formula for the remaining cities.

5 In the **SALES** column, use the **SUM** function to calculate the **OVERALL SALES** figure. This is calculated by adding the **SALES** figures for all of the cities.

6 a In the header enter your **name** and **centre number**.

   b In the footer insert an **automatic date** and an **automatic filename**.

   c Set the spreadsheet to fit on **one page**.

7 Make sure that all data is displayed in full.

8 Save the spreadsheet using the new filename **regsales**.

9 Print one copy of the spreadsheet on **one page** in **landscape** orientation, showing the figures, not the formulae.

Task 2

The manager has asked you to make some changes to the spreadsheet.

Open your saved spreadsheet **regsales**.

1a Delete the **MINIMUM** column and all its data.
  b Make sure blank cells do not remain where the data was deleted.

2a Insert a new column between **NOV** and **TOTAL**.
  b Enter data into the new column as shown below:

CITY	DEC
LONDON	450
BIRMINGHAM	430
MANCHESTER	400
CARDIFF	350
NEWCASTLE	450
CARLISLE	350

3 Make sure that the formulae in the **TOTAL** and **SALES** columns have updated after the DEC column was inserted.

4 Save your spreadsheet using the new filename **decsales**.

5 Apply the following alignments:

  a Centre the column label **REGIONAL SALES**.

  b **All** other text in the first column should be displayed as left-aligned.

  c Display all numeric data as right-aligned.

6 Format the numbers as follows:

  a Display the figures in the **TOTAL** column with a **currency symbol** and in **integer** format (zero decimal places).

  b Display the figures in the **WEIGHTING** column to **2** decimal places with no currency symbol.

  c Display the figures in the **SALES** column with a **currency symbol** and to **2** decimal places.

  d Display the figures in the other columns (SEP to DEC) in **integer** format (zero decimal places).

7 Add a **single outside border** beginning with the row label **OVERALL SALES** and ending with the **OVERALL SALES** figure in the **SALES** column.

8 Save the spreadsheet keeping the filename **decsales**.

Task 3

The manager would like you to make a few more amendments to the spreadsheet.

1 Make the following changes to the spreadsheet file **decsales**.

   a Change the NOV figure for LONDON to **814**.

   b Change the row label LONDON to **LONDON CITY**.

   c Change the WEIGHTING for BIRMINGHAM to **1.39**.

   d Make sure that the TOTAL and SALES figures have been updated as a result of these changes.

2a Save the spreadsheet keeping the filename **decsales**.

   b Make sure **gridlines** will be displayed on the printout.

   c Print one copy of the spreadsheet on **one page** in **landscape** orientation showing the **figures**, not the formulae.

3a Display the formulae. Make sure the formulae are displayed in full.

   b Make sure the page orientation is **landscape** and the spreadsheet fits on one page.

   c Make sure that **gridlines** and **row and column headings** (1, 2, 3, etc. and A, B, C, etc.) will be displayed when printed.

   d Save the spreadsheet formulae using the new filename **regform**.

   e Print the entire spreadsheet on **one page** in **landscape** orientation showing the **formulae**.

   f Make sure all formulae are displayed in full and are readable on your printout.

   g Close the file **regform**.

4 Close all open files.

For this task, you will need the file **grants** from the folder **files_graphs**.

Task 4

Scenario

The manager has asked you to produce a graph to show recent grant allocations.

1   Using suitable software for creating graphs, open the datafile **grants** which contains data on the grants given for the last six months.

2 a   Create a comparative line graph to show the grants given for **Medicine** and **Dentistry** from **April** to **September** inclusive.

  b   Display the months along the *x*-axis.

  c   Title the graph **Grant Allocations**.

  d   Give the *x*-axis the title **Month**.

  e   Give the *y*-axis the title **Number of Grants**.

  f   Use a legend to identify each line. Make sure that the lines and/or data points are distinctive and can be clearly identified when printed.

  g   Display the values (numbers) for each data point on both lines.

  h   Make sure that the chart is created on a full page on a sheet that is separate from the source data.

  i   Set the *y*-axis range from **10** to **45**.

3   In the **footer**, enter your **name**, **centre number**, an **automatic date** and an **automatic filename**.

4   Save the file using the filename **unigraph**.

5   Print one copy of the line graph.

6   Close the file.

7   Check your printout for accuracy.

The solutions for the Build-up tasks can be found in the folder **U2_workedcopies_buildtasks** on the **CD-ROM**. The solutions for the Practice tasks can be found in the folder **U2_workedcopies_practicetask** on the **CD-ROM**.

Assessment guidelines for Unit 2

1 Your tutor will provide you with the file/s you need to create the graph(s) for the assessment.

2 Before an assessment you should create a new folder just for the assessment.

TIP!

Before you start, COPY the folder containing the file(s) into another user area in case you need to open an original file again.

Spreadsheet tasks

There will usually be three tasks covering spreadsheet skills.

- You will create a new spreadsheet, enter data and use formulae and functions.
- You will need to make some changes to your spreadsheet and save it with a different filename.
- You will need to format the updated spreadsheet and display the formulae.

Create a new spreadsheet

1 Make sure that you open a new spreadsheet, do not open an existing spreadsheet that may already have headers and footers or any data.

2 Set the orientation when instructed, do not leave it to be done later.

3 Do not enter the data in bold – it is presented in bold to help you to see what to enter.

4 You may use any font style or size unless otherwise instructed.

5 You will not be penalised if you leave a blank row below the spreadsheet title and/or below the column labels. However, you are advised not to leave a blank row below the column labels.

6 Double-check your work to make absolutely sure that you have entered all numbers with **100 per cent** accuracy.

7 If the instruction is to use a function you MUST use a function e.g. SUM, AVERAGE, etc. Do not use a formula even though this may also give a correct result.

8 Remember to read each instruction to calculate formula carefully. You may need to use brackets in a formula but you will not always be instructed to do so – you are expected to know when to use brackets.

9 Do not enter any additional data in any cells.

10 When asked to insert an automatic date and an automatic filename, do NOT type the date or the filename. You MUST use the automatic date and automatic filename option in Excel.

11 Always use **Print Preview**. Check that the data in all cells is fully displayed and that all headers and footers are correct.

Edit a spreadsheet

1 You will need to edit the spreadsheet that you created earlier.

2 Read through the task to see what the new filename should be.

3 Save your original spreadsheet with the new filename as soon as you open it. This will prevent you from saving over the original spreadsheet.

4 **Deleting a row/column.** You will need to delete either a row or a column.

- Make absolutely sure that you delete the whole row/column not just the data in the cells.
- Do not hide the row/column.
- The remaining rows/columns should 'close up' the gap.
- Check to make sure that the remaining rows/columns are automatically renumbered/relabelled.

5 **Inserting a row/column**. You will need to insert either a row or a column and enter data into the new row/column.

- Make sure that you insert the row/column in the correct position.
- Double-check to make sure all numbers that you enter are **100 per cent** accurate.
- Check to make sure that all formulae automatically recalculate.
- Refer to the printout of your original spreadsheet to check the original calculation results compared to the spreadsheet you are currently working on.

Format a spreadsheet

1 To display figures with a currency symbol, do not use the Currency icon on the toolbar. This displays as Accounting format which places the currency symbol (e.g. £ sign) to the far left of the cell and also moves figures further in from the far right of the cell.

2 When instructed to display gridlines, do not use the border option. Borders are not the same as gridlines. You will also be asked to use borders for selected cells, they should be darker than gridlines. For borders, choose the thick box border option as this will print more clearly.

3 When instructed to right-align numbers, even though they display as right-aligned, it is better to select the cells and the right-align icon (particularly important if your work is to be assessed electronically). The same applies to left and centre alignment of text.

4 Use Print Preview again to check that the data in all cells is fully displayed and that all headers and footers are correct (check for the updated filename).

Display formulae

1 Make sure that all columns containing formulae are wide enough to display formulae in full.

2 Make sure that you have used formulae where instructed. The value(s) must not be displayed in the cell(s).

3 Make sure that the source formulae have been copied where instructed. The formula in the rest of the row/column should be constructed in the same way (only the cell references should be different).

4 Formatting and alignment will not display on the formulae print; this is normal.

Create graphs

1 Use **Print Preview** before printing. After printing check your printout again. For any chart that displays a legend, make sure that the data is clearly distinctive

2 There will not be specific instructions about the points below but as good practice you should:

- remove the grey background from the plot area for bar charts and line graphs
- use a pattern fill for one or both sets of bars on comparative bar charts
- format lines to be thick and dark on line graphs
- use one dotted and one solid line for comparative line graphs
- set the print option to print in black and white to ensure that data is clearly distinctive for all graphs that display a legend (unless you have used pattern fills).

3 Charts with or without gridlines are acceptable.

4 Any intervals are acceptable on the *y*-axis, there is no need to change the default intervals set by Excel.

Good luck!

Contents

More general advice on preparation for the assessment and the Unit 3 Definition of terms can be found on the CD-ROM that accompanies this book.

In Unit 3, you need to open a provided database, make some changes to it, and create queries and reports.

This book is divided into 3 sections:

- *in Section 1 you will learn how to open a provided database, rename the database table, delete records, amend data, add new records and print the updated table*

- *in Section 2 you will learn how to create queries on one and two criteria, sort data and how to display selected fields*

- *in Section 3 you will create a simple tabular report.*

You will use a software program called Microsoft Office Access 2003 which is part of Microsoft Office 2003. Access is a program that saves data as it is entered, allowing different views of data. It lets you search for and present data in many different ways. We will refer to it as Access from now on. Note that default settings are assumed.

A CD-ROM accompanies this book. It contains all the files that you will need for the tasks in this book. The solutions for all the tasks can be found on the CD-ROM in a folder called **dbases_worked_copies**.

> *Note:* There are many ways of performing the skills covered in this book. This book will provide How to... guidelines that are easily understood by learners.

Files for this book

To work through the tasks in this book, you will need the files on the accompanying CD-ROM from the folder called **files_dbases**. Copy this folder into your user area before you begin.

▶▶ How to... *copy the folder files_dbases from the CD-ROM*

1. Insert the CD-ROM into the CD-ROM drive of your computer.

2. Close any windows that may open.

3. From the **desktop**, double-click on the **My Computer** icon. The **My Computer** window is displayed.

4. Under **Devices with Removable Storage**, double-click on the **CD-ROM drive** icon. A window will open displaying the contents of the CD-ROM.

5. Double-click on the **L1_Unit3_DB** folder. Click once on the folder **files_dbases** (Figure 3.1).

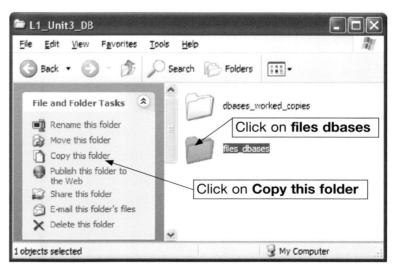

FIGURE 3.1 The File and Folder Tasks box

6   The folder will be highlighted (usually blue).

7   Click **Copy this folder** in the **File and Folder Tasks** box.

8   A **Copy Items** dialogue box will open.

9   In this dialogue box click on the user area that you want to copy the folder **files_dbases** to (Figure 3.2).

10 Click the **Copy** button.

11 The folder **files_dbases** will be copied to your user area.

Access automatically saves changes to data. You are strongly advised to paste a second copy of the folder **files_dbases** to another folder in your user area as backup.

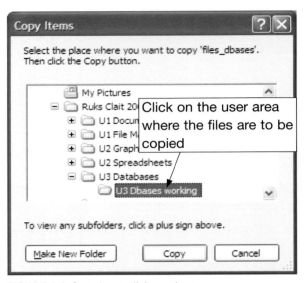

FIGURE 3.2 Copy Items dialogue box

▶▶ How to... *remove the read-only property for provided databases*

The files provided are set to **Read-only**. After you have copied the files to your user area, remove the **Read-only** properties as follows.

TIP!

Do not remove the read-only properties from the backup folder (if you have created one).

1   Right-click on the folder **files_dbases**.

2   Click **Properties** from the drop-down menu.

3   A **Properties** dialogue box opens.

4   Click in the **Read-only** box to remove the tick/square (the box should now be empty).

5   Click **Apply**.

6   A **Confirm Attribute Changes** dialogue box appears (Figure 3.3).

7   Click in the second button to **Apply changes to this folder, subfolders and files**.

8   Click **OK**.

9   Click **OK** to close the **Properties** dialogue box.

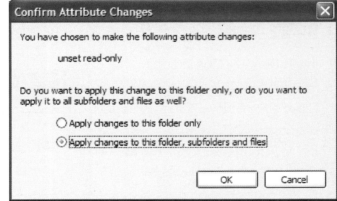

FIGURE 3.3 The Confirm Attribute Changes dialogue box

Preparing your work area

You are advised to prepare your user area to keep your files organised.

An example of a folder structure for all units is shown in Figure 3.4. The main folder in My Documents is called **Ruks Clait 2006 Level 1**. Within this folder are subfolders for each of the units.

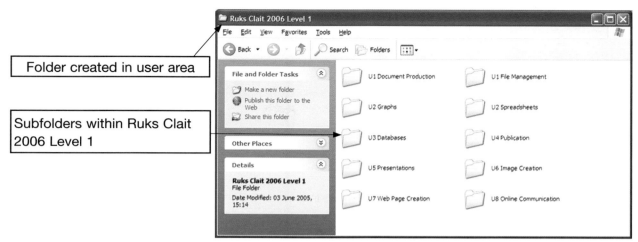

Folder created in user area

Subfolders within Ruks Clait 2006 Level 1

FIGURE 3.4 Folders in the user area

You may not need to create as many folders or you may prefer to create a folder for each unit as you begin it.

Within each unit subfolder, there are further subfolders (Figure 3.5). For example, in the **U3 Databases** subfolder, the subfolders are:

1 **U3 Dbases working** – this is the working folder in which all working files will be saved.

2 **dbases_workedcopies** – this folder has also been copied from the CD-ROM.

3 **files_dbases** – the source files from the CD-ROM have been copied into this folder.

4 **Copy of files_dbases** – a copy of the folder containing the source files has been made.

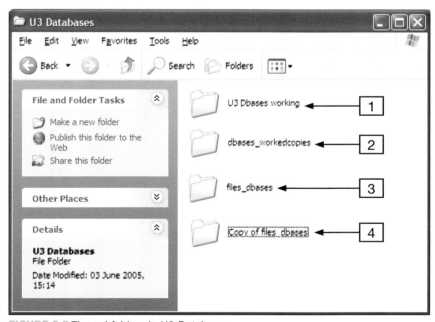

FIGURE 3.5 The subfolders in U3 Databases

LEARNING OUTCOMES

In this section you will learn how to:

- start Access
- open a provided database
- identify the different parts of the database window
- rename a table
- open a database table
- create a backup copy
- identify the parts of a table in datasheet view
- understand database terms (table, field, record, form)
- set the orientation
- change column widths
- save the table layout
- use Print Preview
- print a table
- delete a record
- find and replace data
- amend data in existing records
- create new records
- use spell check
- prepare to print the updated table
- save the updated table
- print the updated table
- close a table
- exit Access.

What is a database?

A database is an organised list of information arranged into **tables** that have rows and columns similar to a spreadsheet. Telephone directories or address books are examples of popular databases.

Spreadsheets can be used to perform some basic database functions – sorting data and searching for information using filters – but a database program like Access allows you more choices.

You can question (**query**) a database more easily than a spreadsheet, and you can use reports to present the data professionally in a variety of ways.

Database terms and actions will be explained throughout this book.

Mouse techniques

Basic computer principles have been dealt with in Unit 1. If you feel that you need to refresh your memory refer to Unit 1. Unless otherwise instructed, always click using the left mouse button.

MOUSE ACTION	DESCRIPTION
Point	Move the mouse on the mousemat until the pointer appears at the required position on the screen.
Click	Press and release the **left** mouse button once.
Double-click	Quickly press the **left** mouse button **twice** then release it.
Right-click	Press the **right** mouse button **once** – a menu displays.
Hover	Position the mouse pointer over an icon or menu item and pause, a **Tool tip** or a further menu item will appear.
Click and drag	Used to move items. Click with the **left** mouse button on an item, hold the mouse button down and move the pointer to another location. Release the mouse button.

Switch on your computer and log in.

▶▶ How to...   start Access

1 Click the **Start** button on the Windows **taskbar**.

2 Click **All Programs**.

3 Click **Microsoft Office**.

4 Click on **Microsoft Office Access 2003**.

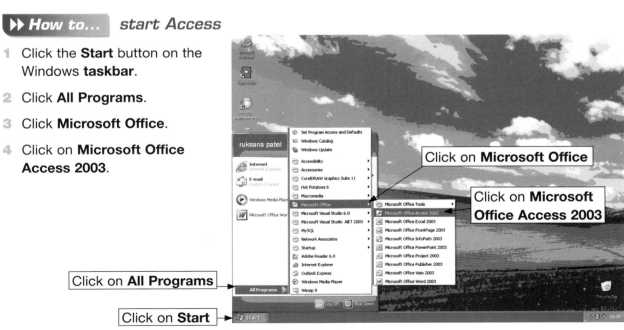

Click on **Microsoft Office**

Click on **Microsoft Office Access 2003**

Click on **All Programs**

Click on **Start**

FIGURE 3.7 Starting Access

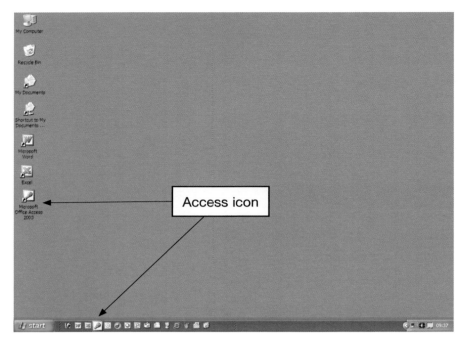

FIGURE 3.8 The Access icon on the taskbar and on the Windows desktop

TIP!

A quicker way to start Access is to double-click on the Access icon on the desktop (if a shortcut has been created). Alternatively, single-click on the Access icon on the taskbar (if a shortcut has been created). See Figure 3.8.

Check your understanding *Start Access*

1 Start Access, either through the Start menu or by using a shortcut icon.

2 The database window will open.

3 Keep this open.

Getting familiar with the Access window

When you open Access on your computer, your screen should look similar to the one shown in Figure 3.9. Access 2003 may open with the task pane on the right, click on the black cross next to **Getting Started** to close the task pane.

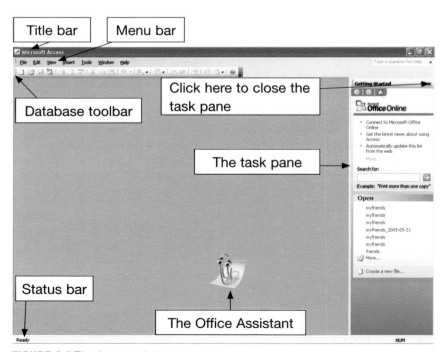

FIGURE 3.9 The Access window

1 Look for the **Menu bar**.

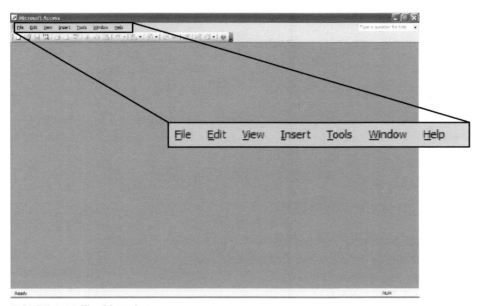

FIGURE 3.10 The Menu bar

2 Click on **File**.

3 A list will drop down with further choices.

4 At first the whole menu may not display, but if you leave it open for a few seconds it will display in full.

5 Click anywhere outside the menu or click on **File** again to close the menu.

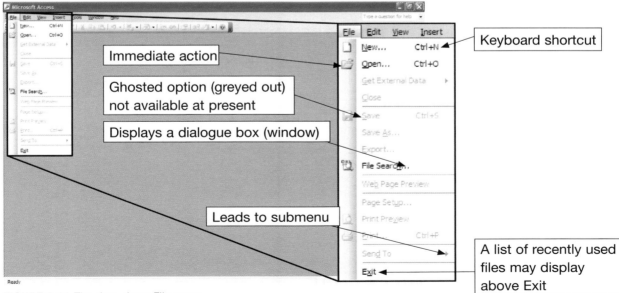

Keyboard shortcut

Immediate action

Ghosted option (greyed out) not available at present

Displays a dialogue box (window)

Leads to submenu

A list of recently used files may display above Exit

FIGURE 3.11 The drop-down File menu

1 In the **Menu** bar, click on **File**.

2 Look for the ghosted (greyed out) options.

3 Look for the keyboard shortcuts listed for some menu options on the right-hand side of the menu.

4 Look for the icons on the left of the menu which show the immediate action.

5 Look for the options that will display a dialogue box (window).

6 Look for the options that lead to a submenu.

7 Click on **File** again to close the menu.

Toolbar buttons

Move your mouse over each toolbar button and pause, a **Tool tip** displays showing the name of the button. Clicking on a toolbar button provides quick ways of carrying out tasks in any program.

In this book, we will usually refer to a toolbar button as an icon.

What does it mean?

Icon
A button (picture) on the toolbar 🖫.

1 Move your mouse over the icons on the toolbar and pause on each button until the Tool tip displays.

▶▶ How to... *open a provided database*

1 In the **Menu bar**, click on **File**.

2 Click **Open** in the drop-down menu.

3 An **Open** dialogue box will display.

4 Click the down arrow to the right of **Look in** (Figure 3.12).

5 A list of user areas will display.

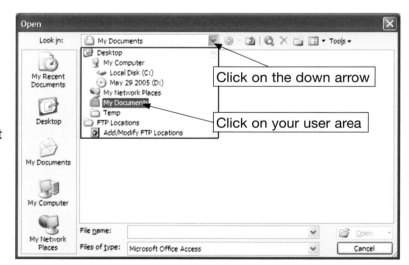

Click on the down arrow

Click on your user area

FIGURE 3.12 User areas in the Open dialogue box

6 Click on your user area.

7 Click **Open**.

8 Select the folder in your user area in which the files are saved. (Figure 3.13).

9 Click **Open**. If the file is saved in a subfolder, select the relevant folder and click **Open** again.

10 Click on the required file.

11 Click **Open**.

12 The **database window** will open.

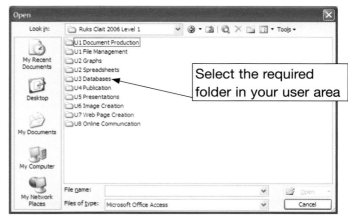

FIGURE 3.13 Subfolders in the user area

TIP!

You may get a warning message asking if you want to open the file. If you do, click **Open**.

FIGURE 3.14 The Security Warning message

TIP!

Before you begin, make sure you have a backup copy of the folder **files_dbases** in a separate folder in your user area. Access saves changes to data automatically, so it is very easy to overwrite the original database unintentionally.

FIGURE 3.15 Access files in the Open dialogue box

Check your understanding *Open a provided database*

1 Open the provided database called **myfriends** from the folder **files_ dbases** in your user area.

2 The database will open in the database window.

Getting familiar with the database window

The different **Objects** in a database (e.g. tables, queries, forms and reports) are stored in different sections of the database (Figure 3.16).

When a database is opened in Access, the **Tables** button (Object) is selected in the **database window**. In the main window (white area), all the tables in the database are displayed under the three standard options preset by Access.

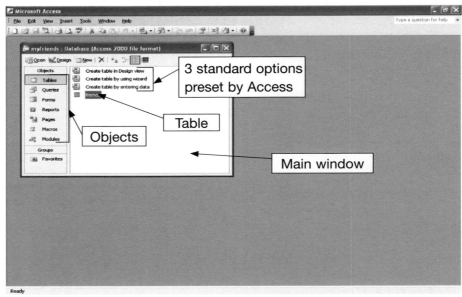

FIGURE 3.16 The Database window

When you create queries they are automatically saved in the Queries section. To view the queries in a database, click on the **Queries** button. Similarly, when you create reports, they are automatically saved in the Reports section. To view the reports in a database, click on the **Reports** button.

Check your understanding *Use the database window*

1 In the **Objects** section, click on **Queries**.

2 There are no queries saved in your database as yet, but there are two or three standard options in all the Objects sections which are preset by Access, these allow you to **Create in Design view** and **Create by using wizard**.

3 Below the standard options will be the name(s) of any queries in your database.

4 Click on **Forms**.

5 There are no forms in your database.

6 Click on **Reports**.

7 There are no reports in your database as yet (you will be creating queries and reports later).

8 Click on **Tables**, you will see one table called **friends** under the three standard options.

Your name

You will often be instructed to name a table, query or report with your name. An example of the instruction is: Name the table **friends (Your Name)**.

You are expected to type your own first and last name, not the words "Your Name". You should not use brackets surrounding your name. You can use any case, but you are advised to use title case or all capitals instead of lower case. Refer to page 257 for an explanation of case.

Rename a database table

In Access you cannot use headers or footers for tables, so a table printout will not display your name. You can add this information to the table name, that way your name will be displayed on the table printout.

▶▶ How to... *rename a database table*

1 In the **database window** with **Tables** selected in the **Objects** section.

2 Click once on the table name (Figure 3.17).

3 In the **Menu bar**, click on **Edit**.

4 Click **Rename** (Figure 3.18).

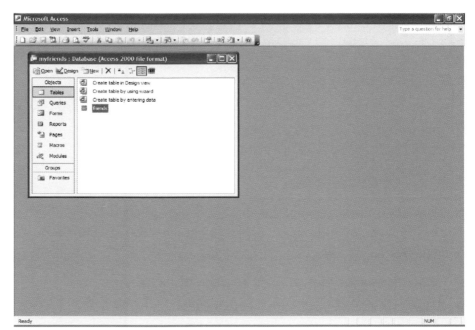

FIGURE 3.17 Table **friends** in the database window

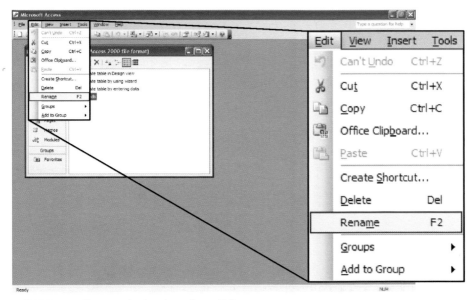

FIGURE 3.18 **Rename** in the drop-down Edit menu

5 A cursor displays after the last character in the filename (Figure 3.19).

6 Click in the highlighted box after the last character.

TIP!

If the table name remains highlighted the name will be deleted when you enter text, if so you should enter the original name followed by your name.

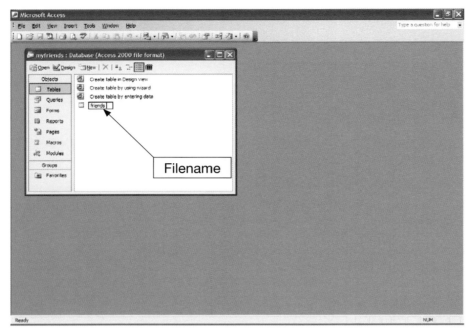

FIGURE 3.19 The filename is highlighted

7 The table name will no longer be highlighted.

8 Press the **spacebar** to insert a space after the table name.

9 Enter your first and last name (Figure 3.20).

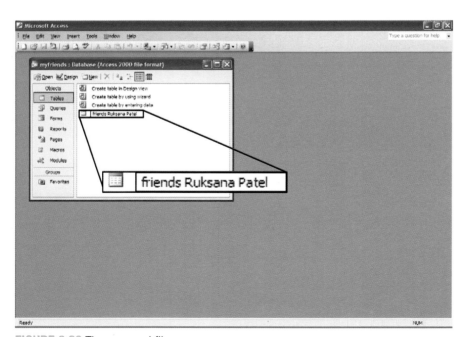

FIGURE 3.20 The renamed file

10 Press the **Enter** key on the keyboard.

11 The table will be renamed to include your name (Figure 3.21).

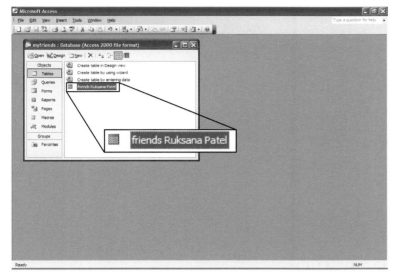

FIGURE 3.21 The Access window will now show the new filename

Check your understanding *Rename a database table*

1 Rename the table **friends** to add **your first and last name**.

2 Press **Enter**.

3 Your name should be displayed after **friends**.

TIP!

Enter **one space** after the table name **friends**.

▶▶ How to... *open a database table*

1 In the **database window** select **Tables** in the **Objects** section (Figure 3.22).

2 Click on the name of the database table that you want to open.

3 Click the **Open** button.

4 The database table will open in the main work area.

TIP!

Double-clicking on the table icon in the main window will also open the table.

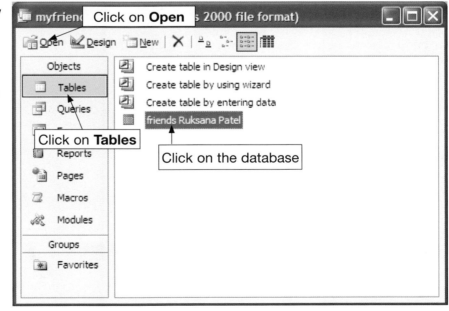

FIGURE 3.22 Opening a database table in the database window

5 Click the **Maximize** icon at the top right of the table window (Figure 3.23).

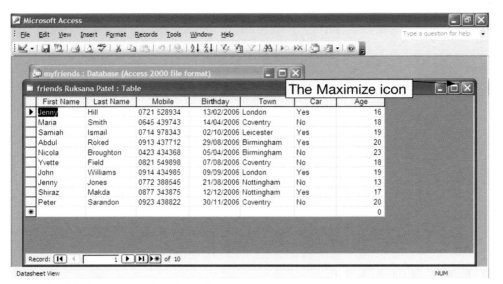

FIGURE 3.23 Maximizing a datasheet view

6 The table name will now display on the Access title bar at the top of the screen and the main work area will be clearer (Figure 3.24).

TIP!

Always maximise your table.

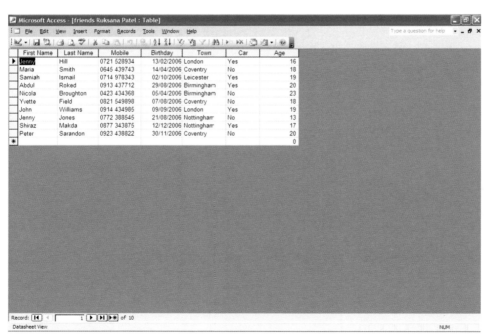

FIGURE 3.24 The maximized table in datasheet view

1 In the database called **myfriends**.

2 Open the table called **friends (Your Name)**.

3 Maximise the table window.

4 Keep the table open until you are instructed to close it.

The task pane

Access 2003 opens with the task pane on the right of the screen. You are advised to change your Access preferences so that the task pane does not display every time that you start Access, this will help to keep the screen clear.

▶▶ How to... *set the option Close the task pane (optional)*

1 In the **Menu bar**, click on **Tools**.

2 Click **Options** in the drop-down menu (Figure 3.25).

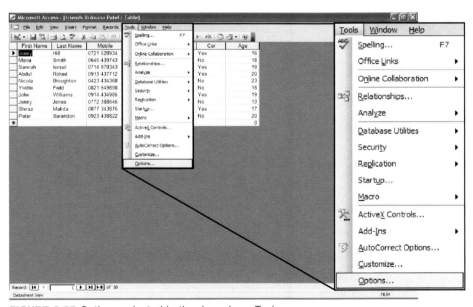

FIGURE 3.25 Options selected in the drop-down Tools menu

3 The **Options** dialogue box will open (Figure 3.26).

4 Select the **View** tab from the Options dialogue box.

5 Click to remove the tick in the box for **Startup Task Pane**.

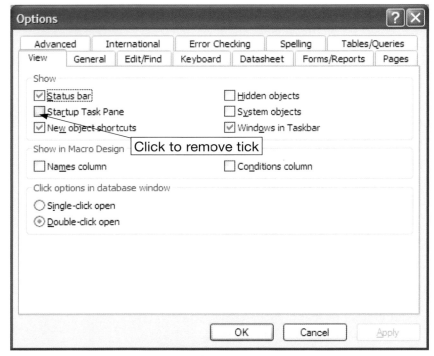

FIGURE 3.26 The View screen in the Options dialogue box

6 Click **Apply**, then click **OK**.

7 The task pane will not display every time you start Access.

▶▶ How to... *create a backup copy of a database (optional)*

1 In the **Menu bar**, click on **File**.

2 Click **Back Up Database** (Figure 3.27).

3 A **Save Backup As** dialogue box will open. Access will save in the same folder as the database that you are working on and will suggest the original name followed by the date in American format (year, month, day).

4 In the **Save Backup As** window, click **Save**.

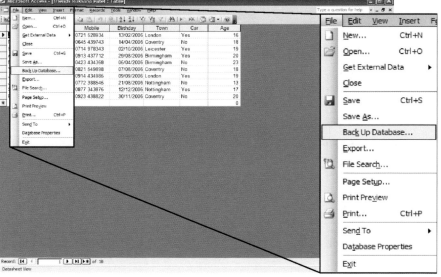

FIGURE 3.27 The Back Up Database option in the drop-down File menu

5 A warning message may display again. If so, click **Open**.

6 The original database will re-open in the database window.

7 In the **Objects** section, check that **Tables** is selected and that the table name is highlighted. Click **Open**.

Getting familiar with datasheet view and the database table

When a database is opened it displays as a table, this is referred to as the **datasheet view**.

Take a few minutes to become familiar with **datasheet view** and the database table (Figure 3.28).

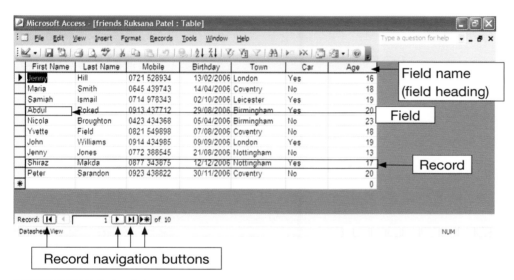

FIGURE 3.28 Datasheet view

What does it mean?	
Database terms	
Table	All data held in a database is stored in a table. Data can be entered, changed or deleted in the table. In Access, when data is entered, amended or deleted, it is automatically saved.
Field name	The name of the field. Think of a field name as a column heading. We will refer to it as field heading from now on. The field headings in the example above are: First Name, Last Name, Mobile, Birthday, Town, Car and Age.
Field	An item of data within a table. Think of a field as each individual block or cell.
Record	Each row is a record. A record runs horizontally across the table. Every record consists of the same number of fields. In the example above there are 10 records.

1 To move between <u>fields</u>, use the **cursor keys** (arrow keys), the **Tab key**, or **click** in the required field.

2 To move between <u>records</u>, use the ***record navigation buttons*** at the bottom left of the table window. Clicking on a record navigation button moves to a record as shown in Figure 3.29.

3 When the cursor is in a field, the **current record marker** ▶ displays to the left of the record.

4 In the **Status bar**, the current record number and the total number of records displays.

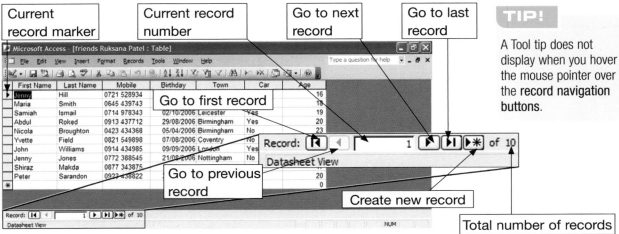

FIGURE 3.29 Record navigation in datasheet view

Check your understanding *Move around a database*

1 In your database table called **friends (Your Name)**.

Use the **cursor keys** or the **mouse** to move to the:

2 **Last Name** field for record 3 (Ismail).

3 **Last Name** field for record 7 (Williams).

4 **Age** field for record 7 (19).

5 **First Name** field for record 9 (Shiraz).

Use the **record navigation buttons** to go to:

6 **Previous** record (Jenny (Jones)).

7 **First** record (Jenny (Hill)).

8 **Next** record (Maria).

9 Click the **New Record** button to move to a new record at the end of the table.

Setting the orientation

The default orientation in Access is portrait. When a database table is printed, it may print on two pages. Changing the orientation to landscape will make the data fit on one page. This makes the table easier to read, saves paper and ensures that the second page is not forgotten on a printer.

TIP!

Access does not retain the orientation settings – you must set the orientation every time.

▶▶ How to... *set the orientation*

1 In the **Menu bar**, click on **File**.

2 Click **Page Setup** in the drop-down menu.

3 A **Page Setup** dialogue box will open (Figure 3.30).

4 Click the **Page** tab.

5 Click on **Landscape** (or Portrait).

6 Click **OK**.

FIGURE 3.30 The Page Setup dialogue box

Check your understanding *Set the orientation*

1 In your database table called **friends (Your Name)**.

2 Set the orientation to **landscape**.

Changing the column width

It is often necessary to change the width of columns so that all data is displayed in full and to make sure that all the fields will fit on one page when printing. Columns will need to be made wider or narrower.

▶▶ How to... *change the column width*

1 In your database table, position your **mouse** on the line to the right of the **field heading**.

2 The mouse pointer will turn into a double-headed arrow ⟨↔⟩.

3 Double-click.

4 Access will adjust the column width to fit the longest line of data visible on screen.

TIP!

You can click and drag the width to reduce/widen columns yourself.

1 In your database table called **friends (Your Name)**.

2 Change the column width of all the columns (data may already be displayed in full but practice the skill anyway).

Saving changes to the layout

Access automatically saves any changes to the data in the database. However, any changes to the layout (e.g. changing column width) are not automatically saved.

▶▶ How to... *save changes to the layout of a database*

1 In the **Menu bar**, click on **File**.

2 Click **Save** (Figure 3.31).

TIP!

Click the **Save** 🔲 icon on the toolbar instead.

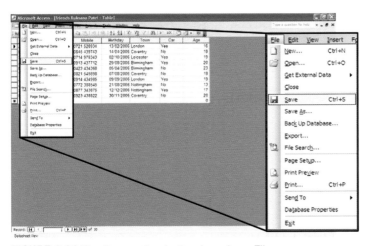

FIGURE 3.31 The Save option in the drop-down File menu

1 Save the database table called **friends (Your Name)**.

Printing a database

Use **Print Preview** to check that all data is fully displayed and that all fields fit on one page, even though you may have changed all column widths.

▶▶ How to... *use Print Preview*

1 Make sure the table is open in **datasheet view** (as a table).

2 In the **Menu bar**, click on **File**.

3 Click **Print Preview**. The table will be displayed as shown below (Figure 3.32).

TIP!

Click the **Print Preview** icon on the toolbar instead.

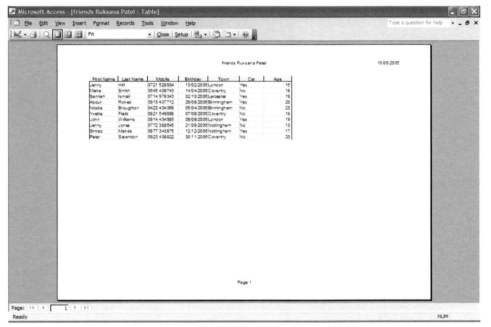

FIGURE 3.32 The Print Preview screen

4 Move your mouse over the page.

5 The pointer changes to a zoom tool.

6 Click in the page to zoom in.

7 Check that all columns are wide enough to display all data in full.

8 If any data is not fully displayed note which fields need to be made wider.

TIP!

Click again to zoom out and click again to zoom in to another part of the table.

9 Click the **Close** button Close to close Print Preview.

10 You will return to the table (datasheet view).

11 If required, adjust any column widths and use Print Preview again.

▶▶ How to... *print a table*

1 In the **Menu bar**, click on **File**.

2 Click **Print** (Figure 3.33).

TIP!

Alternatively, click the **Print** icon on the toolbar instead to skip to step 5.

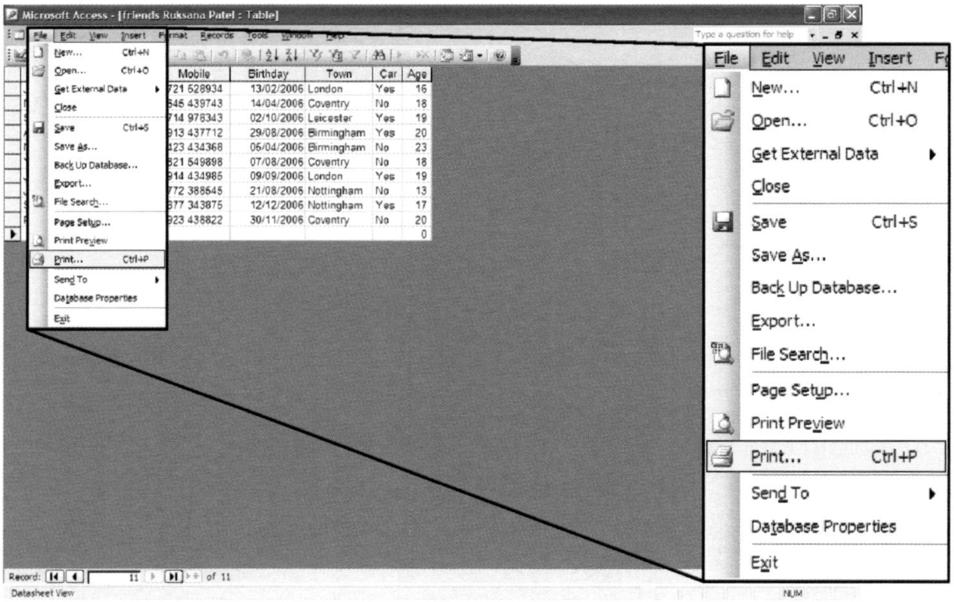

FIGURE 3.33 The Print option in the drop-down File menu

3 A **Print** dialogue box will open (Figure 3.34).

Check that the number
of copies is set to 1.

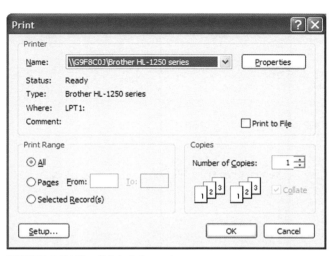

FIGURE 3.34 The Print dialogue box

4 Click **OK**.

5 Check your printout to make sure that all data is fully displayed.

Check your understanding *Print the original database table*

1 Print your database table called **friends (Your Name)**.

2 Check your printout to make sure all data is fully displayed.

Note: if you want to close the table now and exit Access, refer to pages 265–266.

Deleting a record

Deleting a record removes the data from all fields in that record (row)
permanently, leaving no evidence that the record was ever there.

You will delete a record in datasheet view (table view). The remaining
records must "close up" the gap and will be automatically renumbered.
You must make sure that the entire record is deleted and that blank fields
do not remain.

▶▶ **How to...** *delete a record*

1 In the database table, click anywhere in the record to be deleted.

2 In the **Menu** bar, click on **Edit**.

3 Click **Delete Record** (Figure 3.35).

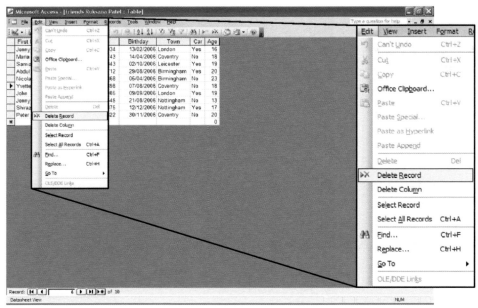

FIGURE 3.35 The Delete Record option in the drop-down Edit menu

4 Access displays a dialogue box prompting you to confirm the deletion.

5 Click **Yes** (Figure 3.36).

6 The record will be deleted and any records below will move up.

TIP!

In Access you cannot undo an action so always double check.

FIGURE 3.36 The prompt to confirm deletion

Check your understanding *Delete a record*

1 In your database table called **friends (Your Name)**.

2 Delete record number 6 for **Yvette Field**.

Points to note when entering data into a database table

Numbers

● *Numbers can be entered using the **number keypad** on the right of the keyboard (make sure the **Num Lock** key is switched on) or by using the number keys above the letters.*

● *When entering digits in a field (column) where the numbers have a fixed amount of decimal places, if you do not type the "trailing zeros" (any zeros after the decimal point) Access will automatically add them.*

Dates

● *Always use UK date format (day, month, year), it does not matter whether you use long date, short date, etc.*

● *When entering dates you may use any date format, Access will automatically convert the date format to match that of other dates in the database.*

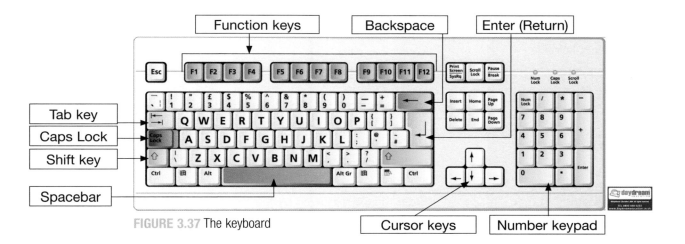

FIGURE 3.37 The keyboard

When you enter text make sure that you type the data exactly as shown and that you use the same case as shown. Examples of case:

CASE	EXAMPLE
lower case	this text is in lower case, there are no capital letters.
Initial Capitals (Title Case)	Each Of These Words Has An Initial Capital, The First Letter Of Each Word Is A Capital. This Is Known As Title Case.
UPPER CASE	THIS TEXT IS IN UPPER CASE, ALL THE LETTERS ARE CAPITAL LETTERS.

For each instance below, ensure that the cursor is in the field that you would like to amend.

HOW TO...	ACTION
Type one capital letter	Hold down the Shift key and press the required letter on the keyboard then let go of the Shift key.
Type word(s) in capital letters	Press down the Caps Lock key, a light may indicate that Caps Lock is on.
Type lower case letters	Check that Caps Lock is switched off. If not press down the Caps Lock key to turn it off.
Insert a space between words	Press the spacebar once.
Delete a letter to the left of the cursor in a field	Press the Backspace key.
Delete a letter to the right of the cursor in a field	Press the Delete key.
Enter numbers	Use the number keys above the QWERTY keys, or press Num Lock and use the number keypad. A light may indicate that Num Lock is on.
Enter a decimal point	Use the full stop key on the keyboard or the decimal point key on the number keypad.
Enter a date	Enter the day followed by the month, followed by the year in any format (long date, short date, etc.). Access will automatically reformat the date to the format set up for the database.

Replacing data

The contents of several records in one field (one column) may be the same. You may need to change the same item of data that appears in several records. To reduce the column width and to save disk space, a code can be used in a field (column) instead of displaying the whole word. Encoding data in this way helps to improve the efficiency of the database.

Access has a **Find and Replace** function which finds and replaces all instances of a word.

1 Click anywhere in the field (column) in which data needs to be replaced.

2 In the **Menu bar**, click on **Edit**.

3 Click **Replace**.

4 The **Find and Replace** dialogue box will open (Figure 3.38).

FIGURE 3.38 The Find and Replace dialogue box

5 In the **Find What** box enter the data to be replaced.

6 In the **Replace With** box enter the new data.

7 Check that the **Match** box displays **Whole Field** (if not press the down arrow and select **Whole Field**).

8 Click to place a tick in the box for **Match Case**.

9 Click the **Replace All** button.

10 Access displays a dialogue box prompting you to confirm the replace (Figure 3.39).

11 Click **Yes**.

12 Click on the cross to close the Find and Replace dialogue box.

TIP!

Do not click the **Replace** button – this will replace only one instance of the data.

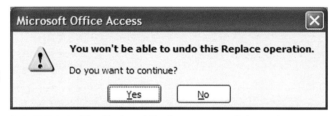

FIGURE 3.39 The Find and Replace prompt dialogue box

Check your understanding *Replace data in a field*

1 In your database table called **friends (Your Name)**.

2 Click anywhere in the **Car** field.

3 Replace all the existing data in the **Car** field as follows:

Replace Yes with **Y**

Replace No with **N**

Amending data in a database

You may need to change the content of some records, this may be done in datasheet view (in the table).

Remember that Access saves changes to data automatically, so it is important to check that you edit the **correct record** (data in one field may be similar or identical for several records) and that each edit is carried out **accurately** before moving on.

TIP!

Remember that you cannot undo previous edits in Access, you can only undo an edit immediately.

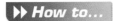 **How to...** *amend data*

1 Click in the field (cell) to be amended.

2 Delete the contents of the field (Figure 3.40).

TIP!

Click at the beginning or the end of the field content instead of in the middle. Use the **Backspace** key to delete data to the **left** of the cursor or the **Delete** key to delete data to the **right** of the cursor.

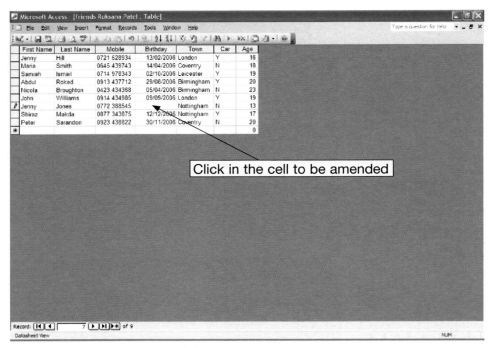

First Name	Last Name	Mobile	Birthday	Town	Car	Age
Jenny	Hill	0721 628934	13/02/2006	London	Y	16
Maria	Smith	0645 439743	14/04/2006	Coventry	N	18
Samiah	Ismail	0714 978343	02/10/2006	Leicester	Y	19
Abdul	Roked	0913 437712	29/08/2006	Birmingham	Y	20
Nicola	Broughton	0423 434368	05/04/2006	Birmingham	N	23
John	Williams	0914 434985	09/09/2006	London	Y	19
Jenny	Jones	0772 388545		Nottingham	N	13
Shiraz	Makda	0877 343875	12/12/2006	Nottingham	Y	17
Peter	Sarandon	0923 438822	30/11/2006	Coventry	N	20
						0

Click in the cell to be amended

Record: 7 of 9
Datasheet View

FIGURE 3.40 The cell to be amended in datasheet view

3 Enter the new data.

4 To amend data in another field, click in the field, delete the contents and enter the new data.

5 Access saves an amendment after you move out of the cell.

6 When you have made all amendments, click in the blank row.

TIP!

Placing the cursor in a blank field avoids any accidental changes to data.

Check your understanding *Amend data*

1 In your database table called **friends (Your Name)**.

2 Make the following amendments:

Change the Birthday for **Jenny Jones** to **21/09/2006**.

For **Samiah Ismail**, change the **Car** field to be **N** and the **Age** to be **21**.

Remember to click in a blank record when you have completed the amendments.

TIP!

There are 2 fields with the first name Jenny!

Create new records

New records can easily be added to a database table. These can only be added at the end of the table below the last record.

Data can be entered, edited or deleted in the table within datasheet view or by using a **form**. Any changes made to data using a form are automatically updated in the table. One record at a time can be viewed in a form.

To use a form, you would click the **Forms** option from the **Objects** section in the database window. Double-click to open the form (if a form has been created) and enter data in the form.

You will add records directly into the table in datasheet view, these will be automatically saved on entry.

▶▶ How to... *create new records*

1 Click the **New Record** button from the **record navigation buttons** at the bottom left of the screen to create a new record, or click in the first column of the last row (the blank row) of the database table.

2 Enter the required data in the first field.

3 Press the **Tab** key to move to the next field.

4 Enter the required data.

5 Press the **Tab** key to move from field to field, enter all the required data for a record.

6 When you have entered data in the last field of a record, press the **Tab** key to move to the next record and enter data in the same way.

7 After entering all the new records, press the Tab key to place the cursor in a blank field at the end of the table.

TIP!

To copy an entry that appears in the field above, press the **Ctrl** and ' (apostrophe) keys at the same time.

1 In your database table called **friends (Your Name)**.

2 Create records for the following four friends:

First Name	Last Name	Mobile	Birthday	Town	Car	Age
Sayed	Mahmed	0723 499982	01/02/2006	Leicester	Y	20
Sophia	Rushton	0983 234213	31/05/2005	Leicester	N	18
Roy	Walker	0941 885449	31/08/2006	Nottingham	N	18
Graham	Crawley-Griffiths	0934 134313	20/03/2006	Nottingham	N	23

TIP!

Note that the Last Name for Graham is long and may not display in full, widen the column so that you can check that all the letters will show. Use **Ctrl** and ' to copy previous entries in the same field, e.g. in the Town field for Sophia Rushton, use this to copy the entry from the record above.

TIP!

Although you can only add records at the end of a database table, you may find that when you close a table and open it again the order of records may have changed (e.g. some new records may no longer be displayed at the bottom). Access does this automatically. You do not need to change the order of records or to sort data in a table.

Spell check

Access has a tool called the spell checker that automatically checks the spelling in a table against a large dictionary. Databases often contain proper nouns and specialist words that are not in the English dictionary. The spell checker in Access has a useful feature that prompts you to instruct Access to ignore particular fields, e.g. fields with names of people.

▶▶ How to... *use spell check*

1 In the **Menu bar**, click on **Tools**.

2 Click **Spelling**.

TIP!

Click the **Spelling** icon on the toolbar instead.

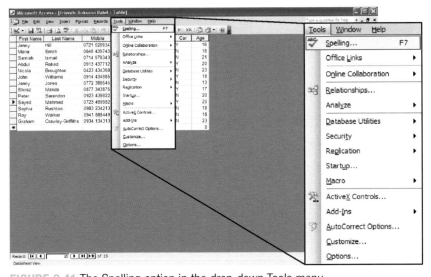

FIGURE 3.41 The Spelling option in the drop-down Tools menu

3 Access will begin a spell check.

4 If a word is found that is not in the English dictionary, this word will display in the Not In Dictionary box (Figure 3.42).

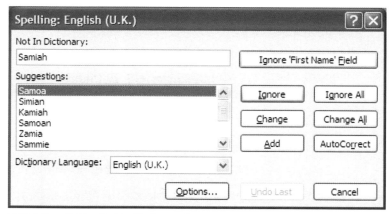

FIGURE 3.42 The Not in Dictionary box

5 Fields containing proper nouns (e.g. names of people and places) will have many words that are not in the dictionary.

6 Access has an option to ignore selected fields. Click the button for **Ignore 'xxx' field** (xxx: the name of the field in your database will display), do the same for other fields if required.

7 If you select **Ignore**, Access will continue the spell checking.

8 If an error is found a dialogue box will display (Figure 3.43).

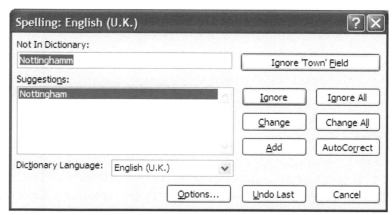

FIGURE 3.43 A suggested correction for a misspelling

9 The incorrect word will display in the top row and a suggestion may be given in the second box.

10 Click **Change** to accept the suggestion, or click **Ignore** to reject it, and enter the correct spelling in the **Not In Dictionary** box and click **Change**.

11 When the spell check is complete a dialogue box will display (Figure 3.44).

12 Click **OK**.

FIGURE 3.44 This dialogue box appears at the end of the spell check

---

Check your understanding *Spell check your database*

1 In your database table called **friends (Your Name)**.

2 Carry out a spell check, correct any errors if necessary.

3 Click on **Ignore First Name field** and **Ignore Last Name field** when prompted by Access.

Use the skills that you have learned on pages 251–255 for How to... set the orientation, How to... change column widths, How to... use Print Preview and How to... print a table.

1 In your database table called **friends (Your Name)**.

2 Set the orientation to **landscape**.

3 Change the column widths, if required, so that all data is fully displayed.

4 Save the changes to the table layout (if necessary).

5 Use **Print Preview** to check:

The orientation.

That all data fits on one page.

That all data is displayed in full.

6 Close Print Preview.

7 If necessary, adjust any field widths and use Print Preview again.

8 Print the database table called **friends (Your Name)**.

Check your printout, it should look similar to the one shown in Figure 3.45.

If there are any errors in your table, open the table in datasheet view, click in the relevant field and correct these before carrying on.

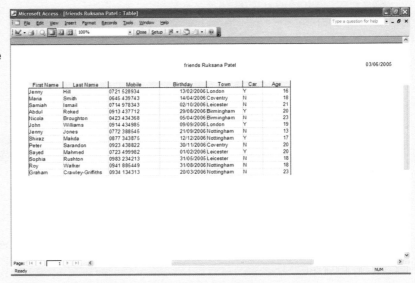

FIGURE 3.45 The database table in Print Preview

How to... *close a database table*

1 In the **Menu bar**, click on **File**.

2 Click **Close** (Figure 3.46).

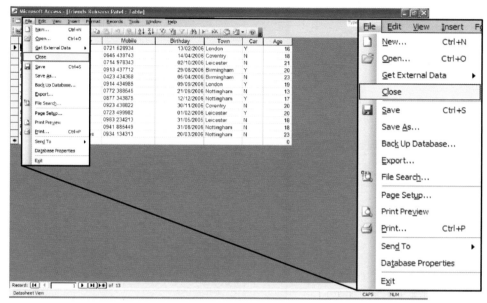

FIGURE 3.46 The Close option in the drop-down File menu

3 You will see the **database window**. The Objects will be on the far left if the window is maximized (Figure 3.47).

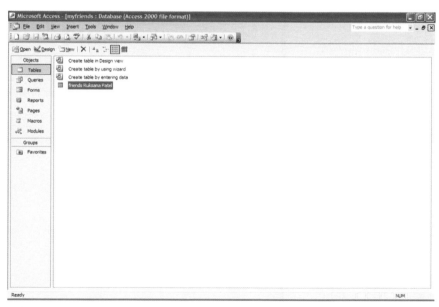

FIGURE 3.47 The database window

1 Close the database table called **friends (Your Name)**.

▶▶ How to... *close Access*

1 In the **Menu bar**, click on **File**.

2 Click **Exit** (Figure 3.48).

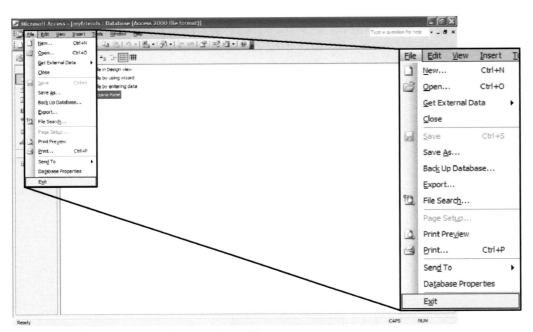

FIGURE 3.48 The Exit option in the drop-down File menu

1 Close the database called **myfriends** and exit Access.

ASSESS YOUR SKILLS – Update a database

By working through Section 1 you will have learnt the skills below. Read each item to help you decide how confident you feel about each skill.

- start Access
- open a provided database
- identify the different parts of the database window
- identify database objects (table, queries, reports)
- rename a table
- open a database table
- identify the parts of a table in datasheet view
- understand database terms (table, field, record)
- move around a database table
- set the orientation
- change column widths
- save the table layout
- use Print Preview
- print a database table
- delete a record
- amend data in existing records
- create new records
- use spell check
- prepare to print the updated table:
  - set the orientation
  - change column widths to make sure that all records are displayed in full and that the table will fit on one page
- save the updated table
- print the updated table
- close the updated table
- exit Access.

If you think you need more practice on any of the skills above, go back and work through the skill(s) again.

If you feel confident, move on to Section 2.

LEARNING OUTCOMES

In this section you will learn how to:

- understand queries
- go to the query design view
- select field names to query
- enter the selection criterion
- understand sorting of data
- sort data
- present (display) selected fields
- run queries
- save queries with specified filenames
- use Print Preview to preview queries
- print queries
- close queries
- understand comparison operators in numeric fields
- create queries using comparison operators in numeric fields
- understand comparison operators in dates
- create queries using comparison operators in date fields
- select data on two criteria.

Understanding queries

A query is used in a database to ask questions about the data in the database table in order to find specific information. To find the specific information, appropriate "selection conditions" are entered into a query design.

The term used to describe the selection conditions is **criteria** (a single criteria is referred to as a **criterion**). You will be creating queries using one criterion and two criteria.

The advantage of a query over other methods of finding specific information (e.g. filters) is that when a database table is amended or updated, a saved query is also automatically updated. This is referred to as **live data handling**.

There are many ways of creating queries, two frequently used ways are:

- *creating a query using the wizard*
- *creating a query in design view.*

You will learn how to create queries in design view.

▶▶ How to... *open the query design view*

There are a number of ways of going to the query design view, one of these methods is shown below.

1. Close the database table.
2. From the database window click on **Queries** in the **Objects** section.
3. Click **Create query in Design view**.
4. Click **Open**.
5. A **Show Table** window opens.
6. Click to highlight the table name.
7. Click **Add**.
8. Click **Close**.

However, using the icons on the toolbar allows you to perform actions much quicker, e.g. save or print. Similarly, it is quicker to use the icon on the toolbar to go to the query design view. You will learn how to use the quicker way.

Creating queries

You will learn how to create a query in 6 steps.

1. Go to the **query design view**.
2. **Select field names** and drag to the query grid.
3. Enter the selection (query) **criteria**.
4. **Sort** data.
5. **Display** (present) selected fields.
6. **Run** the query.

You will then learn how to:

7. **Save** the query with a specified name.
8. Use Print Preview and **print** the query.
9. **Close** the query.

▶▶ How to... *go to the query design view*

1. Open the database table in datasheet view.
2. Click the drop-down arrow next to **New Object: AutoForm** ▾ on the toolbar.

3 A drop-down list will display (Figure 3.49).

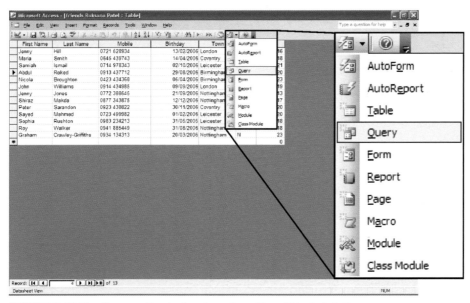

FIGURE 3.49 The Query option in the drop-down New Object: AutoForm menu

4 Click **Query** from the list.

5 A **New Query** dialogue box will open (Figure 3.50).

6 Check that **Design View** is selected.

7 Click **OK**.

8 You will see the query design view (Figure 3.51).

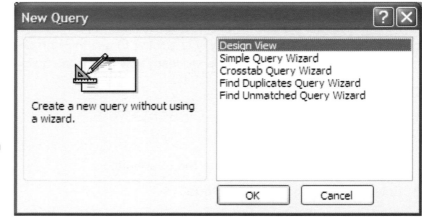

FIGURE 3.50 Design View highlighted in the New Query dialogue box

The New Object button on the toolbar

The first time that you hover with your mouse on the **New Object** button on the toolbar, the Tool tip displays as New Object: AutoForm.

Once you have used this button, Access remembers which option you selected from the drop-down list and changes the button accordingly. If you had selected **Query**, when you hover with your mouse over the button it looks different and the Tool tip now displays as New Object: Query.

You can either click on the button to go straight to the New Query dialogue box, or click the drop-down arrow, a menu displays, click **Query** from this menu.

1 In your database table called **friends (Your Name)**.

2 Ensure the table is open in **datasheet view**.

3 Click the drop-down arrow next to the **New Object** button.

4 Select **Query** from the drop-down list.

5 Click **OK** in the New Query window.

Getting familiar with the query design view

When you go to the query design view of your database table you should
see a screen like the one in Figure 3.51.

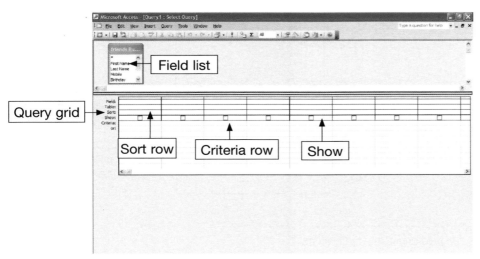

FIGURE 3.51 The query design view

What does it mean?

Field list	Displays the table name at the top in the shaded area (usually blue) and the list of field headings from the database table.	
Query grid	(consists of 6 rows)	
	Field	Displays the field name (field heading).
	Table	Displays the name of the database table.
	Sort	When clicked in, displays a drop-down arrow with 3 sort options.
	Show	If ticked the field (column) will be displayed in the query result.
	Criteria	The selection condition should be entered in this row.
	or	More advanced selection conditions may be entered in this row.

FIGURE 3.52 All items in the field list box are selected

1 Position your mouse pointer on the database **table name** (usually blue) at the top of the **field list** box.

2 **Double-click.**

3 All the field names become highlighted (Figure 3.52).

4 Click in the highlighted area, hold the left mouse button down.

5 The mouse pointer will change 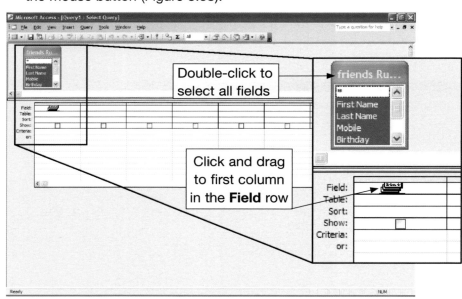 (looks like 3 boxes).

6 Drag to the first column in the **Field** row in the query grid. Release the mouse button (Figure 3.53).

TIP!

This method of selecting fields ensures that no fields are left out (e.g. field names that are at the bottom of the list).

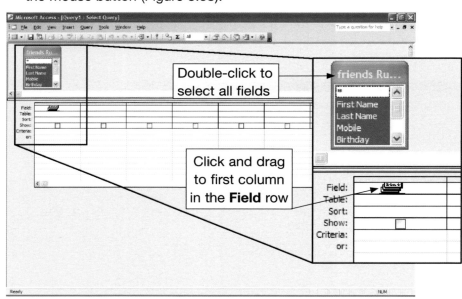

FIGURE 3.53 The selected fields can be dragged into the Field row

TIP!

Another way to select fields to be placed in the query grid is to double-click on each field name.

7 All the field names will be displayed in the **Field** row in all columns (Figure 3.54).

8 The table name will display in the **Table** row in all columns.

9 A tick will display in the **Show** row in each box.

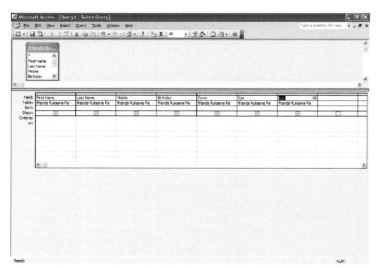

FIGURE 3.54 The selected fields are now all placed and Show is automatically selected

1 In the query design view double-click on the table name **friends (Your Name)**.

2 Drag all the field names into the query grid.

3 Remain in the query design view.

▶▶ How to... *enter the selection (query) criteria*

1 Click in the **Criteria** row of the field (column) to be queried.

2 Enter the required criteria. You must enter the criteria with **100**% accuracy because Access will only find records that are an exact match (Figure 3.55).

TIP!

In the Criteria row text can be entered in upper or lower case.

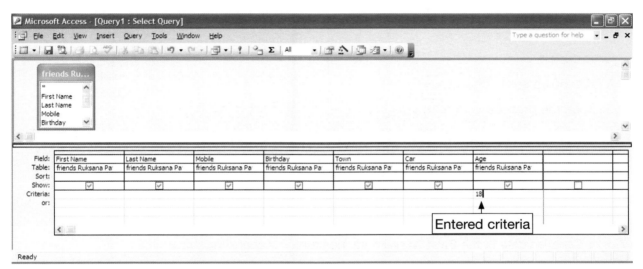

FIGURE 3.55 Entering criteria for a query in query design view

1 Click in the **Age** field (column).

2 Enter the selection criteria **18**.

Understanding sorting of data

The order in which records are displayed in a query can be changed (re-ordered) so that certain data is clearer to identify. For example, in your database table called **friends (Your Name)**, it might help you if the data in the Town field (column) was sorted in alphabetical (ascending) order. This would make it easier for you to see at a glance which of your friends lived in Birmingham, Coventry, Leicester or Nottingham.

Text, numbers and dates can be sorted in ascending or descending order. Look at the table below to help you understand how text, numbers and dates are sorted in ascending and descending order.

TEXT		NUMBERS		DATES	
Ascending (A to Z)	Descending (Z to A)	Ascending (1 to 100)	Descending (100 to 1)	Ascending (01/01/2006 to 31/12/2006)	Descending (31/12/2006 to 01/01/2006)
Alice	Fay	14	34	28/01/2006	30/11/2006
Amanda	Bilkis	21	28	19/03/2006	29/08/2006
Bilkis	Amanda	28	21	29/08/2006	19/03/2006
Fay	Alice	34	14	30/11/2006	28/01/2006

▶▶ How to... *sort data in a query*

1 In the query design view, click in the **Sort** row of the field to be sorted.

2 A drop-down arrow displays.

3 Click on the drop-down arrow.

4 A drop-down list will display (Figure 3.56).

5 Click on **Ascending** or **Descending** from this list.

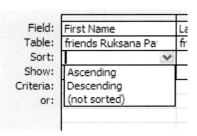

FIGURE 3.56 The drop-down list in the Sort row

Check your understanding *Sort data (text)*

1 Sort the data in the **First Name** field (column) in **Ascending** order.

Display selected fields

When you query a database table only certain records are displayed. Similarly, you may only want to display certain fields (columns).

Look at the **Show** row in your query grid. Ticks are displayed in all columns, this is done automatically by Access. Any field that is ticked will display in the query result.

You may choose to display only some fields in the query result.

▶▶ How to... *display selected fields*

1 Click in the **Show** box to remove the tick for the fields (columns) that you do not want to display.

2 Unless otherwise instructed, fields may be displayed in any order.

TIP!

You do not need to display a field in which you entered selection criteria.

1 Display only the **First Name**, **Last Name**, **Mobile** and **Town** fields.

▶▶ How to... *run the query*

1 Click the **Run** icon ! on the **toolbar**.

2 The results of the query will be displayed as a table in datasheet view.

3 Look at the **record navigation buttons** in the bottom left of your screen. The number of records in the query result displays.

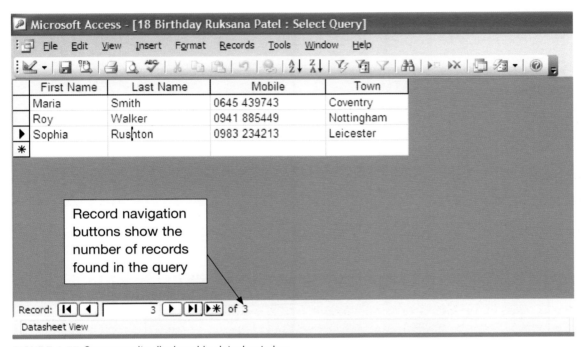

FIGURE 3.57 Query results displayed in datasheet view

1 Run your query.

▶▶ How to... *return to the query design view*

Once you have run your query, check that records found:

● *meet the selection criteria*

● *have been sorted correctly, and that*

● *selected fields are displayed.*

If you need to make changes, you can do these by returning to the query design view.

1 Click the **View** icon ![view icon] on the **toolbar**.

2 You will return to the query design view.

3 Make any changes as needed.

4 To return to the datasheet view, click the **View** ![view icon] icon again.

Check your understanding *Return to the query design view*

1 Click the **View** icon on the toolbar to return to the query design view.

2 If you need to make any changes (e.g. to the number of fields displayed or to the sort order, then make these changes).

3 Return to datasheet view.

Saving queries

It is helpful to use meaningful names for all queries. To display your name on a query printout, you should add your name to the query name.

▶▶ How to... *save a new query with a specified name*

1 In the **Menu bar**, click on **File**.

2 Click **Save**.

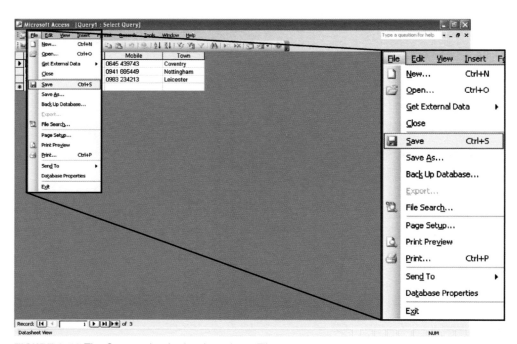

FIGURE 3.58 The Save option in the drop-down File menu

3 A **Save As** dialogue box will open.

4 Delete the text **Query1**.

5 Enter the required query name (Figure 3.59).

6 Click **OK**.

7 The query will be saved and the name will be displayed in the title bar of the query window (or, if the query is maximized, in the title bar at the top of the screen, as shown in Figure 3.60).

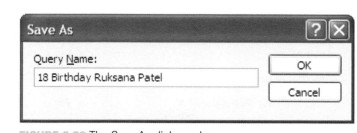

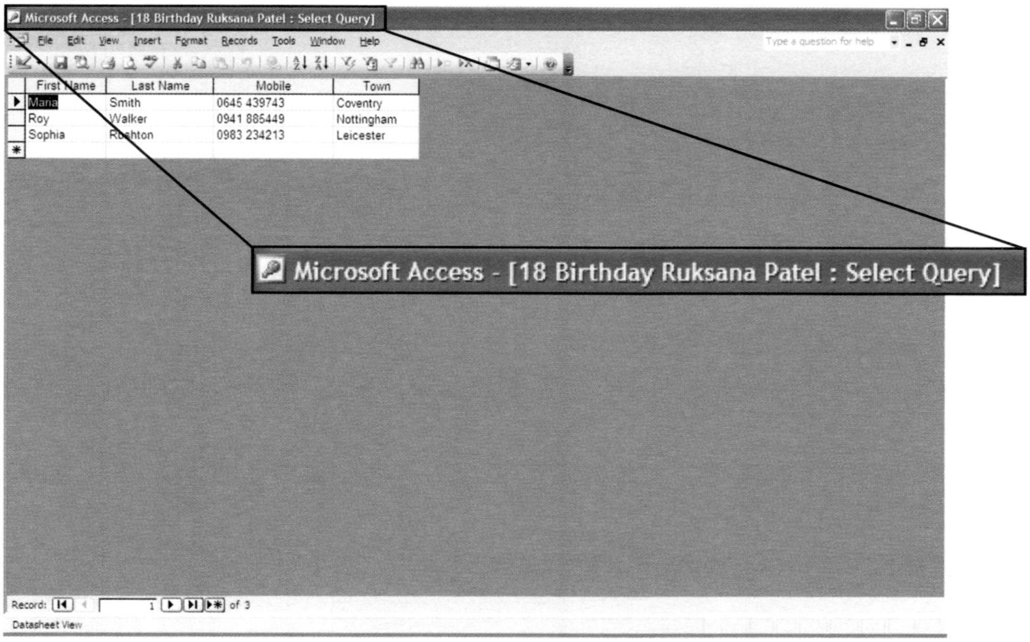

FIGURE 3.59 The Save As dialogue box

FIGURE 3.60 The title of the query now appears in the title bar

Check your understanding *Save a query*

1 Save your query using the filename **18 Birthday (Your Name)**.

Printing a query

Before you print a query you must:

○ use **Print Preview**

○ change the **column widths** (if necessary)

○ change the **orientation** (if necessary). Remember that the default orientation is portrait.

Only then should you print the query. A query is printed in the same way as a table.

The query should be open in datasheet view (as a table).

1 In the **Menu bar**, click on **File**.

2 Click **Print Preview**.

3 Move your mouse over the page.

4 The mouse pointer changes to a zoom 🔍 tool.

5 Click in the page to zoom in.

6 Check that all columns are wide enough to display all data in full.

7 If any data is not fully displayed note which fields need to be made wider.

8 Click the Close button on the Preview toolbar to close Print Preview.

9 You will return to the query (datasheet view).

10 If required, adjust any column widths and use **Print Preview** again.

1 In the **Menu bar**, click on **File**.

2 Click **Print** (Figure 3.61).

TIP!

Alternatively, click the Print Preview 🔍 icon on the toolbar instead to skip straight to step 3.

TIP!

Click again to zoom out and zoom in to another part of the query.

TIP!

Click the **Print** 🖨 icon on the toolbar instead.

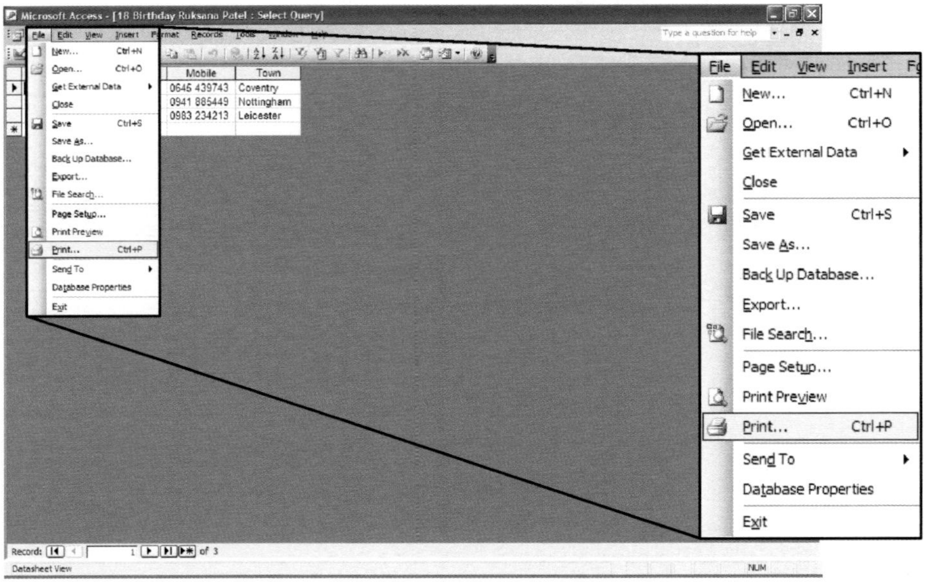

FIGURE 3.61 The Print option in the drop-down File menu

3 A **Print** dialogue box will open (Figure 3.62).

4 Click **OK**.

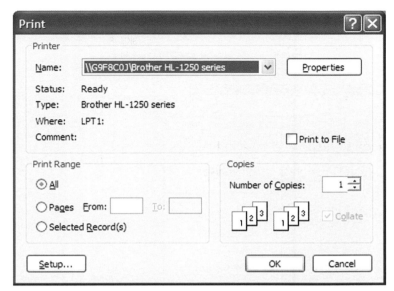

FIGURE 3.62 The Print dialogue box

Check your understanding *Print a query*

1 Print your query **18 Birthday (Your Name)**.

Check your printout, it should look similar to the one shown in Figure 3.63.

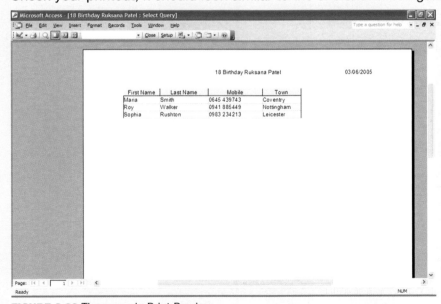

FIGURE 3.63 The query in Print Preview

You should have 3 records and 4 fields.

1 In the **Menu bar**, click on **File**.

2 Click **Close**.

3 You will see the database table.

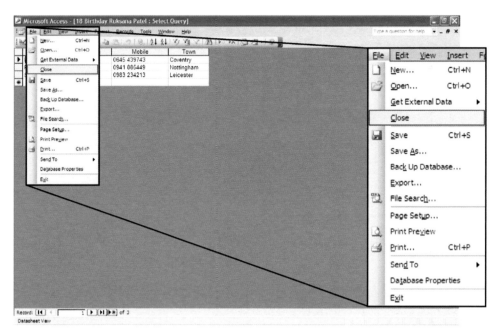

FIGURE 3.64 The Close option in the drcp-down File menu

Check your understanding *Close a query*

1 Close your query **18 Birthday (Your Name)**.

Understanding comparison operators

Where numbers or dates are used in tables, using comparison operators in a query allows you to search for specific numbers or dates.

Comparison operators in numeric fields

Look at your database table called **friends (Your Name)**.

To create a query in the **Age** field (which is numeric), you can use different comparison operators as shown opposite.

TIP!

To find any friends aged exactly 16, you do not need to enter the equals sign, just enter the number 16 in the criteria row. Access will find records that are an exact match.

Using comparison numeric fields

SYMBOL	WHAT IT MEANS	HOW TO ENTER THE CRITERIA	WHAT THE CRITERIA WILL FIND	HOW MANY RECORDS WILL MEET THE CRITERIA
>	More than	>16	All friends that are over 16 years old	11
>=	More than or equal to	>=16	All friends that are 16 and all those that are over 16	12
<	Less than	<16	All friends that are less than 16 years old	1
<=	Less than or equal to	<=16	All friends that are 16 or younger than 16	2

Check your understanding
Create queries using operators in a numeric field

1 In your database table called **friends (Your Name)**.

2 Create a new query.

3 Drag all the fields to the query grid.

4 Select all friends whose **Age** is **over 16**.

5 Display only the **First Name**, **Last Name** and **Birthday** fields.

6 Sort the data in **descending** order of **Last Name**.

7 Run the query.

8 The query will display in datasheet view.

9 Look at the record navigation buttons in the bottom left of the screen.

10 This should display **11** records (Figure 3.65).

11 Save the query using the name **Over 16 (Your Name)**.

FIGURE 3.65 The record navigation panel shows the number of records found

12 Use **Print Preview** and make any necessary adjustments to the query in datasheet view.

13 Print the results of the query.

14 Close the query.

(Continued overleaf)

15 Keep the table open in datasheet view.

Check your printout, it should look similar to Figure 3.66.

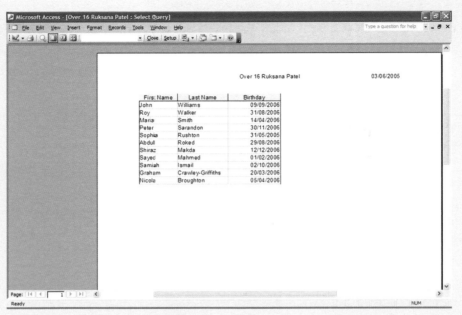

FIGURE 3.66 The query in Print Preview

You should have 11 records and 3 fields.

Check your understanding
Practice creating queries using operators in numeric fields

1 Create a new query.

2 Select all friends whose **Age** is **16 or over**.

3 Run the query.

Look at the record navigation buttons at the bottom of the screen, the number of records found should be **12**. You do not need to save the query – close it without saving.

4 Create a new query.

5 Select all friends whose **Age** is **Under 16**.

6 Run the query.

Look at the record navigation buttons at the bottom of the screen, the number of records found should be **1**. You do not need to save the query – close it without saving

7 Create a new query.

8 Select all friends whose **Age** is **16 or under**.

(Continued overleaf)

9 Run the query.

Look at the record navigation buttons at the bottom of the screen, the number of records found should be **2**. You do not need to save the query – close it without saving.

10 When you close the last query, you should return to the table in datasheet view.

11 Keep the table open.

Comparison operators in date fields

Look at your database table called **friends (Your Name)**.

To create a query in the **Birthday** field (which has dates), you can use different comparison operators.

What does it mean?

Using comparison operators in date fields

SYMBOL	WHAT IT MEANS	HOW TO ENTER THE CRITERIA	WHAT THE CRITERIA WILL FIND	HOW MANY RECORDS WILL MEET THE CRITERIA
>	After	>31/08/2006	All friends whose birthdays are after 31/08/2006	5
>=	On or after	>=31/08/2006	All friends whose birthdays are on 31/08/2006 or after 31/08/2006	6
<	Before	<31/08/2006	All friends whose birthdays are before 31/08/2006	7
<=	On or before	<=31/08/2006	All friends whose birthdays are on 31/08/2006 or before 31/08/2006	8

1 In your database table called **friends (Your Name)**.

2 Create a new query.

3 Select all friends whose **Birthday** is **on or after 31/08/2006**.

4 Sort the query in **ascending** order of birthday.

5 Display only the **First Name**, **Mobile** and **Age** fields.

6 Run the query.

7 Save the query as **Parties (Your Name)**.

8 Use **Print Preview**, make any necessary changes to column widths in datasheet view.

9 Print the query.

10 Close the query.

Check your printout, it should look similar to Figure 3.67.

You should have 6 records and 3 fields.

> **TIP!**
>
> In the query design view, if you click in another column after entering the date criteria, you will see that Access displays a # (hash) sign before and after the date.

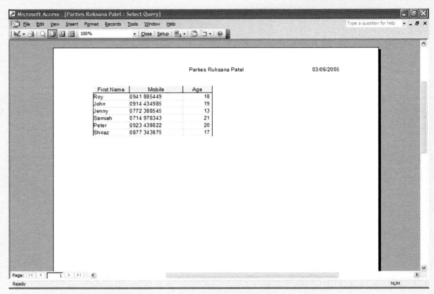

FIGURE 3.67 The query displayed in Print Preview

Practice creating queries using operators in date fields

11 Create a new query.

12 Select all friends whose birthday is **after 31/08/2006**.

13 Run the query.

Look at the record navigation buttons at the bottom of the screen, the number of records found should be **5**. You do not need to save the query – return to the query design view and change the query criteria.

14 Select all friends whose **Birthday** is **before 31/08/2006**.

(Continued overleaf)

15 Run the query.

Look at the record navigation buttons at the bottom of the screen, the number of records found should be **7**. You do not need to save the query – close it without saving.

16 Create a new query.

17 Select all friends whose **Birthday** is **on or before 31/08/2006**.

18 Run the query.

Look at the record navigation buttons at the bottom of the screen, the number of records found should be **8**. You do not need to save the query – close it without saving.

19 When you close the last query, you should return to the table in datasheet view.

20 Close the database table and exit Access.

Selecting data on two criteria

You may need to find records that meet selection criteria in two fields. For example, if you are organising a party in Birmingham, you may want to know which of your friends that live in Nottingham do not have a car. You would need to enter selection criteria in the **Town** field and in the **Car** field.

▶▶ How to... *create a query using two criteria*

1 Open the database table in datasheet view.

2 Create a new query.

3 Drag all the fields into the query grid.

4 Click in the **Criteria** row of the first field to be queried.

5 Enter the selection criteria.

6 Click in the **Criteria** row of the second field to be queried.

7 **Sort** the data as required.

8 Click in the **Show** box to remove the display of fields as required.

9 **Run** the query.

10 **Save** the query.

1 In your database table called **friends (Your Name)**.

2 Create a new query.

3 Drag all the fields to the query grid.

4 Select all the records where the **Town** is **Nottingham** and **Car** is **N**.

5 Sort the query in ascending order of **First Name**.

6 Display only the **First Name**, **Mobile**, **Town** and **Car** fields.

7 Run the query.

8 Save the query using the name **Notts No Car (Your Name)**.

9 Use **Print Preview**, make any necessary changes to column widths in datasheet view.

10 Print the query.

11 Close the query.

12 Close the database window.

13 Exit Access.

Check your printout, it should look similar to Figure 3.68.

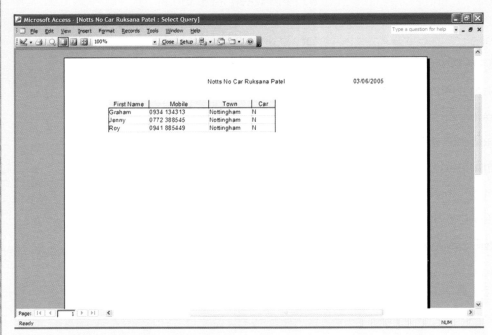

FIGURE 3.68 The query in Print Preview

You should have 3 records and 4 fields.

ASSESS YOUR SKILLS – Create queries

By working through Section 2 you will have learnt the skills listed below. Read each item to help you decide how confident you feel about each skill.

- understand queries
- go to the query design view
- understand how to use the New Object button
- select field names to query
- enter the selection criterion
- understand sorting of data
- sort data
- present (display) selected fields
- run queries
- save queries with specified filenames
- use Print Preview to preview queries
- print queries
- close queries
- understand comparison operators in numeric fields
- create queries using operators in numeric fields
- understand comparison operators in date fields
- create queries using operators in date fields
- select data on two criteria.

If you think you need more practice on any of the skills above, go back and work through the skill(s) again.

If you feel confident, move on to Section 3.

LEARNING OUTCOMES

In this section you will learn how to:

- understand reports
- open a saved query
- create a simple tabular report
- check that data is displayed in full
- go to the report design view
- enter a report title
- move fields
- widen fields
- check headers and footers
- save a report with a specified filename
- print a report
- view the objects in a database
- close and exit Access.

Understanding reports

Reports are used to produce professional-looking printouts of the data in a database table or in a query. There are many different report styles and layouts available in Access.

A tabular report displays field names (column headings) at the top of the page with records in rows across the page. There are more formatting and layout options available for reports than there are for tables or queries in datasheet view. You will only be required to create a simple, tabular report.

An **AutoReport** can be generated directly from the table or query in the database. It is one of the quickest ways to create a simple, tabular report.

▶▶ How to... *start Access and open a database*

1. Click the **Start** button, click **All Programs**, click **Microsoft Office**, then click **Microsoft Office Access 2003**.

2. In the **Menu bar** click on **File**, then click **Open**.

3 From your user area, open your updated database.

4 The database will open in the database window.

Make sure that you open the updated database, not any original ones or backups.

▶▶ How to... *open a saved query*

1 In the **Objects** section click on **Queries**. The saved queries will display (Figure 3.69).

2 Click on the name of the query you want to open.

3 Click **Open**.

4 The query will open in datasheet view.

5 Click **Maximize** in the query window.

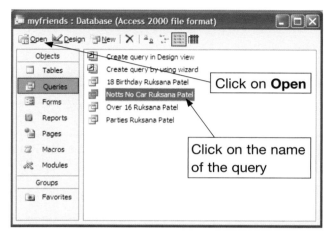

FIGURE 3.69 The Queries in the Objects section of the database window

▶▶ How to... *create a simple report*

1 Make sure the query is open in datasheet view (as a table).

2 Click the drop-down arrow next to **New Object button** on the toolbar.

3 A drop-down list will display (Figure 3.70).

4 Click **Report** from the list.

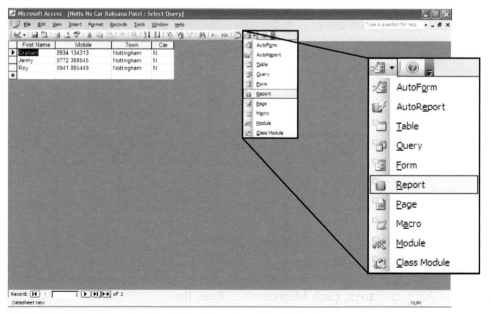

TIP!

If you have used the New Object: AutoForm icon once, the next time it may display as New Object: Query or New Object: Report.

FIGURE 3.70 The Report option in the drop-down New Object menu

5 A **New Report** dialogue box will open (Figure 3.71).

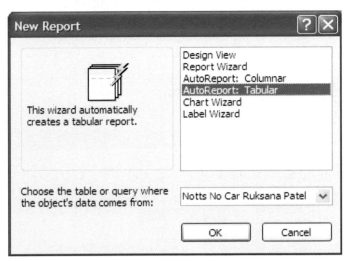

FIGURE 3.71 The AutoReport: Tabular option in the New Report dialogue box

6 Click on **AutoReport: Tabular**.

7 Click **OK**.

8 Access will create the report automatically and will display it in Print Preview.

Check your understanding *Create a simple report*

1 Start Access.

2 Open the database called **myfriends**.

3 From the database window, click on **Queries** in the **Objects** section.

4 Open your saved query called **Notts No Car (Your Name)**.

5 With the query open in datasheet view, click the down arrow next to the **New Object** icon and select **Report** from the drop-down list.

6 From the **New Report** window, click **AutoReport**: **Tabular**.

7 Click **OK**.

▶▶ How to... *check that all data is displayed in full on a report*

1 Display your report in **Print Preview**, move your mouse over the report.

2 It changes to a zoom tool 🔍.

3 Click once in the report to zoom in.

4 Check that all columns are wide enough to display all data in full.

5 Click again to zoom out and then zoom in to other parts of the report.

6 If any data is not fully displayed note which columns need to be widened.

TIP!

Notice that Access automatically displays the date and the page numbers at the bottom of the report.

TIP!

Do not click the ☒ icon in Print Preview. This will close the report.

Check that all data is fully displayed on a report

1 In **Print Preview**, view your report titled **Notts No Car (Your Name)**.

2 Use the **zoom tool** to zoom in to the report title, each of the field headings and all the records to make sure that all data is displayed in full.

3 Click again to zoom out and view the whole report.

4 Make a note of any changes that need to be made to your report (e.g. report title, field width).

Check your screen, the Print Preview of your report should look similar to Figure 3.72.

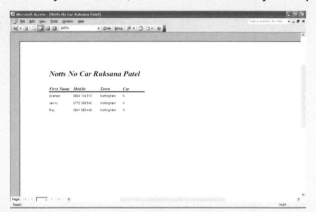

FIGURE 3.72 The Notts No Car (Your Name) report displayed in Print Preview

▶▶ How to... *go to the report design view*

1 Click on the **View** icon in the **toolbar**.

2 The report will display in design view.

1 Click the **View** icon on the toolbar to go the design view of your report titled **Notts No Car (Your Name)**.

2 Check the headers and footers, make sure that the date and page number are displayed (Figure 3.73).

Understanding the report design view

The design view of a report can appear to be confusing. Not all of the records in your query (or table, if the report is based on a table) display and the report has different sections.

In Level 1 you will not need to make many amendments in the design view so do not be concerned if you think that it appears difficult to understand.

Have a look at the boxes (called controls) in the white areas of your report and the labels in Figure 3.73. These should help you to understand the parts of a report.

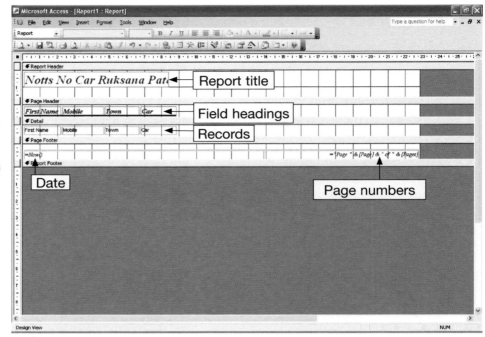

FIGURE 3.73 The report design view

Displaying data in full in a report

When you create an AutoReport it displays automatically in Print Preview. You should make a note of any parts of the report that need to be made wider and any changes that you need to make. While you are in Print Preview, check that the report title, the field headings and all of the records are fully displayed.

In the report design view, if you need to widen the report title or the last field, this is quite straightforward to do. However, if you need to widen any other field (i.e. one between two other columns that display data), you will need to move any fields that are to the right of that field before you can widen it. If your report is based on a query, there will not be many fields displayed and all field headings and records are likely to be fully displayed in the report. However, it is useful to learn how to widen fields and how to move fields.

Headers and footers in reports

Access automatically displays the date and the number of pages in a report, therefore you will not have to insert these in the headers or footers. However, when you preview the report, you should check that these are displayed. In the report design view, the date displays as =Now().

Page orientation

Access automatically displays AutoReports in landscape orientation. If you need to change the orientation, from the **Menu bar** click on **File**, click **Page Setup** and choose **Portrait** in the **Page** tab. Margins can also be changed in this window.

1 In the report design view.

2 Click anywhere in the report title text (in the **Report Header** section).

3 Square handles will appear around the title.

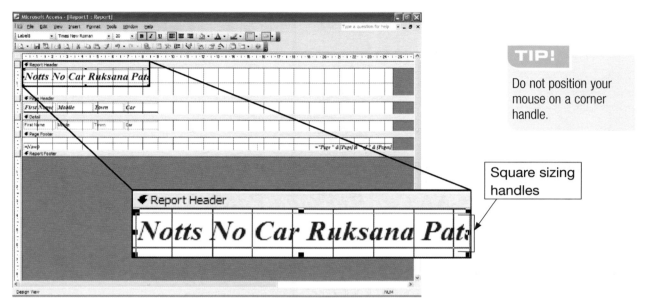

TIP!

Do not position your mouse on a corner handle.

Square sizing handles

FIGURE 3.74 The report title in the Report Header box

4 Position your mouse on the square handle on the right-hand side of the title.

5 The mouse pointer will change to a double-ended arrow.

6 Click and drag the square handle further to the right to make the box (control) for the report title wider.

7 Release the mouse button.

Check your understanding
Make the report title control (box) wider

Your report title may have been fully displayed when you previewed your report, work through this task as practice because you may need to widen the report title in another task.

1 In the **design view** of your report titled **Notts No Car (Your Name)**.

2 Click in the report title box (control) to display the square handles.

3 Drag the right-hand side of the box further to the right.

4 Once the box (control) is wide enough, release the mouse button.

1 In the report **design view** click in the box for the report title.

2 A cursor will display.

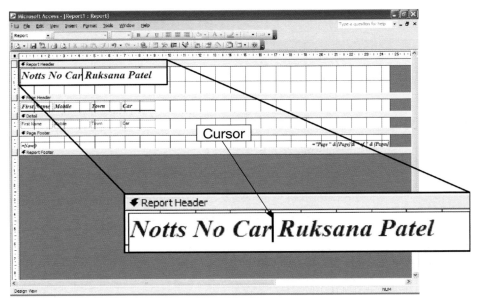

FIGURE 3.75 Editing the report title

3 Delete the word(s) that is/are not required.

4 Enter the required word(s).

5 Click in the grey work area below the report (so that you don't accidentally select or change any part of the report).

6 The report will be titled with the new name.

Check your understanding *Title a report*

1 In the **design view** of your report titled **Notts No Car (Your Name)**.

2 Delete the text **No Car** and enter the word **Friends** so that the report title is **Notts Friends (Your Name)**.

3 Click in the grey area below your report.

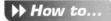 **How to...** *select field heading(s) and records (field detail)*

Before you can move fields you need to select the field heading(s) and the records (field detail).

1 In the report **design view**, click once on the box (control) for the first field name (below **Page Header**).

2 Square handles display around the field heading (Figure 3.76).

3 Hold down the **Shift** key on the keyboard.

4 Click on the field name in the **Detail** section.

5 Square handles display around the field heading **and** the field content (Figure 3.77).

6 If you need to move another field repeat this: keep the **Shift** key held down and click in the box for the **Field Heading** and for the **Detail**.

7 Release the **Shift** key.

8 You have now selected the field heading(s) and records (field detail) to be moved further to the right (Figure 3.78).

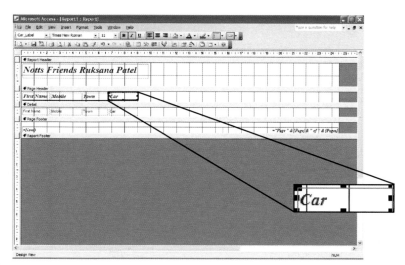

FIGURE 3.76 Square sizing handles in design view

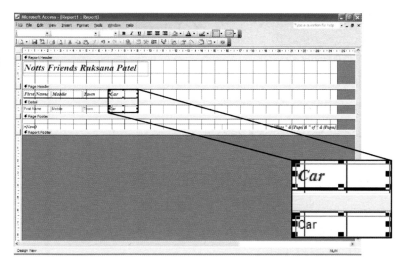

FIGURE 3.77 Square sizing handles in both the field heading and field content sections

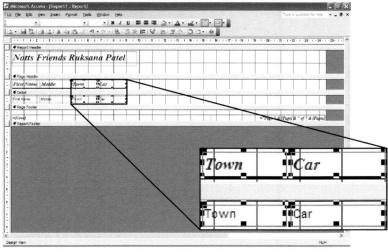

FIGURE 3.78 Field headings and records are selected for movement

TIP!

Once you have made your selection do not click on any part of the screen, you may deselect any boxes (controls) if you click.

All the records in your report may have been fully displayed when you viewed the report in Print Preview, but work through this task as practice because you may need to select, move and widen fields in another task.

1 In the **design view** of your report titled **Notts Friends (Your Name)**.

2 Select the field headings **Town** and **Car** and the detail boxes for **Town** and **Car**.

▶▶ *How to...* **move field headings and records in a report**

1 Position your mouse anywhere in the boxes that you have selected (don't click!).

2 The mouse pointer changes to a hand.

You are going to move the fields to the right by clicking and dragging the boxes (controls).

3 Click and drag the mouse to move the selected boxes to the right.

4 Release the mouse button.

5 The fields will be moved.

1 In the **design view** of your report titled **Notts Friends (Your Name)**.

2 You should have four boxes (controls) selected.

3 Move these boxes to the right so that there will be enough room to make the **Mobile** field wider.

4 Release the mouse button.

▶▶ *How to...* **widen a field**

1 In the report **design view**, click once on the field name in the Page Header section.

2 Hold the **Shift** key down and click once on the field detail in the Detail section.

3 Release the mouse button.

4 Position your mouse on the handle on the right-hand side of either one of the selected boxes (field heading or field detail box).

5 The mouse changes to a double-ended arrow.

6 Drag the mouse to the right.

TIP!

Do not use the corner handle.

7 Both the field heading and the content (the records) will be widened.

8 Click the **Print Preview** icon to check that all data will display in full when printed.

If you need to make any changes, click the **View** icon  to return to design view. Make any necessary changes and click the **Print Preview** icon to return to Print Preview.

Check your understanding
Select a field heading and detail and make the field wider

All the numbers in the Mobile column of your report may have been fully displayed when you viewed the report in Print Preview, but work through this task as practice because you may need to widen field(s) in another task.

1 In the **design view** of your report titled **Notts Friends (Your Name)**.

2 Select the **Mobile** field heading and the **Detail** of the Mobile field.

3 Make the field wider.

Saving reports

It is helpful to use meaningful names for all reports.

▶▶ **How to...** *save a report with a specified name*

1 In the **Menu bar**, click on **File**.

2 Click **Save** (Figure 3.79).

3 A **Save As** dialogue box will open.

4 The name of the query that the report was based on will display.

5 Delete the query name.

6 Enter the required report name (Figure 3.80).

7 Click **OK**.

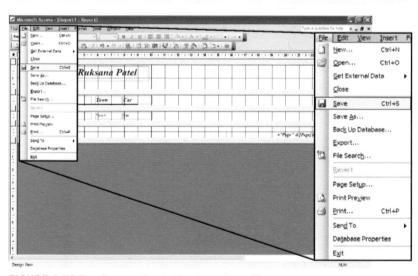

FIGURE 3.79 The Save option in the drop-down File menu

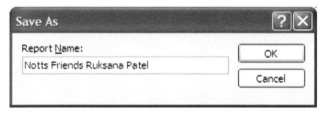

FIGURE 3.80 The Save As dialogue box

Check your understanding *Save a report*

1 Save your report using the filename **Notts Friends (Your Name)**.

▶▶ How to... *print a report*

1 Display your report in **Print Preview** and ensure that all the data displays in full.

2 Click the **Print** icon on the toolbar (or click the **File** menu, click **Print**, then **OK**).

3 The report will be printed.

4 Check your printout to make sure that all data is fully displayed.

Check your understanding *Print a report*

1 Use **Print Preview** to make sure that the title, field headings and all records are fully displayed.

2 Print your report titled **Notts Friends (Your Name)**.

Check your report, it should look similar to Figure 3.81. Note that when you create reports using the AutoReport method, the Access title bar will display the name of the query that the report was based on, this does not print and is acceptable. The report title that you entered will display correctly on the printout.

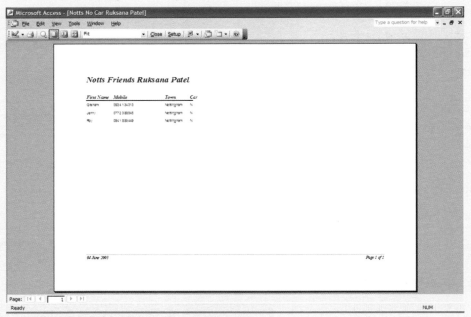

FIGURE 3.81 The report in Print Preview

▶▶ How to... *close a report*

1 In the **Menu bar,** click on **File**.

2 Click **Close**.

3 You will see the database window.

1 Close your report **Notts Friends (Your Name)**.

2 Exit Access.

ASSESS YOUR SKILLS – Create a report

By working through Section 3 you will have learnt the skills below. Read each item to help you decide how confident you feel about each skill.

- understand reports
- open a saved query
- create a simple tabular report
- check that data is displayed in full
- go to the report design view
- enter a report title
- move fields
- widen fields
- check headers and footers
- save a report with a specified name
- print a report
- check the objects in your database
- close and exit Access.

If you think you need more practice on any of the skills above, go back and work through the skill(s) again.

If you feel confident, do the Build-up and Practice tasks.

Remember, you can refer to the **Quick reference** guides when doing any tasks and during an assessment.

Click means click with the left mouse button

QUICK REFERENCE – *Update a database*

HOW TO...	METHOD
Start Access	Click Start button → select Programs → Microsoft Office → Microsoft Office Access 2003. If shortcuts have been created single click on the Access icon on the Quick Launch bar, or double-click on the Access icon on the desktop.
Open a provided database	In the Menu bar, click on File → click Open → Open window displays → click down arrow next to Look in → click on your user area → go to the folder containing the required file → click once on the file → click Open.
Rename a database table	In the database window → check that Tables is selected in the Objects section → in the right-hand section click once on the table name (unless it is already highlighted) → click Edit menu → click Rename → a cursor will display in the table name → click in the table name after the last letter → table name should no longer be highlighted → enter your own first and last name → press Enter.
Open a database table	In the database window, check that Tables is selected from the Objects section on the left → in the right-hand section click once on the name of the table → click Open → the table will open in datasheet view (as a table). Maximize the table window.
Move between fields	Use the cursor keys, or the Tab key, or click in a field.
Move between records	Use the record navigation buttons at the bottom left of the screen in datasheet view.
Set orientation	In the Menu bar, click on File → click Page Setup → click the Page tab → click on Landscape (or Portrait) → OK. Access does not remember the orientation set, so this needs to be set each time.
Change column width	Position the mouse on the line to the right of the field heading → the mouse pointer will change to a double-ended arrow → double-click or click and drag the field heading to change the field width.
Save changes to layout	Remember that any changes to data are saved automatically, but any changes to layout (e.g. column width) must be saved. To save: in the Menu bar, click on File → click Save or click the Save icon on the toolbar.
Use Print Preview	Click the Print Preview icon on the toolbar, or click File menu → click Print Preview.
Print a database table	Check/set the orientation → use Print Preview → check all data fits on the printout → click the File menu → click Print → in the Print dialogue box → check Print Range is set to All → set Number of copies to 1 → click OK.

HOW TO...	METHOD
Delete a record	Click anywhere in the record to be deleted → click Edit menu → click Delete Record → Access displays a dialogue box asking you to confirm the delete → check that the correct record is selected → click Yes.
Replacing data (using codes)	Click anywhere in the field (column) in which data needs to be replaced → click Edit in the Menu bar → click Replace → a Find and Replace dialogue box opens → enter data to be replaced in the Find What box → enter new data (the code) in the Replace With box → check that the Match box displays Whole Field → click to place a tick in the Match Case box → click Replace All → Access displays a dialogue box asking you to confirm the replace → click Yes → click the cross to close the Find and Replace dialogue box.
Amend data	Click in the field (cell) to be edited → delete the unwanted data → enter the new data. Remember, when entering dates, to use UK English format (day, month, year).
Create new records	Click the New Record button in the record navigation buttons on the bottom left of the screen, or click in the first column of the first blank row of the database → enter the new data → use the Tab key to move from field to field → use the Tab key to move to the next record → click in a blank row once you have entered the new records.
Spell check	In the Menu bar, click on Tools → click Spelling → click Change to accept any suggestions → click Ignore to reject suggestions or, if there are no suggestions, enter the correct data in the top box of the Spelling dialogue box → click Ignore XXXX field if a field contains words not in the English dictionary.
Prepare to print an updated table	Set the orientation again → change column widths → save changes to table layout → click the Print Preview icon on the toolbar → use the zoom tool to zoom in to different parts of the table → check that the longest line in each column is fully displayed (not truncated) → check that all fields (columns) fit on one page → click the Close button to close Print Preview → make any changes if necessary.
Print an updated table	In the Menu bar, click on File → click Print (or click the Print icon on the toolbar) → check that Print Range is set to All in the Print dialogue box → set Number of copies to 1 → Click OK.
Close an updated table	Click the File menu → click Close.

QUICK REFERENCE – Create queries

Keep a copy of this page next to you. Refer to it when working through tasks and during any assessments.

HOW TO...	METHOD
Go to the query design view	Method 1 (quicker method): Open the database table → click the drop-down arrow next to the New Object icon on the toolbar → a drop-down menu will display → click Query from the list → a New Query dialogue box opens → check that Design View is highlighted → click OK → you will see the query design view. Method 2: Close the table → click Queries from the Objects section in the database window → click Create Query in Design View → click Open → a Show Table dialogue box opens → click to highlight the table name → click Add → click Close.
Select all fields to place them into the query grid	Double-click on the table name in the field list box in the top section of the query design view → all field headings (field names) become highlighted → position your mouse within the highlighted field names → click and drag the field names to the query grid below → release the mouse button in the field row of the first column → all the field headings will be placed in separate columns.
Select certain fields and place into the query grid	In the field list box → double-click on each field heading → each field that you double-click on will be placed in the query grid.
Enter the selection criterion	Click in the Criteria row of the field to be queried → enter the required criterion. Make sure that you enter the criterion 100% accurately. It is good practice to enter dates in the same format as in the database, but Access will change the date format to the format set up for the database if you do not.
Enter comparison operators for numbers	> more than, >= more than and equal to, < less than, <= less than and equal to.
Enter comparison operators for dates	> after, >= after or on, < before, <= before or on.
Enter selection criteria in two fields	In the query grid → click in the Criteria row of the field to be queried → enter the required criterion → click in the next field → enter the required criterion.
Sort data in queries	Click in the Sort row of the field to be sorted → a drop-down arrow displays in the field → click on the down arrow → click Ascending or Descending.
Display selected fields	In design view, click in the Show box to remove the tick for the fields (columns) that should not be displayed. Check that a tick is displayed in the check box for all fields to be displayed.

HOW TO...	METHOD
Run a query	Click the Run icon on the toolbar in design view → results of the query will be displayed as a table in datasheet view → check the record navigation buttons at the bottom left of datasheet view → the number of records found displays.
Save a query with a specified name	In the Menu bar, click on File → click Save → a Save As dialogue box will open → delete the text Query1 → enter required query name → click OK.
Return to query design view to make amendments	Click the View button on the toolbar → make any changes in the query grid as required → click Run to run the query → save the query.
Prepare to print a query	Click the Print Preview icon on toolbar → use zoom tool to zoom in to different parts of the table → check longest line in each column is fully displayed (must not be truncated) → check that all fields (columns) fit on one page → click Close button to close Print Preview → make any changes to the layout in datasheet view → use Print Preview again. Change the orientation if required (refer to Set orientation).
Print a query	In the Menu bar, click on File → click Print → in the Print dialogue box → click OK, or click the Print icon on the toolbar.
Close a query	Click the File menu → click Close.

Click means click with the left mouse button

QUICK REFERENCE – *Create a tabular report*

Keep a copy of this page next to you. Refer to it when working through tasks and during any assessments.

HOW TO...	METHOD
Create a tabular report	Open the query in datasheet view (as a table) → click the down arrow next to New Object on toolbar → a list will display → click Report → a New Report dialogue box opens → click on AutoReport: Tabular → click OK. Access will create the report automatically and will display it in Print Preview.
Check the report in Print Preview	Use the zoom tool to zoom in to different parts of the report → check the report title is fully displayed → check longest line in each column is fully displayed → check that all fields (columns) fit on one page.
Go to the report design view	Click on the View icon on the toolbar → the report will display in design view.
Headers and footers in reports	Access automatically displays the date and the number of pages, so these do not have to be inserted. When you preview the report, you should check that these are displayed, the date displays as =Now() in design view.
Set the report orientation	From Print Preview or from Design View → in the Menu bar, click on File → click Page Setup → click the Page tab → click on Landscape (or Portrait) → OK.
Widen the report title	In the report design view → click on the report title → square handles appear around title → position mouse on the square handle on the right side of the title box (not on a corner handle) → mouse changes to a double-ended arrow → click and drag the square handle further to the right to make the box (control) for the report title wider → release the mouse button.
Enter or amend a report title	Click in the box for the report title → a cursor will display → delete word(s) not required → enter required title → click in the grey work area below the report (to avoid accidental changes to the report). The report will be titled with the new name.
Select field heading(s) and records (field detail)	Click once on the box (control) for the first field name (below Page Header) → square handles display around field heading → hold the Shift key down → click on the field name in the Detail section → square handles display around the field heading and the field content → repeat by holding the Shift key and selecting for another field if required.
Move field headings and records in a report	Position your mouse anywhere in the boxes that you selected → don't click → the mouse pointer changes to a hand → click and drag the mouse to move the selected boxes to the required position → release the mouse button → the fields will be moved.

HOW TO...	METHOD
Widen a field	Click once on the field name in the Page Header section → hold the Shift key down → click once on the field detail in the Detail section → release the mouse button → position your mouse on the handle on the right-hand side of one of the selected boxes (field heading or field detail box) → do not use the corner handle → the mouse changes to a double-ended arrow → drag the handle to the right → the field heading and the content (the records) will be widened. Click the Print Preview icon to check.
Save a report with a specified name	In the Menu bar, click on File → click Save → a Save As dialogue box will open → the name of the query that the report was based on will display → delete the query name → enter the required report name → click OK.
Print a report	From Print Preview → click the Print icon on the toolbar.
Close a report	Click the File menu → click Close.
Check the Objects (tables, queries, reports) in a database	Open the database window → click on Tables in the Objects section → the tables in the database will display → click on Queries in the Objects section → the queries in the database will display → click on Reports in the Objects section → the reports in the database will display.
Exit Access	Click the File menu → click Exit.

Scenario

You are working as an Assistant for the organisers of leisure activities. You have been asked to update a database containing information about Saturday swimming classes held in the local area.

1 a Start Access.
  b Open the database provided called **SAT_CLASSES**.

2 a Rename the database table **CLASSES** to add your name to the table name.
  b Open the database table **CLASSES (YOUR NAME)**.

For your information only, the database table that you will be working on consists of the following fields:

FIELD HEADING	DESCRIPTION OF DATA
COURSE	The type of swimming course
CENTRE	The location where the class will take place
LEVEL	The level of swimmer that the course is suitable for
CATEGORY	Who the course is suitable for
STARTS	The date the course will start
HOURS	The length of time a class will run for
MAXIMUM	The maximum number of people in that class

3 a Set the page orientation to **landscape**.
  b Print all the records in table format, making sure that all data is fully visible.

4   The **DIVING** course in **EDGBASTON** will not be offered. Delete this record from your database table.

5   Replace the existing entries in the **LEVEL** field with the three letter codes listed below.

  a Replace TASTER with **TST**
  b Replace BEGINNERS with **BEG**
  c Replace RETURNERS with **RET**
  d Replace INTERMEDIATE with **INT**
  e Replace ADVANCED with **ADV**

Four new CLASSES will be offered.

6   Create records for the following four classes:

COURSE	CENTRE	LEVEL	CATEGORY	STARTS	HOURS	MAXIMUM
DIVING	BOURNVILLE	INT	LADIES ONLY	29/01/2008	1.0	8
WATER POLO	EDGBASTON	BEG	BOYS ONLY	29/01/2008	2.5	14
RELAYS	HARBORNE	BEG	BOYS ONLY	05/04/2008	3.0	24
DISTANCE SWIMMING	EDGBASTON	ADV	BOYS ONLY	19/03/2008	2.5	15

Check the new records to make sure you have entered all the data accurately. Make sure that all data is fully displayed.

7 Make the following amendments in your database table called **CLASSES (YOUR NAME)**.

  a Change the STARTS date for the BACKSTROKE in SELLY OAK to be **16/10/2007**.

  b For the FRONT CRAWL course in BOURNVILLE, change the LEVEL to **ADV** and the MAXIMUM to **10**.

8 a Set the page orientation to **landscape**.

  b Print all data in table format, making sure that all data is displayed in full.

  c Make sure that fields are wide enough to display all data in full on the printout.

9 Save the database table keeping the name **CLASSES (YOUR NAME)**.

10 Close the database table **CLASSES (YOUR NAME)**.

11 Close the database **SAT_CLASSES**.

12 Exit Access.

BUILD-UP TASK ❷ *Create queries*

Before you begin this task make sure you have the database you updated in Build-up task 1 called **SAT_CLASSES**.

1 Start Access and open the database called **SAT_CLASSES** that you updated.

2 Open your updated database table called **CLASSES (YOUR NAME)**.

There have been many requests for classes for those who cannot swim.

3 Set up the following database query.

  a Select all courses where the level is **TST**.

  b Sort the data in descending order of **MAXIMUM**.

  c Display only the **COURSE, CENTRE, CATEGORY** and **MAXIMUM** fields.

  d Save the query as **TASTER (YOUR NAME)**.

  e Print the results of the query in table format.

The Leisure Services Manager would like to make sure that there are enough swimming teachers available for courses to be offered in 2008.

4 Set up the following database query.

  a Select all courses with a STARTS date **after 03/01/2008**.

  b Sort the data in ascending order of **STARTS**.

  c Display only the **COURSE, CENTRE, CATEGORY, STARTS** and **HOURS** fields.

  d Save the query as **JAN HARBORNE (Your Name)**.

  e Print the results of the query in table format.

5 Close the database table called **CLASSES (YOUR NAME)**.

6 Close the database called **SAT_CLASSES**.

7 Exit Access.

BUILD-UP TASK 3 Create a query

Before you begin this task make sure that you have the database you updated in Build-up task 1 called **SAT_CLASSES**.

1 Start Access and open the database called **SAT_CLASSES**.

2 Open your updated database table called **CLASSES (YOUR NAME)**

Information about swimming courses for children has been requested.

3 Set up the following database query.

  a Select all courses with HOURS of **more than or equal to 1.5** and with a CATEGORY of **CHILDREN**.
  b Sort the data in ascending order of **CENTRE**.
  c Display only the **COURSE, CENTRE, LEVEL** and **HOURS** fields.
  d Save the query as **CHILD SWIM (YOUR NAME)**.
  e Print the results of the query in table format.

BUILD-UP TASK 4 Create a report

1 Using the query saved in Build-Up task 3.

  a Create a tabular report in **landscape** orientation.
  b Title the report **SWIM REPORT (YOUR NAME)**.
  c Save the report as **SWIM REPORT (YOUR NAME)**.
  d Print the report on **one page** in **landscape** orientation.

2 Make sure you check all your printouts for accuracy.

3 Exit the software with all updated data saved.

PRACTICE TASK 1

Scenario

You are a trainee Travel Agent for First Travel Shop. One of your duties includes maintaining a database of holidays planned for 2009.

TASK 1 – Update a database

1 Open the database provided called **holidays**.

2 a Rename the database table **hols** to add your name to the table name. For example: **hols Fozia Roked**.

 b Open the database table **hols (Your Name)**.

3 The database table consists of the following fields:

FIELD HEADING	DESCRIPTION OF DATA
DESTINATION	The location of the holiday
BOOKING REF	The reference number of the holiday package
LEAVES	The date of departure
NIGHTS	The number of nights that the holiday will last
TRANSPORT	How the holiday party would travel
DEPARTS	Where people will leave from
COST	The price of the package
NUMBER	The number of people in the group

4 a Set the page orientaion to **landscape**.

 b Print all the records in table format, making sure all data and field headings are fully visible.

5 The holiday to the destination **MINORCA** has been cancelled. Delete this record from the database table.

6 Replace the existing entries in the TRANSPORT field with the three letter codes below:

 a Replace MINIBUS with **MNB**

 b Replace COACH with **CCH**

 c Replace FLIGHT with **FLT**

 d Replace CRUISE with **CRS**

(Continued overleaf)

Four new records need to be added to the database.

7 Create records for the following four holidays:

DESTINATION	BOOKING REF	LEAVES	NIGHTS	TRANSPORT	DEPARTS	COST	NUMBER
MADRID	4334MA	21/04/2009	7	FLT	BIRMINGHAM	275	112
DUBLIN	4983DU	20/03/2009	3	FLT	EAST MIDS	179	54
EDINBURGH	9897ED	21/05/2009	4	CCH	BULL RING	145	65
EDINBURGH	8734ED	21/04/2009	2	FLT	BIRMINGHAM	300	35

Check the new records to make sure that you have entered all the data accurately. Make sure that all data is fully displayed.

Some changes need to be made to your database.

8 Make the following amendments.

   a Change the date that the Paris flight LEAVES to be **25/05/2009** and the COST to **165**.

   b For the Lake District holiday change the number of NIGHTS to **5**.

9 Save the database table keeping the name **hols (Your Name)**.

10 a Set the page orientation to **landscape**.

   b Print all data in table format, making sure that all data and field headings are displayed in full.

   c Make sure fields are wide enough to display all data in full on the printout.

TASK 2 – Create queries

Your Line Manager would like more information about flights.

1 Set up the following database query.

   a Select all holidays of **7 NIGHTS** where DEPARTS is **BIRMINGHAM**.

   b Sort the data in descending order of **COST**.

   c Display only the **DESTINATION, LEAVES** and **COST** fields.

   d Save the query as **Birm Flights (Your Name)**.

   e Print the results of the query in table format.

Your Line Manager is considering an April promotion.

2 Set up the following database query.

   a Select all holidays where the LEAVES date is **21/04/2009**.

   b Sort the data in ascending order of **DESTINATION**.

   c Display only the **DESTINATION, BOOKING REF** and **NIGHTS**.

   d Save the query as **April (Your Name)**.

   e Print the results of the query in table format.

TASK 3 – Create a query

There have been some enquiries about short city breaks.

1 Set up the following database query.

  a Select all holidays that are for **3 nights or less**.
  b Sort the data in ascending order of **LEAVES**.
  c Display only the **DESTINATION, LEAVES, NIGHTS, DEPARTS** and **COST** fields.
  d Save the query as **Weekend Breaks (Your Name)**.
  e Print the results of the query in table format.

TASK 4 – Create a report

1 Using the query saved in Task 3.

  a Create a tabular report in **landscape** orientation.
  b Title the report **City Breaks (Your Name)**.
  c Save the report as **City Breaks (Your Name)**.
  d Print the report on one page in **landscape** orientation.

2 Make sure you check your printouts for accuracy.

3 Exit the software with all updated data saved.

You should have six printouts in the following order:

hols (Your Name) – the original database table

hols (Your Name) – the updated database table

Birm Flights (Your Name)

April (Your Name)

Weekend Breaks (Your Name)

City Breaks (Your Name).

Assessment guidelines for Unit 3

1 Your tutor will provide you with the database files that you will need.

2 Before an assessment you should create a new folder just for the assessment.

TIP!

Before you start, **COPY** the folder containing the files into another user area in case you need to open an original file again.

Database tasks

There will usually be four tasks.

○ You will rename the provided database table, open it, change the page orientation, display all data in full and print it. You will then update the database by deleting a record, use **Find and Replace**, add about four new records and amend existing data (approximately 3 fields).

○ You will create 3 queries, one on a numeric field, one on a text field and one on a date field.

○ One of the queries will be using two criteria, and at least one query will be using a comparison operator. You will be required to save each query with a specified name, each filename will include your first and last name.

○ You will create a simple tabular report, usually based on a query. You may need to amend the report title. You will be required to save the report using a specified filename which will include your name.

Open an existing database table and print it

○ Use File ⇒ Back Up Database to create a backup copy of the database table when you open it. You are advised not to copy and paste the original table in the same database because you may run queries accidentally from the original, unamended table.

○ Remember that Access saves any changes to data automatically and that you cannot use the **Undo** tool to undo previous actions.

○ You will need to rename the original table name to include your name. Enter the filename accurately as it will display on each printout. You will be penalised for errors in a filename (but not for errors in your name).

○ Set the orientation when instructed. Even though you may not be instructed to fit all the data on one page, you are advised to do so.

○ Make sure that you widen all fields to ensure that all data is displayed in full, then use Print Preview. In Print Preview, zoom in to the longest data item in each column to make sure that all data is displayed in full.

○ Check the printout to make sure that all data in all columns is fully displayed, especially the longest line in each column.

Update the database table

○ You will need to delete at least one record, replace data in at least one field using **Find and Replace**, amend data in at least three fields and add approximately four new records.

- Remember that you can only add new records to the end of the database table.
- Do not attempt to enter any data in bold unless specifically told to do so – it is presented in bold to help you to see what to enter. You cannot format selected fields to be bold in a database table anyway.
- Use the same case as shown in the assignment. However, if you do not, inconsistent use is penalised once only per assignment.
- Double check to make absolutely sure that you have entered all data 100% accurately.
- Do not enter any additional data in any fields, e.g. your name. Including your name in the table as a new row may interfere with queries.
- When deleting a record, make sure that you delete the whole record not just the data in the fields. The remaining records should 'close up' the gap.
- Use the updated table for all the subsequent tasks.
- Always use **Print Preview** before you print a table.
- Check the printout again to make sure that all data in all columns is fully displayed, especially the longest line in each column.

Remember, Access sometimes changes the order of records when you close a table. The order of records on the table printouts is not specified in the assignment (sort order is only assessed on the query prints). If you close your table and open it again, do not be concerned if the new records that you added are no longer displayed at the bottom of the table. The records in the table are acceptable in any order.

Create queries

- You will usually need to create three queries, one on a numeric field, one on a text field, and one on a date field.
- For at least one of the queries you will need to use a comparison operator.
- You will usually need to display selected fields only. Unless otherwise instructed, fields can be displayed in any order.
- You will need to sort the data in all queries. Usually you will need to sort one query on a date field, one on a numeric field and one on a text field.
- When you run each query, check the number of records found against your printout of the updated data. Make sure that the number of records found is correct.
- Check to make sure that only the selected fields are displayed.
- Check that the data in the correct field is sorted, and that it is sorted in ascending or descending order correctly.
- You will need to save each query with a specified name (this will include your name). Enter this data accurately as it will display on each query printout. You will be penalised for errors in a filename.
- Always use Print Preview before you print a query.
- Check the printout again to make sure that all data in all columns is fully displayed, especially the longest line in each column.

Create a report

- You will usually need to create one simple, tabular report.
- You may need to amend the report title.
- You will need to save the report with a specified name to include your name.
- Zoom in to the report in Print Preview to check what amendments are required. Make a note of these, then switch to design view and make the amendments.
- Check that any specified headers (e.g. page number, date, etc.) are displayed in Print Preview. Remember that the date and page number(s) will be displayed automatically.
- You will probably need to amend the title of the report in design view. Make sure you enter the title exactly as shown in the assignment.
- Use Print Preview again before you print.
- Check all your printouts before you close the database and exit Access.

Check all printouts for accuracy.

Good Luck!

Index